Taylor's Guides to Gardening

Barbara W. Ellis

FRANCES TENENBAUM, Series Editor

Taylor's Guide to

Annuals

HOW TO SELECT AND GROW MORE THAN 400 ANNUALS, BIENNIALS, AND TENDER PERENNIALS

HOUGHTON MIFFLIN COMPANY
BOSTON NEW YORK 1999

Library of Congress Cataloging-in-Publication Data

Ellis, Barbara W.

Taylor's guide to annuals.

p. cm.—(Taylor's guides to gardening)

ISBN 0-395-94352-3

1. Annuals (Plants) I. Title. II. Series.

SB422.E44 2000

635.9'312—dc21 99-33188 CIP

Cover photograph by Jerry Pavia

Drawings by Steve Buchanan

Book design by Anne Chalmers

Typefaces: Minion, News Gothic

Printed in Singapore

TWP 10 9 8 7 6 5 4 3 2 1

Contents

Introduction

GROWING ANNUALS, BIENNIALS, AND TENDER PERENNIALS

Annuals, biennials, and tender perennials offer gardeners a staggering array of options. Look at a dozen gardens and talk to a dozen gardeners — or take a minute to spin through the pages of this Guide — and you'll discover an amazing variety of plants to grow, in a multitude of colors, sizes, shapes, and forms. You'll also find that there are a number of options for how they can be grown and used — a fact that can be confusing to beginners. Take hollyhock *(Alcea rosea),* for example. It can be grown as an annual, a biennial, or a short-lived perennial. And while some gardeners start new hollyhocks from seed each year, others simply let them self-sow and enjoy them year after year, essentially as perennials.

In the entries of this encyclopedia, you'll find information on hundreds of annuals, biennials, and tender perennials. Both the photographs and the individual entries are listed in alphabetical order by botanical name — see the index if you need to locate a plant by its common name. The photographs are accompanied by captions that summarize essential information about the plants and give page numbers for the text entries where they are covered in more detail. The text entries are organized by genus — *Begonia, Celosia, Gomphrena,* and so forth — and include descriptions of outstanding species and cultivars, page references corresponding to the photographs, and a "How to Grow" section for each genus. The "How to Grow" information covers site and soil requirements, as well as various growing options. Do you sow the seed indoors or out? When should you sow seeds—spring, summer, or fall? What other care is essential? Can the plants be grown in more than one way—as annuals sown indoors in spring, or as biennials sown in midsummer, or as tender perennials overwintered indoors? Other propagation options are included for plants that can be treated as tender perennials. That's because they can be overwintered in several different ways: as container plants or as cuttings taken in late summer, for example.

The entries also mention some options for using annuals in the landscape to help you start experimenting with these fascinating and versatile plants. Use them to completely change the color scheme of your garden for a single season, to add summer-long color to a spring-blooming perennial border, or to fill a container with a mix of textures and colors, for example. Don't miss the fun of combining various plants in containers—or even right in beds and borders—to create "bouquets" that last all summer long. Look for flowers and foliage colors that will highlight one another, for example, as well as shapes and textures that will create interesting contrast. In "How to Grow," you'll also find suggestions on which plants make good cut or dried flowers, as well as plants that attract butterflies, moths, and hummingbirds.

The choice of how to grow these plants is largely up to you: the best techniques for a particular plant in a particular garden will vary from region to region because of climate, length of growing season, soil, and other variables. For example, gardeners in an area with hot, humid summers grow many annuals differently from those who live in regions where cool temperatures prevail. Southern gardeners avoid some plants altogether, because they just won't grow well in heat and humidity. Then, too, some plants northerners grow as annuals or tender perennials overwintered indoors are hardy and can be grown outdoors year-round in southern gardens. To determine the best way to grow plants in your own backyard, talk to other gardeners in your area and experiment with different schedules and techniques.

The best growing techniques for a particular plant also depend on the gardener. Some people enjoy starting plants from seeds or rooting cuttings, and can't resist the challenge of trying out different methods for overwintering plants. Others are happy to start anew with plants from the local garden center each spring. Pick the approach that works best for you.

In the section below, you'll find general growing guidelines for annuals—both cool-weather and warm-weather ones—as well as biennials

Popular cool-weather annuals, pansies (Viola × wittrockiana) *come in a range of colors and patterns. These are 'Melody Purple and White'.*

and tender perennials. Use these guidelines with the specific information in the text entries. Don't confuse the botanical description of a particular species with how it's grown. For example, botanists classify pansies *(Viola × wittrockiana)* as perennials, but gardeners grow them as annuals or biennials. And wax begonias are perennials, but tender ones, hardy only from Zone 10 south; most gardeners grow them as annuals. The entries in this book emphasize how plants are grown, not their botanical designations.

Annuals

True annuals germinate, flower, set seed, and die within a single season, but gardeners use the term in a more general way. For them, annuals are plants that grace the garden for a single season and are killed by frost in fall (whether they set seed or not). Gardeners recognize two general types of annuals—cool-weather and warm-weather—that are useful for determining a general growing schedule to try with a particular species. Not every annual falls neatly into one category or the other, so be prepared to experiment a bit to determine what works best in your area.

COOL-WEATHER ANNUALS Sometimes called hardy or half-hardy annuals depending on how much frost they will tolerate, these are plants that thrive in cool conditions. They are grown for winter or early-spring bloom in the South but die out or stop blooming when the weather gets warm. In areas with cool summers—the Pacific Northwest, New

Sweet peas (Lathyrus odoratus) *are cool-weather annuals available in both climbing and bushy forms.*

England, mountainous areas, or more northerly areas, such as Zone 4 and north—they can last the entire summer. Pansies, sweet peas *(Lathyrus odoratus)*, larkspur *(Consolida ajacis)*, and pot marigolds *(Calendula officinalis)* are popular cool-weather annuals.

In warmer zones, plant or sow cool-weather annuals in fall for bloom in winter or the following spring. Or sow seeds or move transplants in late winter or early spring for bloom from late spring until the plants begin to languish in summer's heat. After that, pull them up and replace them with heat-tolerant plants.

In the North, cool-weather annuals normally are sown in late winter or early spring for spring to summer bloom. Some can be sown as soon as the soil can be worked (meaning it is no longer frozen and is dry enough for you to dig without compacting or otherwise damaging it). Others are best sown just before or on the last frost date (see "Scheduling and Frost Dates" on page 7 and the individual text entries for more specific information). They can also be started indoors and moved to the garden as hardened-off transplants on or around the last frost date. If in doubt about whether it's too early to sow or plant, wait a week or two—seeds that sit in soil that is too cold will often rot, and transplants can be damaged or killed by a hard late freeze.

Yellow-flowered Cosmos (Cosmos sulphureus) *is a warm-weather annual that blooms all summer.*

WARM-WEATHER ANNUALS
Also called tender annuals, these are the annuals that thrive in summer heat and fill gardens with color from early summer to fall. They aren't sown or planted outdoors until after the last spring frost date, because they don't tolerate cool temperatures. Sensitivity to cold varies: some can be sown or transplanted to the garden on the last spring frost date, but others are so cold-sensitive they are best kept inside until the soil warms up or the weather has settled and temperatures remain above 45° or 50°F. Warm-weather annuals can be sown outdoors in spring after the last frost date, provided the growing season is long enough, but they're also commonly purchased as transplants or started indoors and moved to the garden after the last spring frost date. Moving purchased or homegrown plants to the garden gives them a head start on the growing season, but not all plants tolerate transplanting well. Zinnias, marigolds, cosmos, and petunias are all warm-weather annuals that do.

Biennials

In their first year, true biennials produce foliage and other growth that overwinters, such as thick roots or stems. The second year, they flower, set seed, and die. (Cool-weather annuals, which are sometimes planted in late summer or fall, overwinter as small seedlings or seeds, not nearly full-size plants as do biennials.) Many short-lived perennials are grown as biennials because their first flowering is abundant, but they peter out in subsequent years. Gardeners thus pull them up and replace them after that first flowering. Some true biennials can be grown as annuals if they are started indoors early enough.

Biennials can be sown indoors or out. Outdoors, sow seed in a prepared seedbed in spring or summer up to 2 months before the first fall frost for bloom the following year. Indoors, sow in individual pots 6 to 8 weeks before plants are scheduled to go into the garden. That translates to midsummer sowing for plants that are to be moved to the garden in early fall, winter sowing to produce seedlings for spring planting. Plants grown as biennials are normally pulled up after they have bloomed to make room for new transplants or self-sown seeds. Keep in mind that you'll need to start new plants every year (or let them self-sow) to ensure blooms every summer.

Tender Perennials

While a perennial is a plant that lives for three or more years, a tender perennial is one that normally would be perennial, but in the area where it is being grown is killed by freezing temperatures at the end of the season. Gardeners treat a variety of plants as tender perennials, including herbaceous (nonwoody) perennials, subshrubs (plants with a somewhat or slightly shrubby habit), woody plants such as shrubs and trees, and

While Snapdragons (Antirrhinum majus) *are actually tender perennials, they are most often grown as cool-weather annuals.*

herbaceous and woody vines. Wax begonias, coleus, impatiens, salvias, and zonal geraniums (*Pelargonium* spp.) are all tender perennials grown as annuals. Some gardeners overwinter them indoors; others replace them each spring, either by starting new seeds or buying plants. Snapdragons *(Antirrhinum majus)*, too, are tender perennials grown as cool-weather annuals, but they are rarely overwintered indoors. They will overwinter in Zones 8 to 11 and will even survive mild Zone 7 winters.

SCHEDULING AND FROST DATES

Where you live has a significant effect on how you grow many annuals. For example, in areas with a long growing season (the number of days from the last spring frost to the first fall frost), marigolds, which are warm-weather annuals, can be sown outdoors where the plants are to grow and still have plenty of time to flower. Farther north, where the growing season is shorter, transplants are a better bet. In southern zones, summers are commonly too hot for most cool-weather annuals, and you'll want to plan on late-spring replacements for them.

To determine optimum scheduling and to find out the best way to grow specific plants in your region, ask your local Cooperative Extension agent or experts at a local public garden or garden center. Neighbors who garden can also advise you. Watching public plantings sometimes works, too. If gardeners plant display beds of pansies in fall in your city, for example, it's a good bet you can do likewise.

You'll also need to know the last spring and first fall frost dates for your area. Most annuals, biennials, and tender perennials are sown in relation to the date of the average last spring frost. Marigolds are sown indoors 6 to 8 weeks before that date and transplanted outdoors after it, for example. Petunias, which take longer from seed, are sown indoors 10 to 12 weeks before the last frost.

To keep track of what you want to sow when, count back the required number of weeks for each plant and jot it down on a calendar; or make a list of annuals to be sown on a particular date. Also note outdoor sowing dates as well as dates when you think plants will be ready for transplanting. Keep track of when you need to sow biennials on the same calendar—late spring and early summer are common times to start the seeds for bloom the following year.

Use the first fall frost date to determine the length of your growing season (count the days from last spring to first fall frost). Then use the growing season length to determine if a slow-growing annual will have time to flower before frost. The fall frost date also is helpful for scheduling when to transplant biennial seedlings to their permanent location. They should generally be in place a few weeks before the first frost date to give them time to put down roots before the onset of winter.

PLANTING AND GROWING TECHNIQUES

For most annuals, cool-weather or warm-weather, along with many biennials and tender perennials, the ideal site is in full sun with well-drained soil rich in organic matter. (This also describes the ideal site for a vegetable garden, but then tomatoes, basil, and peppers are all grown as warm-weather annuals.) There are, however, some annuals and biennials that prefer partial or full shade. Annuals for shade include impatiens, wax begonias, ageratums, pansies, Johnny-jump-ups, coleus, garden balsam *(Impatiens balsamina),* and sweet alyssum *(Lobularia maritima).* Money plant *(Lunaria annua)* and Canterbury bells *(Campanula medium)* are two biennials that will grow in partial shade.

Before sowing seeds or moving transplants to the garden, prepare the site for planting. Loosen the soil to a depth of 10 to 12 inches to accommodate the roots—most annuals have shallow, fibrous root systems, while biennials and tender perennials tend to have deeper ones. Spread 2 to 3 inches of compost or other organic matter over the site and work it into the soil. If your soil is poor, work a balanced organic fertilizer into the soil before planting as well. Rake the bed smooth and you are ready to plant. If you're planting in an existing bed, simply loosen up the soil surface, add a little organic matter, and rake smooth. For an early start on spring planting (when there are already too many garden chores to keep up with), prepare the soil the previous fall. If you have heavy clay soil or are gardening in a low, damp spot, consider installing raised beds to improve drainage. Loosening the soil more deeply and working in more organic matter is also helpful.

Direct Sowing

This technique is used for annuals that grow so quickly that indoor sowing isn't necessary, as well as for plants that do not transplant well. Like seeds started indoors, direct-sown seeds are scheduled according to the last spring frost date. Warm-weather annuals are usually sown on or just

Canterbury bells (Campanula medium) *can be sown indoors before the last frost date and grown as an annual. Most often, it is grown as a biennial and sown outdoors in late spring or early summer.*

after the last spring frost date. Cool-weather annuals are sown on or before that date.

Sow annual seeds in the garden where the plants are to grow by sprinkling them thinly over the site. If you like, draw shapes in the soil with a stick to guide your sowing. In a cutting garden or formal bed, you'll want to sow in rows. Keep in mind that the more sparingly you spread the seeds, the less thinning they'll require later on. Mix a small amount of white sandbox sand in with very fine seeds to make it easier to see where they've been sown. Label the areas you've sown so you can find them easily: you'll need to keep the seedbed evenly moist until seedlings appear, and that can be especially difficult if you've sown seeds in among perennials. A daily session with a watering can is about all it takes if spring rains don't water the plants for you.

When seedlings have one or two sets of true leaves (these look like the leaves the plant will have at maturity, only smaller), thin them to the spacing recommended on the seed packet by pulling them up or cutting them off with scissors. Although destroying perfectly healthy seedlings seems like the antithesis of gardening, thinning is necessary to give the remaining plants the room they need to grow.

Starting Seeds Indoors

Sowing seeds indoors offers several advantages, not the least of which is that it gives you a jump on the season over direct-sown seeds. Setting out

Money plant (Lunaria annua) *is a biennial that self-sows.*

purchased transplants also gives you an early start, but you'll have a wider choice of annuals if you start from seeds, especially if you order by mail. Sowing seeds indoors also makes it easier to control their environment in order to provide ideal germination conditions, such as just the right amount of soil moisture. Using clean containers and a special germination medium reduces pest and disease problems as well.

For indoor sowing, use 2½- to 4-inch plastic pots and/or market packs, depending on the size of the plants you'll be growing. You'll also need flats to carry them in, enough wooden or plastic plant labels to have one for each pot, and a marking pen or pencil. If you are sowing annuals that are difficult to transplant, use individual pots. Many gardeners use peat pots for this because the transplants can be set in the garden pots and all. Another option is newspaper pots, which are easily made by rolling newspaper around a form. These also can be planted right into the

Sweet alyssum (Lobularia maritima) *is an easy-to-grow cool-weather annual that can be sown indoors or out.*

garden. Conventional pots work, too, provided the seedlings are handled carefully at transplant time: gently tip them from their containers with minimal disturbance to the roots; plant immediately into moistened, prepared soil; and water in place.

Fill the containers with premoistened seed-starting mix. (To premoisten the mix, pour it into a large bucket and add a quart of warm water. Knead the mix with your hands to help it absorb the water, and keep adding water until the mix is evenly moist. When you squeeze a handful of mix, it should stay in a ball but break apart easily if you tap it lightly. If you add too much water, just add more dry mix.) Press the medium down lightly with your fingers. The final surface of the mix should be ½ to ¼ inch below the top of the pot. If you are germinating very small seeds or seeds prone to damping off (a fungal disease that rots the stems right at the soil line and kills the seedlings), sterilize the soil

*For best results with African daisy (*Arctotis *spp.) seedlings, keep them on the dry side and water from below.*

surface before sowing. To do this, pour boiling water over the surface, then let the pots drain and cool before sowing.

To sow, scatter the seeds evenly over the surface of the mix. Handle large and medium-size seeds with your fingers or tweezers, sowing three or four seeds per pot. For smaller seeds, fold a card or stiff piece of paper in half, pour the seeds onto the card, and then tap the paper lightly to scatter the seeds. Resist the temptation to sow too thickly, because that results in overcrowded seedlings that are difficult to thin and to transplant. Crowded seedlings are also more likely to be sickly. Either spread the seeds out over several containers or don't sow the entire packet.

The ideal sowing depth for each kind of seed will be listed on the seed packet. Once you've spread out the seeds, cover them with the correct amount of mix. A general guideline is to cover them with a layer of mix that's about two to three times the thickness of the seed. Don't cover very small seeds; just press them into the surface. Some seeds require light to germinate, and these shouldn't be covered regardless of seed size. You'll find specifics for each plant in the text entries.

Label each pot with the plant name and date sown. Using premoistened mix eliminates the need to water the seeds immediately after sowing. To keep the medium moist and the conditions humid, set the pots in flats and loosely cover them with plastic suspended on a wire frame. (Dry-cleaner's bags suspended on a frame made from coat hangers work well.) Keep the flats out of direct sunlight, because temperatures under the plastic can quickly build up and kill seeds and seedlings. The optimum setup is to place the flats on an old table with fluorescent lights suspended several inches above it.

CARING FOR SEEDLINGS

Check the mix in the containers daily—ideally more than once a day—and never let it dry out. When you need to water, water from below by setting the pots in a pan filled with an inch or so of room-temperature or warmer water; capillary action will draw the water up through the mix. When the surface of the mix looks moist (usually within 10 to 20 minutes), remove the pots and let them drain. This system also works well for watering seedlings; just allow the top of the mix to dry slightly between soakings. Watering from below takes a little more time than top watering, but it's worth it. You won't have to worry about washing out the seeds or knocking over the seedlings, and the mix will stay evenly moist, promoting good root growth. Watering from below helps prevent damping off and also keeps other diseases from getting started, because the seedlings don't get wet.

Once seedlings appear, begin venting the plastic, leaving it open for a longer period each day and finally removing it entirely. The first leaves the seedlings will produce are the seed leaves, or cotyledons, which are generally oval. Once the first set of true leaves (the ones that look like miniature versions of the leaves the plant will have at maturity) appears, the seedlings are ready for thinning or transplanting. If you have sown only a few seeds per pot, use scissors to remove all but the strongest seedling. (Leave two widely spaced seedlings if you plan on transplanting them into separate pots once they've gotten a little larger. Some gardeners thin to a small clump of two or three seedlings, which they then treat as a single plant.) Once they have been thinned, most annuals can be grown on in the same pots until it's time to move them to the garden. If the seedlings become too crowded before they can be transplanted outdoors, move them to larger pots so their growth won't be checked.

If you want to save a large number of the seedlings that are growing in a single pot, you'll need to transplant them into individual containers. To do this, water the seedlings several hours in advance, and premoisten a light growing (not seed-starting) mix. Fill individual 2- to 4-inch pots or market packs with mix, and gently tamp it down. Next, carefully turn the pot of seedlings on its side and tip them into your hand. Carefully separate individual seedlings, using a pencil or plant label to tease the roots apart. With the pencil or label, make a hole in the medium that's deep enough to accommodate the roots. Then lower the seedling into place so that the point where the roots join the stem is even with the top of the growing mix. Always handle seedlings by holding a leaf, because the stem is very easy to crush, and a crushed stem is fatal. Gently push the medium back around the roots. Don't press the soil down around the seedling; just lightly tap the bottom of the pot once or twice on your work surface to settle the mix around the roots. Add a little more mix, if needed, to support the seedling, and label the pot. Water as soon as possible after transplanting. Keep transplanted seedlings out of direct light for a day or so, then return them to bright light.

Start fertilizing your seedlings once they've developed their first pair of true leaves. Use a liquid houseplant fertilizer diluted to half its regular strength, or a fertilizer specially blended for seedlings mixed according to the directions on the label. Feed once a week for 3 to 4 weeks. (Supply it from below, as you would water.) After that, you can use the fertilizer full strength every 10 to 14 days until the seedlings are ready for transplanting into the garden.

China asters (Callistephus chinensis) *are showy cool-weather annuals. For best results, start with seeds or plants of disease-resistant cultivars.*

Buying Transplants

Of course, loading up at the local garden center is an easy way to fill your garden with plants. (Avoid sidewalk displays at grocery stores and home centers, where plants receive minimal care and often are stressed by heat and drought.) Always inspect plants before you buy. Well-grown transplants will be compact and well branched and have healthy-looking leaves. Scorched or brown leaf edges indicate that the plants have dried out in bright sunlight or have been exposed to too much heat. Look for signs of disease such as black or brown spots or moldy or powdery patches. Plants starved for nutrients typically have yellowed lower leaves or yellow patches between veins. Check under the leaves for signs of pests (wear glasses if you need them for reading!) such as aphids, spider mites, or whiteflies. Tip a plant out of its pot to see if the roots are excessively

Love-in-a-mist (Nigella damascena) *is best direct-sown outdoors, as plants resent transplanting. They thrive in cool weather.*

crowded. Plants that are not yet blooming are generally a better buy. They recover from transplanting more quickly, because they can direct energy to growing roots rather than to supporting flowers.

Transplanting

Most annuals, biennials, and tender perennials are moved to the garden on or just after the last frost date. (Some cool-weather annuals, such as pansies and Johnny-jump-ups, go in earlier.) With warm-weather annuals and tender perennials that are cold-sensitive, you generally don't gain much if you move them out too early, especially in a cold, wet spring. Until the soil warms up, they'll often sit and do nothing, and cool weather will check their growth; a late frost can damage or even kill them. Don't worry if you're not the first person on your block to plant; plants that haven't been stressed by cold weather will catch up quickly to those that have.

Hardening Off

Plants that have been carefully tended indoors aren't ready for the garden: they need to be hardened off before they're transplanted. (Plants on outdoor display in a garden center have already been hardened off.) Hardening off is the process of gradually toughening up seedlings so they will be able to withstand conditions outdoors. About a week before you're ready to transplant, move seedlings outdoors for a few hours every day. Set them in a shaded location that is protected from wind. Leave them out for a few more hours each day, and gradually move them into a more exposed location. Be sure to keep them well watered during this process. The night before you transplant, leave them out all night. Gardeners who must be away from home all day should start this process on the weekend, and then leave the plants in a very protected location the first full day they'll be away.

If possible, transplant on a cloudy day—a sprinkle of rain is ideal weather for moving plants. To transplant, dig a hole large enough to accommodate the roots, tip the plant out of its pot, set it in place, and firm the soil over the root ball. If a plant has roots that wind around the inside of the pot, use a knife to score the root ball on each side to encourage branching. Water each new transplant with a weak solution of compost or manure tea after you've set it in the soil. If the weather promises to be cloudy for a few days, you're all finished. If it's going to be sunny, shade the plants with pieces of burlap, bushel baskets, or boards propped over the plants for a few days.

Watch the weather for the first week or two after transplanting. If a late frost threatens, cover warm-weather annuals with bushel baskets, sheets, or other coverings in late afternoon and remove the protection the following morning. Cool-weather annuals that have been properly hardened off will generally withstand a light frost, but they may need protection in freezing weather.

CARE THROUGH THE SEASON

Water annuals, biennials, and tender perennials regularly to keep the soil evenly moist but not wet. Most need about 1 inch of water per week—by rainfall or watering—for best growth. An efficient way to water is to snake a soaker hose through the planting. It can be covered with mulch or just left on the soil surface until the plants fill in. Container-grown plants are especially susceptible to drying out: check the pots regularly to see if the top inch or so of soil has dried out. If it has, water thoroughly, until water comes out the bottom of the container. In hot weather, you may need to check pots daily or even twice a day.

One way to reduce watering frequency is to incorporate water-storing polymer crystals into the soil at planting time. Another option is to sink a jar or other water container into the soil right to the rim and run one or two long, thin strips of pantyhose material from the bottom of the jar over the edge and into the soil. Keep the jar filled with water, and the wick(s) will pull water into the soil. Watch wicked pots closely at first to make sure the water is being pulled out into the soil.

WEEDING, MULCHING, AND FEEDING It is important to weed plantings regularly until they fill in, especially direct-sown ones. Otherwise weeds will overwhelm the plants before they've had a chance to get started for the season. Mulch beds with shredded bark, chopped leaves, or other organic mulch to retain soil moisture and control weeds. (Weed before mulching.) Keep the mulch away from plant stems. In direct-sown plantings, don't mulch until the plants have several sets of true leaves and have been thinned to their final spacing.

Most annuals, biennials, and tender perennials will grow just fine without supplemental feeding, provided organic matter and a balanced fertilizer were incorporated into the soil at planting time. If your soil is poor, or your annuals aren't growing vigorously, feed monthly with a balanced organic fertilizer. Plants growing in containers are another matter: feed them at least monthly, and better yet every other week, with a weak solution of a balanced fertilizer.

SUCCESSION PLANTING To lengthen the bloom season for annuals that flower for a short period of time, consider succession plant-

Hollyhocks (Alcea rosea) *will stand on their own, provided they're grown in average soil. Stake the stems individually if they begin to lean.*

ings. The easiest way to succession-plant is to sow seed at 2-week intervals where the plants are to grow. You can also start an extra-early crop indoors and follow it with outdoor sowings. This technique is most frequently used with fast-growing, cool-weather annuals such as China asters *(Callistephus chinensis)* and love-in-a-mist *(Nigella damascena)*. In the North, these plants are sown from spring to early summer, and sowing is timed so they will flower before the onset of summer heat. In areas with long, cool falls, try sowing again beginning in late summer for fall bloom. A site with afternoon shade will protect late-summer plantings from heat. In the South, try making succession plantings from late winter to early spring; many cool-weather annuals can also be sown in fall for bloom over winter.

DEADHEADING Deadheading is another technique that lengthens bloom, because removing spent blooms before they form seeds encourages many annuals to produce more flower buds. To deadhead, pinch flowers between thumb and forefinger or snip them off with pruning shears. Never tug at the plant to remove a flower; this damages the roots and checks growth. Some plants—sweet alyssum *(Lobularia maritima)* is one—can simply be sheared, or cut back by one-third or one-half with hedge shears or garden scissors. Deadheading prevents self-sowing, which may or may not be a problem depending on what you are growing.

ENDING THE SEASON Many annuals, biennials, and tender perennials will continue to bloom right up to the first hard frost. If an early frost threatens, cover plants with sheets, bushel baskets, or other coverings in the afternoon and remove the covering the following morning once temperatures have risen. In many years, after protecting plants for a night or two, you will be rewarded by a return of late-summer weather and will be able to enjoy your flowers for several more weeks. When fall sets in for good, pull up annuals and any biennials that have flowered and add them to the compost pile. (First-year biennials don't need any special care to overwinter in areas where they are hardy.) To encourage reseeding, crumble a few seedpods over sites where you'd like the plants to grow next season. To protect the soil over winter, spread a layer of chopped leaves or other organic mulch.

If you're growing tender perennials you want to overwinter indoors, you may begin preparing for the end of the season weeks before the last frost date. Start taking cuttings of tender plants in late summer to early fall, before they're stressed by cold temperatures. (Unstressed cuttings are better bets for rooting.) Dig plants that you are planning to pot up around the last frost date, too—you'll want to keep track of which ones are more tender than others, and move the least cold-tolerant ones indoors first. You can wait to move container-grown plants indoors until the night before frost threatens, but it's generally easier if you move these plants in gradually as time and space permit. Again, move the most tender ones indoors first. Plants with fleshy roots usually are fine in the garden until the tops are killed by a light frost.

Inevitably, you'll have to make decisions: most gardeners limit the number of plants they overwinter because of the space they have available indoors. Cuttings have an obvious advantage for space-stressed gardeners. Give priority to plants that are hard to replace or are slow to grow from seeds. It doesn't pay to crowd them with lots of plants that are simple to replace from seeds next spring.

OVERWINTERING TENDER PERENNIALS Options vary for keeping these plants from year to year: you can move container-grown plants indoors, take cuttings in late summer to early fall (before cool weather sets in), or dig entire plants and pot them up. A few plants have fleshy roots that can be dug and stored nearly dry over winter. Where the plants are marginally hardy, selecting a protected (generally south-facing) site and/or covering them with a dry mulch such as salt marsh hay, weed-free straw, or evergreen boughs may keep them warm enough to make it through the winter. Some gardeners cover plants that are marginally hardy with plywood boxes or other structures filled with insulating material such as leaves. These aren't attractive to look at all winter, but they can be effective, especially because they keep the roots dry in areas with wet winters. More overwintering perennials are killed by wet feet than by cold.

Indoors, a sunny, cool (60° to 65°F) spot is generally best for holding tender plants over the winter months. Plant preferences vary, however, and many are better off in considerably cooler conditions. When holding plants over the winter, always be careful with watering, even with species that require moist soil during the growing season. Plants are dormant or at least growing much more slowly than in summertime, and usually are best kept on the dry side. You'll find specific recommendations in the individual entries.

Move overwintered perennials back outdoors after the last frost date. Repot specimens that are kept in containers from year to year. This is a good time to prune, too. Set container-grown plants on terraces or decks,

To encourage gloriosa daisies (Rudbeckia hirta) *to self-sow, crumble some seedheads over the site when cutting back the plants in fall.*

or sink their pots to the rim in the garden; this latter approach makes them easy to bring indoors in fall. Spring also is a good time to take cuttings of many tender perennials: if your plants are getting woody and didn't bloom as well as expected last year, propagate them to grow replacements. Many gardeners use the overwintered plants simply as stock plants. In late winter or spring, they take all the cuttings they'll need for the garden, then either discard the stock plant or plant it out with the others.

ROOTING CUTTINGS Cuttings offer a fast, easy way to propagate many tender perennials. You'll find recommendations for the best times to collect them in the text entries. Mid- to late summer is a great time to gather cuttings for overwintering plants, and many tender perennials root well from cuttings taken in mid- to late spring from stem tips or shoots that arise from the base of the plant. If you don't have luck rooting certain plants from midsummer cuttings, try gathering them earlier the following year.

For best results with soft-stemmed cuttings, it's important to keep them from drying out before they can establish a new root system. (If you are taking cuttings of woody tender perennials in mid- to late summer, treat them just as you would soft-stemmed plants.) Before collecting the cuttings, fill pots (4-inch ones are fine) with a moistened rooting medium such as a 50-50 mix of perlite and vermiculite or peat moss and perlite. Also set up a system for maintaining high humidity around the cuttings. Possibilities include a wooden or wire frame draped with plastic, a large clear plastic sweater box, or an old aquarium with a piece of glass over the top. All will accommodate several pots of cuttings.

Gather cuttings early in the day, while the stems are full of moisture. Cuttings from wilted or water-stressed plants are much less likely to recover and root well. In fact, if the weather has been dry, water the day before gathering cuttings. Take cuttings from strong-looking growth, with leaves that have fully expanded and growth that has hardened a bit. Avoid spindly shoots or ones that are growing very rapidly. To judge if the growth is at the best stage for cutting, try bending one of the plant's stems firmly. If it snaps off cleanly, it's a good time to collect cuttings. Growth that just bends over is too soft, while growth that crushes or partially breaks is old and may be slow to root. Snip off 2- to 6-inch shoots with a sharp, clean pair of pruning or garden shears. Make sure each shoot has at least two nodes (the joints where the leaves or leaf pairs emerge from the stem). Collect cuttings in a plastic bag to prevent them from drying out, and keep them out of direct sun. As soon as you have all the cuttings you need, take them indoors and prepare them for planting. If you can't plant them immediately, wrap them in a moist paper towel and keep them in the plastic bag in a cool, shady spot until you are ready for them.

Use a sharp, clean pair of shears or a utility knife to trim each shoot to its final size—2- to 4-inch-long cuttings are ideal. Whenever possible, trim each cutting so there are at least two nodes left, and make the bottom cut just below a node. Trim the leaves off the bottom half of the cut-

Commonly called butterfly flower or poor-man's orchid, Schizanthus pinnatus *is a cool-weather annual that can be staked with twiggy brush.*

ting, and remove any flowers or flower buds. Use a pencil to poke a hole in the growing medium, then insert the cutting about halfway into the medium, to just below the lowest leaves. If you've had trouble rooting cuttings of a particular plant in the past, you may want to dip the base of each cutting in a rooting hormone to encourage roots to form; many tender perennials will root just fine without it, though. Push the medium back around the stem to support the cutting. Repeat with the remaining cuttings, spacing them 1 to 4 inches apart. The cuttings shouldn't touch, so if the leaves are large, either space the cuttings farther apart or trim their leaves slightly (by no more than one-half). A 4-inch pot will usually hold several cuttings. Different plants root at different rates, so it's best to use separate pots for each species or cultivar. Label each pot with the name of the plant and the date. After planting, water all cuttings thoroughly.

Set the cuttings in a warm (65° to 75°F) spot in the sweater box or other enclosure you prepared. The growing medium should be a steady 70° to 75°F, so use a heated propagating mat if necessary. Good light, but not direct sun, is also essential. Outdoors, set covered cuttings at the base of a north-facing wall or in a spot that's lightly shaded all day by trees or shrubs. Cuttings also root well under fluorescent lights such as those used for starting seeds.

Within a day, condensation should build up on the inside of the propagation enclosure. If you don't see condensation, water again thoroughly. Otherwise, leave the cuttings covered and water only when the condensation thins or disappears; don't let the pots sit in water. Remove the cover for an hour or so two or three times a week to allow some air circulation around the leaves. To discourage diseases, remove any dropped leaves or obviously dead cuttings immediately. Most soft-stemmed plants start rooting in 2 to 5 weeks. Resist the urge to check for roots until you see the cuttings producing new growth, then tug lightly on the stems. When the cuttings feel firmly anchored in the medium, they are ready to be transplanted to individual, larger pots. Gradually remove or open the enclosure over a period of a few days to increase ventilation and to decrease humidity. This will help the new growth harden off and reduce the chance of wilting.

Move the rooted cuttings into pots filled with moistened potting soil. Lightly tap the base of each pot against a hard surface two or three times to settle the mix around the roots, then water thoroughly. Set potted cuttings in a shady spot and mist them a few times with a hand sprayer daily for 2 or 3 days. Then move them to their preferred light conditions, and water and fertilize as usual.

FOILING INSECTS AND OTHER PESTS

On the whole, annuals, biennials, and tender perennials present few problems once they're planted out in the garden. Most diseases are fairly easy to control, especially if you spot them in the early stages. Pick off leaves that have yellow, brown, or black spots or blotches as they appear. For information on controlling damping off, which can devastate seedling crops by rotting them at the soil line, see "Starting Seeds Indoors" and "Caring for Seedlings" on pages 9 and 13. Below, you'll find information on some of the more common pests you may encounter and safe, organic ways to control them.

Silhouettes show actual size.

APHIDS. These are tiny green, black, brown, or reddish, pear-shaped, soft-bodied insects. Some have wings. Look for these pests in clusters on buds, shoots, and undersides of leaves, where they suck plant juices, causing stunted or deformed blooms and leaves. They also exude a sticky substance called honeydew, which produces a shiny coating on leaves and supports the growth of black sooty mold fungus. Aphids also transmit plant viruses. To control them, encourage or introduce natural predators, including lacewings and ladybugs. Pinch off and destroy infested plant parts, or knock the pests off plants with a strong spray of water. Spray serious infestations with insecticidal soap or pyrethrins.

BEETLES. While some of these hard-shelled, oval to oblong insects are beneficial in the garden, others are pests, especially Japanese beetles, which are metallic-looking green insects with coppery brown wings; the larvae are brown-headed white grubs. Beetles chew holes in leaves, stems, and flowers during the growing season. The larvae of some kinds feed on roots. To control them, handpick adult beetles early in the morning and drop them into a container of soapy water. Apply parasitic nematodes to the soil to control grubs. You can also apply spores of

milky disease to lawns to control Japanese beetle grubs. Treat seriously infested plants with neem, pyrethrins, or rotenone.

CATERPILLARS. These soft-bodied, wormlike creatures have several pairs of legs and smooth, hairy, or spiny bodies. Adults are moths or butterflies. They chew holes in leaves, flowers, fruit, and shoots through the growing season. To control, handpick and destroy them. (Wear gloves to prevent possible skin irritation.) Or move them to other plants—many caterpillars are the larvae of butterflies that most gardeners welcome to their gardens. The larvae of swallowtail butterflies, for example, feed on parsley, dill, and other related plants.

CUTWORMS. Gardeners seldom see these plump, smooth, brown, gray, or green, 1-inch-long caterpillars, but their presence is evident when they chew through the stems of seedlings and transplants near the soil line. The larvae are active only at night and are most troublesome in spring. The adults are brown or grayish moths. Prevent damage by surrounding stems with cardboard collars extending 2 inches above and below the soil line. Apply parasitic nematodes to the soil around the base of young plants.

LEAFHOPPERS. Adult leafhoppers are small, greenish, wedge-shaped, soft-bodied insects that hop quickly when disturbed. Nymphs look similar to the adults but lack wings. Both feed on stems and the undersides of leaves. They suck plant juices, causing discoloration and stunted or distorted growth. The tips and sides of affected leaves may turn yellow or brown and curl upward. Leafhoppers exude sticky honeydew on leaves and also transmit plant diseases.

Use a strong spray of water to wash nymphs off plants. Spray serious infestations with insecticidal soap or pyrethrins; use rotenone or sabadilla as a last resort.

MITES. Often called spider mites, these very tiny, golden, red, or brown spiderlike pests spin fine webs around leaves or between leaves and stems. They suck plant juices from leaves, producing a light-colored stippling on leaf surfaces. Whole leaves become pale and dry and may drop. Rinsing or spraying leaves frequently with water can suppress mite populations. Pollen- and nectar-rich plants attract natural predators, such as ladybugs and lacewings. Spray serious infestations with insecticidal soap, superior oil, neem, or pyrethrins.

PLANT BUGS. Adult plant bugs are fast-moving, oblong, flattened insects, ¼ to ⅓ inch long. Four-lined plant bugs are greenish yellow and have four black stripes on the back. The wingless nymphs are reddish with black dots. Tarnished plant bugs are greenish to brownish and have brown or black mottling on the back. Nymphs are smaller and pale yellow with black dots; they lack wings. Plant bugs suck plant juices, causing sunken brown or black spots on leaves and deformed leaves, buds, and shoots. Handpick adults and nymphs in early morning (while they are still sluggish) and drop them in a container of soapy water. Grow pollen- and nectar-rich plants to attract natural predators. Treat serious infestations with neem, sabadilla, or rotenone. To prevent damage to future crops, clean up garden debris in fall and spring to remove overwintering sites for adults.

SLUGS AND SNAILS. These are gray, tan, or black, slimy, soft-bodied mollusks. Snails have a hard outer shell and may be up to 1½ inches long. Slugs lack shells; they may be ⅛ inch to 6 inches or more in length. Both leave slime trails on leaves and rasp large holes in leaves, stems, and fruit; they may completely devour seedlings. Slugs are usually most active at night and in damp places; snails are less dependent on moisture. Trap slugs and snails under fruit rinds, cabbage leaves, or boards set on the soil, or in shallow pans of beer set into the soil surface; check traps daily and destroy pests. If slugs or snails are a major problem, eliminate mulches and garden debris; these materials provide ideal hiding places. Use barriers of copper screen or sheeting to repel slugs and snails. Plant ground covers to attract ground beetles and other predators.

WHITEFLIES. Sometimes called "flying dandruff," adult whiteflies are tiny flies with white powdery wings. They cluster on the undersides of leaves and fly up in great numbers when disturbed. Both the adults and the tiny, flattened larvae suck plant juices through the season outdoors and all year indoors. Infested plants look yellow, sickly, and stunted. As they feed, whiteflies exude a sticky honeydew that supports the growth of black sooty mold. Indoors, catch whiteflies on sticky yellow cards or use a handheld vacuum to suck pests off plants. Spray serious infestations with insecticidal soap, superior oil, pyrethrins, or rotenone.

FLOWERS FOR BUTTERFLIES

Marigolds, sunflowers, and zinnias are just three of the many annuals, biennials, and tender perennials that will attract butterflies—along with some fascinating moths—to your garden. The individual entries in the back of this book mention whether a species is known to attract butterflies, but for the best results, plan for other features to attract these winged beauties to your garden. Start with a sunny spot that is protected from prevailing winds—a barrier of trees and shrubs is ideal for giving butterflies a relatively windless spot where they can fly without being buffeted about.

Successful butterfly gardens include nectar plants (flowers) for adults as well as food to feed caterpillars (the larvae). Annuals help ensure a steady supply of nectar all summer long and let you plant an "instant" garden, but many perennials also attract butterflies. A variety of trees, shrubs, and vines are very important plants for larvae. Willows (*Salix* spp.) and aspens and poplars (*Populus* spp.) host the larvae of western tiger swallowtails, mourning cloaks, white admirals, red-spotted purples, and viceroys. Hackberries (*Celtis* spp.) host hackberry butterflies, question marks, and mourning cloaks.

Plan a sunning spot in your garden—an area covered with low ground covers, grasses, clovers, or even a flat rock. Since butterflies are cold-blooded, sunning helps them regulate their temperatures. Butterflies need water, too. One easy way to provide it is to fill a conventional birdbath or other shallow container with flat stones before topping it off with water. The stones should emerge from the water, allowing butterflies to alight and drink without getting wet. A low spot that remains moist (or that you keep moist by regular watering) also provides a suitable drinking spot. Butterflies also will visit muddy or sandy spots along streams and pools. Finally, the more types of habitats your yard provides, the more species of butterflies you are likely to attract.

Members of a few plant families are especially important to butterflies, either as nectar sources, larval plants, or both. (You'll find the plant family listed at the beginning of each entry in the encyclopedia section.) If you include some plants from each of the families below, you will be well on your way to attracting a variety of butterflies.

ASTER FAMILY, ASTERACEAE. A wide variety of butterflies visit daisies and asters looking for nectar, including sulphurs, question marks, painted ladies, skippers, buckeyes, and fritillaries. Painted ladies, pearl crescents, and blues use them as food for larvae. Aster-family plants include cornflowers or bachelor's buttons *(Centaurea cyanus),* cosmos (*Cosmos* spp.), sunflowers *(Helianthus annuus),* marigolds (*Tagetes* spp.), Mexican sunflowers *(Tithonia rotundifolia),* and zinnias (*Zinnia* spp.)

PEA FAMILY, FABACEAE. Pea-family plants are good nectar sources for many butterflies and are valuable food plants for butterfly larvae. Sulphurs, blues, and skippers are among the butterflies that use them as food for their larvae. Sweet pea *(Lathyrus odoratus)* is a popular annual in this family.

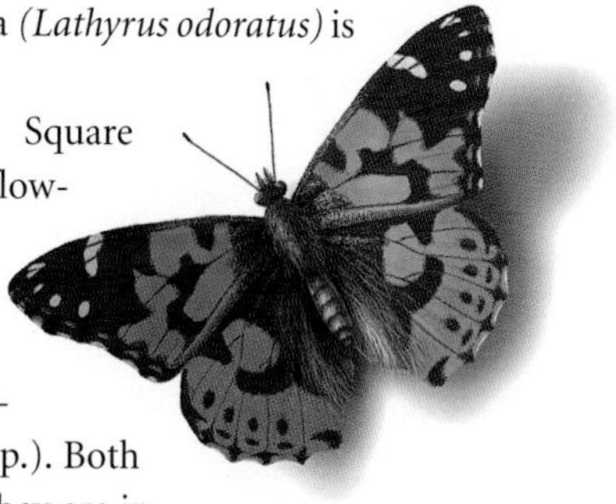

MINT FAMILY, LAMIACEAE. Square stems and spikes of small two-lipped flowers characterize mint-family plants, which attract both butterflies and beneficial insects. Annual members of this family include hyssops (*Agastache* spp.) as well as salvias (*Salvia* spp.). Both are as at home in the herb garden as they are in the flower garden.

MILKWEED FAMILY, ASCLEPIADACEAE. Monarch butterflies are the best-known visitors to milkweeds, but queens also lay eggs on milkweeds, and other species dine on their nectar. Bloodflower *(Asclepias curassavica)* is an annual milkweed.

CARROT FAMILY, APIACEAE. Swallowtails are perhaps the best-known butterflies that frequent carrot- or parsley-family plants. Eastern black swallowtails and anise swallowtails, as well as several other species, lay their eggs on parsley *(Petroselinum crispum),* dill *(Anethum graveolens),* and Queen-Anne's-lace *(Daucus carota).*

VIOLET FAMILY, VIOLACEAE. Several species of fritillaries lay eggs on violets and pansies, and spring azures visit the flowers for nectar.

MUSTARD FAMILY, BRASSICACEAE. The mustard family, Brassicaceae, presents something of a battleground between the goals of conventional gardening and butterfly gardening. The cabbage white butterfly feeds on cabbages and other mustard-family plants. Other species of whites and long-tailed skippers visit other mustard-family members, including basket-of-gold wallflowers (*Erysimum* spp.), dame's rocket *(Hesperis matronalis),* and sweet alyssum *(Lobularia maritima).*

Gallery of Plants

Abelmoschus manihot

Sunset Hibiscus

SIZE: Shrubby, to 5 or 6 feet

Full sun

Rich, well-drained soil

Large, lush leaves and lemon yellow, 5- to 6-inch-wide flowers from midsummer to frost

Tender perennial

P. 203

Abelmoschus moschatus

Musk Mallow

SIZE: 1½ to 2 feet

Full sun

Rich, well-drained soil

Showy, 3-inch-wide flowers in shades of pink, orange-red, and scarlet from midsummer to frost

Tender perennial

P. 204

Abutilon × hybridum

Flowering Maple

SIZE: Shrubby, to 15 feet

Full sun or partial shade

Rich, well-drained soil

Maplelike leaves and colorful bell- to cup-shaped flowers from spring to fall

Tender perennial

P. 204

Abutilon megapoticum

Trailing Abutilon

SIZE: Shrubby, reaching 6 feet high and wide

Full sun or partial shade

Rich, well-drained soil

Pendent flowers with red, heart-shaped calyxes and yellow petals from summer to fall

Tender perennial

P. 205

Abutilon pictum 'Thompsoni'

Variegated Abutilon

SIZE: Shrubby, to 15 feet

Full sun or partial shade

Rich, well-drained soil

Pale orange flowers from spring to fall and handsome yellow-mottled leaves

Tender perennial

P. 205

Acalypha hispida

Chenille Plant, Red-hot-cat's Tail

SIZE: Shrubby, to 6 feet or more

Full sun or partial shade

Fertile, well-drained soil

Fiery-colored, tail-like flower clusters from summer to frost

Tender perennial

P. 205

Acalypha wilkesiana

Copperleaf, Joseph's Coat

SIZE: Shrubby, to 6 feet

Full sun or partial shade

Fertile, well-drained soil

Foliage plant grown for its variegated leaves marked with bronze, copper, red, white, and green

Tender perennial

P. 206

Agapanthus hybrid

Agapanthus

SIZE: 1 to 4 feet

Full sun

Fertile, well-drained, evenly moist soil

Rounded clusters of trumpet-shaped flowers in blues, purples, or white in mid- to late summer

Tender perennial

P. 207

Agastache barberi 'Tutti-Frutti'

SIZE: 2 feet

Full sun or very light shade

Rich, well-drained soil

Loose spikes of red-purple to raspberry red flowers from midsummer to fall

Tender perennial or annual

P. 207

Agastache foeniculum

Anise Hyssop

SIZE: 3 to 5 feet

Full sun or very light shade

Rich, well-drained soil

Anise-scented foliage topped by spikes of blue flowers from midsummer to fall

Tender perennial or annual

P. 208

Agastache mexicana 'Heather Queen'

Mexican Giant Hyssop

SIZE: 2 to 3 feet

Full sun or very light shade

Rich, well-drained soil

Lemon-scented foliage topped by spikes of rose-red flowers in mid- to late summer

Tender perennial or annual

P. 208

Ageratum houstonianum 'Blue Horizon'

Ageratum, Floss Flower

SIZE: Dwarf types, 6 to 8 inches; standard types, up to 18 inches

Full sun or light shade

Rich, moist, well-drained soil

Lavender-blue, lilac, white, or pink flowers from midsummer to frost

Warm-weather annual

P. 208

Agrostemma githago

Corn Cockle

SIZE: 2 to 3 feet

Full sun

Poor to average, well-drained soil

Gray-green leaves and 2-inch-wide, magenta to cerise-pink flowers in summer

Cool-weather annual

P. 209

Alcea rosea

Common Hollyhock

SIZE: 4 to 5 feet or more

Full sun to light shade

Average, well-drained soil

Erect spikes of 2- to 4-inch-wide flowers in many colors from early to midsummer

Short-lived perennial grown as a biennial

P. 210

Alcea rosea 'Chatter's Double'

Double Hollyhock

SIZE: 4 to 5 feet or more

Full sun to light shade

Average, well-drained soil

Erect spikes of carnation-like flowers in many colors from early to midsummer

Short-lived perennial grown as a biennial

P. 210

Alternanthera ficoidea

Joseph's Coat, Parrot Leaf

SIZE: 4 inches to 1 foot

Partial shade to full sun

Moist, well-drained soil

A foliage plant with leaves variously marked with green, brown-purple, red, and orange

Tender perennial

P. 211

Amaranthus caudatus

Love-lies-bleeding

SIZE: Bushy, from 3 to 5 feet

Full sun to partial shade

Evenly moist, average soil

Deep red or green tassel-like clusters of flowers from summer to early fall

Warm-weather annual

P. 212

Amaranthus hypochondriacus

Prince's Feather

SIZE: Bushy, from 3 to 4 feet

Full sun to partial shade

Evenly moist, average soil

Erect, plumelike flower clusters in reds, yellows, orange-yellow, and yellow-green

Warm-weather annual

P. 212

Amaranthus tricolor 'Illumination'

Joseph's Coat

SIZE: 1½ to 4½ feet

Full sun to partial shade

Evenly moist, average soil

A foliage plant with leaves marked with flaming red, rose-pink, gold, yellow, or brown

Warm-weather annual

P. 212

Amberboa moschata

Sweet Sultan

SIZE: 2 feet

Full sun

Average, well-drained soil

Fragrant, 2-inch-wide flowers in white, yellow, pink, and purple from spring to summer

Cool-weather annual

P. 213

▲ *Ammi majus*

Lace Flower, Bishop's Flower, White Dill

SIZE: 3 feet

Full sun or partial shade

Average to rich, well-drained soil that is evenly moist

Bears rounded, 6-inch-wide umbels of tiny white flowers in summer

Cool-weather annual

P. 214

▼ *Ammi visnaga*

SIZE: 3 feet

Full sun or partial shade

Average to rich, well-drained soil that is evenly moist

Bears rounded, 6-inch-wide umbels of tiny chartreuse flowers in summer

Cool-weather annual

P. 214

Ammobium alatum

Pearly Everlasting, Winged Everlasting

SIZE: 1½ to 3 feet

Full sun

Light, well-drained, average soil

Bears 1-inch-wide flower heads with orange or yellow centers surrounding papery white bracts in summer

Tender perennial grown as a cool-weather annual

P. 214

Anagallis monellii

Blue Pimpernel

SIZE: 1 to 1½ feet

Full sun

Average, light to sandy, well-drained soil

Bears deep blue, ½-inch-wide flowers in summer

Tender perennial grown as a warm-weather annual

P. 215

Anchusa capensis

Bugloss, Summer Forget-me-not

SIZE: ½ to 1½ feet

Full sun to very light shade

Average to rich soil that is evenly moist but well drained

Bears sprays of tiny, ¼-inch-true blue flowers with white throats in summer

Biennial grown as a cool-weather annual

P. 216

Anethum graveolens

Dill

SIZE: 2 feet

Full sun

Fertile, well-drained soil

Feathery, aromatic leaves and lacy yellow flower clusters in summer

Cool-weather annual

P. 217

Anisodontea × *hypomandarum*

Rose Mallow

SIZE: Shrubby, from 3 to 5 feet

Full sun in areas with cool summers, afternoon shade where summers are warm

Rich, well-drained soil

Pale pink, 1- to 1¼-inch-wide flowers with darker purple veins borne from spring to fall

Tender perennial

P. 217

Antirrhinum majus

Common Snapdragon

SIZE: 8 inches to 3 feet

Full sun

Rich very well drained soil high in organic matter

Produces spikes of two-lipped flowers in many colors from early summer to fall

Tender perennial usually grown as a cool-weather annual

P. 219

Arctotis fastuosa

Monarch of the Veldt

SIZE: 1 to 2 feet

Full sun

Light, very well drained soil that remains evenly moist

Silver-white leaves and 4-inch-wide daisylike flowers from midsummer to early fall

Tender perennial grown as a warm-weather annual

P. 220

Arctotis × *hybrida* 'Flame'

Hybrid Arctotis

SIZE: 18 to 20 inches

Full sun

Light, very well drained soil that remains evenly moist

Bears silver-green leaves and 3- to 3½-inch-wide daisylike flowers from midsummer to early fall

Tender perennial grown as a warm-weather annual

P. 220

Arctotis venusta

Blue-eyed African Daisy

SIZE: 2 feet

Full sun

Light, very well drained soil that remains evenly moist

Produces white, 3-inch-wide, daisylike flowers with blue centers from midsummer to early fall

Tender perennial grown as a warm-weather annual

P. 220

Argemone grandiflora

SIZE: 2 feet, spreading to 5 feet

Full sun

Poor, well-drained soil

Showy, 4-inch-wide, white or yellow flowers are borne singly or in small clusters all summer long

Warm-weather annual

P. 221

▲ *Argemone mexicana*

Mexican Prickly Poppy

SIZE: 2 to 3 feet, spreading as far

Full sun

Poor, well-drained soil

Spiny, blue-green leaves topped by solitary, pale lemon to deep yellow flowers from midsummer to frost

Warm-weather annual

P. 221

▼ *Argyranthemum frutescens* 'Vancouver'

Marguerite Daisy, Boston Daisy

SIZE: Shrubby, to 2 feet

Full sun

Well-drained, moderately fertile soil

Bears single, white, daisylike flowers or double chrysanthemum-like ones from late spring to fall

Tender perennial

P. 222

Artemisia annua

Sweet Wormwood, Annual Artemisia, Sweet Annie

SIZE: Bushy, from 1 to 5 feet

Full sun

Average to fertile soil that is well-drained

Sweetly fragrant, featherlike leaves and tiny yellow flowers from summer to fall

Cool-weather annual

P. 222

Asclepias curassavica

Bloodflower

SIZE: 2½ to 3 feet

Full sun

Average to fertile soil that is well drained

Rounded, 2- to 4-inch-wide clusters of red-orange and yellow flowers from summer to fall

Tender perennial or warm-weather annual

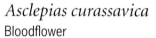

P. 223

Asparagus densiflorus 'Myersii'

Asparagus Fern

SIZE: 2 to 3 feet

Light shade or full sun; afternoon shade where summers are hot

Rich, well-drained soil

A foliage plant with plumlike leaves, tiny white flowers in summer, and red berries

Tender perennial

P. 224

Asperula orientalis

Annual Woodruff

SIZE: To 1 foot

Light shade

Rich, moist, well-drained soil

Produces rounded clusters of small, fragrant flowers in summer

Cool-weather annual

P. 225

▲ *Atriplex hortensis*

Orach, Mountain Spinach, Sea Purslane

SIZE: 1 to 4 feet

Full sun

Rich, well-drained, evenly moist soil

A foliage plant with edible, spinachlike, green, red, or yellow leaves

Cool-weather annual

P. 225

▼ *Bacopa* sp. 'Snowflake'

Bacopa

SIZE: 3 inches tall, spreading to 1½ feet

Full sun to partial shade

Rich, well-drained soil

A spreading or trailing plant bearing small white flowers from early summer to fall

Tender perennial

P. 226

▲ *Ballota pseudodictamnus*

False Dittany

SIZE: Mounding to 2 feet

Full sun

Poor, dry, well-drained soil

Fuzzy gray-green leaves and clusters of small, two-lipped, white flowers in late spring and early summer

Tender perennial

P. 227

▼ *Bassia scoparia* forma *trichophylla*

Burning Bush, Summer Cypress

SIZE: Shrublike, from 1 to 5 feet

Full sun

Rich, well-drained soil

A fast-growing species grown for its narrow, lacy-looking leaves that turn scarlet in fall

Warm-weather annual

P. 227

Begonia semperflorens

Wax Begonia

SIZE: Mounding, from 8 to 12 inches

Full sun to shade, but partial shade is best

Average to rich, well-drained soil

Green or bronze leaves and abundant white, pink, red, or bicolor blooms from early summer to frost

Tender perennial or warm-weather annual

P. 228

Bellis perennis

English Daisy

SIZE: 2 to 8 inches

Full sun or light shade

Average to rich, well-drained soil; best in areas with cool summers

Single or double daisylike blooms in shades of pink, red, and white in spring and summer

Perennial grown as a biennial

P. 229

Beta vulgaris Cicla Group

Swiss Chard, Leaf Beet

SIZE: 18 inches

Full sun to light shade

Rich, well-drained soil

A foliage plant with clumps of green, red, or red-purple leaves with colorful stems and veins

Biennial grown as a cool-weather annual

P. 230

Bidens ferulifolia

SIZE: 12 inches

Full sun

Evenly moist, average to rich, well-drained soil

Lacy, deeply divided leaves and golden yellow daisylike flowers from summer to fall

Tender perennial or cool-weather annual

P. 231

▲ *Borago officinalis*

Common Borage

SIZE: 2 feet

Full sun to partial shade

Average, well-drained soil

Hairy, grayish green leaves and small, star-shaped, blue flowers in summer

Cool-weather annual

P. 231

▼ *Bouvardia ternifolia*

Scarlet Trompetilla

SIZE: Shrubby, from 2 to 3 feet

Full sun; midday shade where summers are hot

Average to rich, evenly moist, well-drained soil

Showy clusters of tubular scarlet flowers from late summer to frost

Tender perennial

P. 232

▲ *Brachyscome iberidifolia*

Swan River Daisy

SIZE 1 to 1½ feet

Full sun

Rich, well-drained soil

Fernlike gray-green leaves and purple-blue, white, or pink flowers in summer

Cool-weather annual

P. 233

▼ *Bracteantha bracteata*

Strawflower

SIZE: Dwarf types, to 1 foot; standard types, from 3 to 5 feet

Full sun

Average to dry, well-drained soil

Bears papery, 1- to 3-inch-wide, daisylike flowers in many colors from late spring to fall

Warm-weather annual

P. 234

Brassica oleracea

Flowering Cabbage, Flowering Kale

SIZE: 10 to 14 inches

Full sun

Rich, well-drained soil

Foliage plants grown primarily in fall for their rosettes of colorful leaves

Biennial grown as an annual

P. 235

Briza maxima

Big Quaking Grass

SIZE: 1½ to 2 feet

Full sun to light shade

Average to rich, well-drained soil

Nodding flower clusters from late spring to late summer that last to fall

Warm-weather annual

P. 235

Browallia speciosa

Browallia, Bush Violet, Sapphire Flower

SIZE: 1 to 2 feet, taller in frost-free areas

Full sun or partial shade

Rich, well-drained soil

Bears clusters of 2-inch-wide, white, blue-violet, or purple flowers in summer

P. 236

Brugmansia arborea

Common Angel's Trumpet

SIZE: Shrubby or treelike, from 6 to 12 feet

Full sun or very light shade

Rich, well-drained soil

Bears fragrant, white, 6-inch-long flowers from late spring to fall

Tender perennial

P. 237

Brugmansia sanguinea

Red Angel's Trumpet

SIZE: Shrubby or treelike, from 10 to 30 feet

Full sun or very light shade

Rich, well-drained soil

Bears orange-red, 6- to 10-inch-long flowers, which are not fragrant, from late spring to fall

Tender perennial

P. 237

Brugmansia suaveolens

Angel's Trumpet

SIZE: Shrubby or treelike, from 10 to 15 feet

Full sun or very light shade

Rich, well-drained soil

Bears white, yellow, or pink ,8-inch-long flowers that are fragrant at night from late spring to fall

Tender perennial

P. 237

Bupleurum rotundifolium

Thorow Wax, Thorough Wax

SIZE: Shrubby, from 1½ to 2 feet

Full sun

Average to poor soil

Rounded leaves and clusters of small yellow-green flowers in summer

Cool-weather annual

P. 238

Calceolaria Herbeohybrida Group

Pouch Flower, Slipper Flower, Slipperwort, Pocketbook Plant

SIZE: ½ to 1½ feet

Full sun to partial shade

Light, average to rich, well-drained soil that is evenly moist; best in areas with cool summers

Clusters of pouched, yellow, orange, red, and bicolor flowers in spring or summer

Biennial

P. 239

Calendula officinalis

Pot Marigold

SIZE: 1 to 2½ feet

Full sun or light shade

Average, well-drained soil; best in areas with cool summers

Daisylike flowers in yellows and oranges from summer to fall in areas with cool summers

Cool-weather annual

P. 240

Callistephus chinensis 'Early Charm Choice'

China Aster, Annual Aster

SIZE: Dwarf types, 8 inches; standard types, 1½ to 3 feet

Full sun or partial shade

Rich, well-drained, evenly moist soil

Single or double flowers in pinks, purples, and white from summer to fall in areas with cool summers

Cool-weather annual

P. 241

Callistephus chinensis 'Rainbow'

China Aster, Annual Aster

SIZE: Dwarf types, 8 inches; standard types, 1½ to 3 feet

Full sun or partial shade

Rich, well-drained, evenly moist soil

Single or double flowers in shades of pink, purple, and white from summer to fall in areas with cool summers

Cool-weather annual

P. 241

Calocephalus brownii

Cushionbush

SIZE: Shrubby, 1 foot

Full sun

Sandy, well-drained soil

A wiry-branched shrub with woolly white leaves and small silvery flower heads in summer

Tender perennial

P. 242

▲ *Campanula isophylla*

Italian Bellflower, Star of Bethlehem, Falling Stars

SIZE: Trailing, from 6 to 8 inches tall

Full sun to partial shade

Rich, well-drained, evenly moist soil; best for areas with cool summers

Bears loose clusters of saucer-shaped, pale blue or white flowers in midsummer

Tender perennial or biennial

P. 243

▼ *Campanula medium*

Canterbury Bells

SIZE: 1½ to 3 feet

Full sun to partial shade

Rich, well-drained, evenly moist soil; best for areas with cool summers

Showy clusters of bell-shaped flowers in purples, white, or pink from late spring to midsummer

Biennial

P. 243

Campanula pyramidalis

Chimney Bellflower

SIZE: To 10 feet

Full sun to partial shade

Rich, well-drained, evenly moist soil; best for areas with cool summers

Showy clusters of fragrant, pale lilac-blue or white flowers from late spring to summer

Biennial

P. 243

Canna × generalis 'Pretoria'

Canna

SIZE: 5 to 6 feet

Full sun

Well-drained, evenly moist soil rich in organic matter

Bears stunning yellow-striped leaves and foot-tall clusters of orange-yellow blooms in summer

Tender perennial or warm-weather annual

P. 245

Canna × *generalis* 'Tropical Rose'

Canna

SIZE: 2 feet

Full sun

Well-drained, evenly moist soil rich in organic matter

Bears large green leaves and showy rose-pink flowers in summer

Tender perennial or warm-weather annual

P. 245

Capsicum annuum

Ornamental Pepper

SIZE: 10 to 36 inches

Full sun

Average to rich, well-drained, evenly moist soil

White flowers and showy fruit in many colors including violet, red, and yellow from summer to frost

Warm-weather annual, tender perennial, or winter annual

P. 246

Cardiospermum halicacabum

Balloon Vine, Love-in-a-puff

SIZE: Vine, can reach 10 to 12 feet

Full sun

Rich, well-drained, evenly moist soil

Fernlike leaves and tiny greenish white flowers followed by inflated seedpods in summer

Warm-weather annual

P. 247

Carthamus tinctorius

Safflower, False Saffron

SIZE: 1 to 2 feet

Full sun

Light, dry, poor soil

Spiny gray-green leaves and thistlelike orange or yellow flower heads in summer

Cool-weather annual

P. 247

Catharanthus roseus

Rose Periwinkle, Madagascar Periwinkle

SIZE: 1 to 2 feet

Full sun to partial shade

Average to rich, well-drained, evenly moist soil

Bears showy, flat-faced flowers in pale to hot pink, red, or white from spring to fall

Tender perennial or warm-weather annual

P. 248

Celosia argentea 'Century Yellow'

Cockscomb, Plumosa Group

SIZE: Dwarf types, 6 to 8 inches; standard types, 2 to 3 feet

Full sun or very light shade

Rich, well-drained, evenly moist soil

Erect, plumelike flower heads in oranges, reds, yellows, and creams in summer

Warm-weather annual

P. 249

Celosia argentea 'Floradale'

Cockscomb, Cristata Group

SIZE: Dwarf types, 6 to 8 inches; standard types, 2 to 3 feet

Full sun or very light shade

Rich, well-drained, evenly moist soil

Rounded, cauliflower-like flower heads in oranges, reds, yellows, and creams in summer

Warm-weather annual

P. 249

Celosia spicata 'Flamingo Feather'

Wheat Celosia

SIZE: 2 feet

Full sun or very light shade

Rich, well-drained, evenly moist soil

Erect, wheatlike flower heads in silver-cream and pink in summer

Warm-weather annual

P. 249

Centaurea americana

Basket Flower

SIZE: 3 to 5 feet

Full sun

Average to rich, well-drained, evenly moist soil

In summer, bears flower heads in shades of pink, rosy lilac, or white

Cool-weather annual

P. 250

Centaurea cineraria

Dusty Miller

SIZE: 8 to 24 inches

Full sun

Average to rich, well-drained, evenly moist soil

A foliage plant grown for its woolly, white fern-like leaves

Tender perennial or cool-weather annual

P. 250

Centaurea cyanus

Bachelor's Buttons, Blue Bottle

SIZE: ½ to 2½ feet

Full sun

Average to rich, well-drained, evenly moist soil

A foliage plant grown for its woolly, white fern-like leaves

Tender perennial or cool-weather annual

Produces dark blue, mauve, pink, rosy red, or white flowers from spring to early summer

Cool-weather annual

P. 250

Ceratotheca triloba

South African Foxglove

SIZE: 4 to 6 feet

Full sun or light shade

Rich, moist soil

Bears two-lipped, lilac flowers commonly striped with purple from midsummer to frost

Warm-weather annual

P. 251

Cerinthe major 'Purpurascens'

Honeywort

SIZE: 1 to 2 feet

Full sun

Average, well-drained soil; best in areas with cool summers

Bears gray-green leaves and clusters of yellow flowers with maroon and purple bracts in summer

Cool-weather annual

P. 251

Chrysanthemum carinatum 'Court Jesters'

Painted Daisy, Tricolor Chrysanthemum

SIZE: 2 to 3 feet

Full sun

Average to rich, well-drained soil

Daisylike, red, orange, yellow, maroon, or white flowers in spring or fall; in summer with cool conditions

Cool-weather annual

P. 252

Chrysanthemum coronarium 'Primrose Gem'

Crown Daisy, Garland Chrysanthemum

SIZE: 2½ to 4 feet

Full sun

Average to rich, well-drained soil

Fernlike leaves and yellow, single or double flowers in spring or fall; all summer with cool conditions

Cool-weather annual

P. 253

Cirsium japonicum

Plumed Thistle

SIZE: 3 to 6 feet

Full sun

Poor to rich, moist but well-drained soil

Deeply cut, soft, thistlelike leaves and brushlike, rose- to lilac-pink flower heads in late summer and fall

Cool-weather annual

P. 253

▾ *Clarkia amoena*

Farewell-to-spring, Satin Flower

SIZE: 2 to 2½ feet

Full sun

Average, moist but well-drained soil

Showy, 2-inch-wide flowers in lavender or rose-pink in summer

Cool-weather annual

P. 254

Clarkia unguiculata ▸

Farewell-to-spring

SIZE: 1 to 3 feet

Full sun

Average, moist but well-drained soil

Single or double ½- to 2-inch flowers in shades of lavender, pink, purple, red, and white

Cool-weather annual

P. 254

Cleome hasslerana 'Violet Queen'

Spider Flower

SIZE: 3 to 5 feet or more

Full sun

Light, rich, well-drained soil

Airy, erect clusters of pink, purple, or white flowers all summer

Warm-weather annual

P. 255

Clianthus formosus

Glory Pea, Desert Pea

SIZE: To 4 feet with a trellis or other support

Full sun

Light, sandy, very well drained soil

Clusters of showy crimson blooms with purple-black centers in summer

Warm-weather annual

P. 256

Cobaea scandens

Cup-and-saucer Vine, Cathedral Bells

SIZE: Vine, can reach 40 feet

Full sun

Average soil

Produces fragrant, bell-shaped flowers sitting in ruffled green cups from summer to fall

Tender perennial or warm-weather annual

P. 257

Coix lacryma-jobi

Job's Tears

SIZE: 1½ to 3 feet

Full sun or light shade

Rich, well-drained soil

Ornamental grass bearing rounded "tears" that turn from green to creamy white, gray, or purplish in fall

Warm-weather annual

P. 258

▲ *Collinsia bicolor*

Chinese Houses

SIZE: 2 feet

Partial shade, especially during the heat of the day

Rich, moist, well-drained soil

Clusters of two-lipped flowers with white upper lips and rose-purple lower ones in summer

Cool-weather annual

P. 259

◄ *Consolida ajacis*

Larkspur, Annual Delphinium

SIZE: 1 to 4 feet

Full sun to very light shade

Average to rich, well-drained soil

Lacy, erect flower spikes all season in areas with cool summers; in early summer in hot regions

Cool-weather annual

P. 260

Convolvulus cneorum

Silverbush

SIZE: Shrubby, to 3 feet

Poor to average or moderately fertile soil

Clusters of white flowers with yellow centers in spring and summer

Tender perennial

P. 260

Convolvulus sabatius

SIZE: Trailing, to 6 inches tall

Full sun

Poor to average or moderately fertile soil

Lavender-blue, funnel-shaped flowers from summer to early fall

Tender perennial

P. 260

Convolvulus tricolor

Dwarf Morning Glory

SIZE: 1 to 1½ feet

Full sun

Poor to average or moderately fertile soil

Solitary, 1½-inch-wide trumpets in rich blue with yellow-and-white throats in summer

Warm-weather annual

P. 261

Coreopsis grandiflora 'Early Sunrise'

Large-leaved Coreopsis

SIZE: 1 to 3 feet

Full sun

Average to rich, well-drained soil

Single, semidouble, or double, yellow to yellow-orange flowers from spring to late summer

Hardy perennial or warm-weather annual

P. 261

▲ *Coreopsis tinctoria*

Calliopsis, Plains Coreopsis

SIZE: 1 to 4 feet

Full sun

Average to rich, well-drained soil

Bears solitary, yellow, daisylike flowers with petals marked with maroon, dark red, or purple-brown in summer

Warm-weather annual

P. 262

▼ *Coriandrum sativum*

Cilantro, Coriander

SIZE: 1 to 2 feet

Full sun or partial shade

Average to rich, well-drained soil

Aromatic leaves and lacy white or pale purple flower heads from summer to fall

Cool-weather annual

P. 262

Cosmos atrosanguineus

Chocolate Cosmos, Black Cosmos

SIZE: 2½ feet

Full sun

Poor to average, evenly moist, well-drained soil

Slightly fragrant, cup-shaped, daisylike flowers with maroon petals from midsummer to fall

Tender perennial or warm-weather annual

P. 263

Cosmos bipinnatus 'Sonata Pink'

Cosmos

SIZE: Dwarf types, to about 2½ feet; standard types, to 5 feet

Full sun

Poor to average, evenly moist, well-drained soil

Showy daisylike flowers in shades of pink, maroon, crimson, and white all summer long

Warm-weather annual

P. 263

Cosmos sulphureus 'Ladybird'

Cosmos

SIZE: Dwarf types, about 1 foot; standard types, to 6 feet

Full sun

Poor to average, evenly moist, well-drained soil

Daisylike flowers in shades of yellow, orange, and orange-red all summer long

Warm-weather annual

P. 263

Craspedia globosa

Bachelor's Buttons, Drumsticks

SIZE: 2 to 3 feet

Full sun

Average, well-drained soil

Woolly white leaves and stiff flower stems with rounded, mustard yellow flower heads in summer

Tender perennial or warm-weather annual

P. 264

▲ *Crepis rubra*

Hawk's Beard, Hawkweed

SIZE: 1 to 1½ feet

Full sun

Poor to average, well-drained soil

Showy, 1- to 1½-inch, pinkish red flowers from spring to summer

Cool-weather annual

P. 265

▼ *Cucurbita pepo* 'Jack Be Little'

Mini Pumpkin

SIZE: 10 inches tall, spreading 8 to 15 feet

Full sun

Rich, well-drained soil

Large yellow-orange flowers followed by orange pumpkins from midsummer to frost

Warm-weather annual

P. 265

Cuphea hyssopifolia

Mexican Heather, Hawaiian Heather, Elfin Herb

SIZE: Shrubby, from 1 to 2 feet

Full sun or light shade

Average to fertile, well-drained soil

Small clusters of pale pinkish purple, pink, or white flowers from summer to fall

Tender perennial or warm-weather annual

P. 266

Cuphea ignea

Cigar Flower, Firecracker Plant

SIZE: Shrubby, from 1 to 2½ feet

Full sun or light shade

Average to fertile, well-drained soil

Showy, tubular, red to red-orange flowers that resemble lit cigarettes from early summer to fall

Tender perennial or warm-weather annual

P. 266

▲ *Cynoglossum amabile*

Chinese Forget-me-not

SIZE: 1½ to 2 feet

Full sun to partial shade

Average, moist but well-drained soil

Gray-green leaves and clusters of blue or sometimes pink or white flowers in mid- to late summer

Biennial or cool-weather annual

P. 267

▼ *Dahlia* Hybrid 'Diablo'

SIZE: Dwarf types, 1 to 1½ feet; standard types, 3½ to 6 feet

Full sun

Rich, well-drained, evenly moist soil

Flowers in many colors and forms, from 2 to 10 inches wide, from midsummer to frost

Tender perennial or warm-weather annual

P. 269

Datura wrightii 'Cornucopaea'

SIZE: 3 to 5 feet

Angel's Trumpet

Full sun

Average, well-drained soil

Showy, night-blooming trumpets in white, lilac, or purple from early summer to fall

Warm-weather annual

P. 270

Dianthus barbatus

Sweet William

SIZE: 1 to 2 feet

Full sun; afternoon shade in areas with hot summers

Dry to evenly moist, well-drained soil

Bears showy, flat-topped clusters of flowers from late spring into early summer

Hardy, short-lived perennial or biennial

P. 272

▲ *Dianthus caryophyllus*

Wild Carnation

SIZE: 2½ to 3 feet

Full sun; afternoon shade in areas with hot summers

Dry to evenly moist, well-drained soil

Fragrant, 2-inch-wide flowers in summer

Cool-weather annual

P. 272

▼ *Dianthus chinensis* 'Telstar Picotee'

China Pink

SIZE: 6 to 12 inches

Full sun; afternoon shade in areas with hot summers

Dry to evenly moist, well-drained soil

Bears small clusters of fringed, scentless flowers from midsummer to fall

Cool-weather annual

P. 272

Diascia barberae

Twinspur

SIZE: Creeping, to 10 inches tall; spreading to 20 inches

Full sun

Rich, well-drained, evenly moist soil

Loose, erect clusters of pink flowers from summer to fall

Tender perennial or cool-weather annual

P. 273

Diascia barberae 'Ruby Field'

SIZE: Creeping, to 10 inches tall; spreading to 20 inches

Full sun

Rich, well-drained, evenly moist soil

Loose, erect clusters of salmon pink flowers from summer to fall

Tender perennial or cool-weather annual

P. 273

▲ *Digitalis ferruginea*

Rusty Foxglove

SIZE: 4 feet

Full sun or partial shade

Rich, evenly moist, well-drained soil

Bears erect spikes of 1½-inch-long, golden brown flowers in summer

Biennial or short-lived perennial

P. 275

◂ *Digitalis purpurea*

Common Foxglove

SIZE: 2 to 6 feet

Full sun or partial shade

Rich, evenly moist, well-drained soil

Showy spikes of flowers in rose-purple, white, pink, and creamy yellow from early to mid-summer

Cool-weather annual, biennial, or short-lived perennial

P. 275

Dimorphotheca pluvialis

Rain Daisy, Weather Prophet

SIZE: 1 to 1½ feet

Full sun

Average to poor, light, well-drained soil

Aromatic leaves and white daisylike flowers with a ring of purple around a darker eye in summer

Warm-weather annual

P. 276

Dimorphotheca sinuata

Star of the Veldt

SIZE: 1 foot

Full sun

Average to poor, light, well-drained soil

Aromatic leaves and daisylike flowers with white, yellow, orange, or pink petals in summer

Warm-weather annual

P. 276

Dorotheanthus bellidiformis

Livingstone Daisy

SIZE: 6 inches tall; spreading to 1 foot

Full sun

Poor to average, very well drained soil

Fleshy leaves and pink, purple, orange, red, cream, or yellow flowers in summer

Warm-weather annual

P. 277

Dracocephalum moldavicum

Moldavian Balm, Dragon's Head

SIZE: 1 to 2 feet

Full sun to light shade

Average to rich, well-drained soil

Narrow spikes of violet-blue or white flowers in summer

Warm-weather annual

P. 277

Eccremocarpus scaber

Chilean Glory Vine

SIZE: Vine, can reach 10 to 15 feet

Full sun

Fertile, well-drained soil

Bears clusters of orange-red, orange, red, pink, or yellow flowers from summer to fall

Tender perennial or warm-weather annual

P. 278

Echium candicans

Pride of Madeira

SIZE: 5 to 8 feet

Full sun

Poor to average, well-drained soil

Silvery-hairy leaves and dense clusters of bluish purple or white flowers in spring and summer

Biennial

P. 279

▲ *Echium vulgare*

Viper's Bugloss

SIZE: 2 to 3 feet

Full sun

Poor to average, well-drained soil

Dense clusters of violet-blue flowers in late summer

Cool-weather annual

P. 280

▼ *Emilia coccinea*

Flora's Paintbrush

SIZE: 1½ to 2 feet

Full sun

Average, well-drained soil

Loose clusters of red to red-orange flowers in summer

Cool-weather annual

P. 280

Eryngium giganteum

Giant Sea Holly, Miss Willmott's Ghost

SIZE: 3 feet

Full sun

Average, well-drained soil

Spiny leaves topped by branched stems of steel blue flowers and silvery bracts in summer

Biennial or cool-weather annual

P. 281

Erysimum cheiri

Common Wallflower

SIZE: 6 to 30 inches

Full sun to partial shade

Poor, average, or somewhat rich, well-drained soil

Clusters of fragrant flowers in shades of yellow, scarlet, orange-red, and pale pink in spring

Cool-weather annual

P. 282

Eschscholzia californica

California Poppy

SIZE: Mat-forming, from 8 to 12 inches

Full sun

Poor to average, well-drained soil

Showy, 3-inch-wide, four-petaled flowers in orange, yellow, or red in summer

Cool-weather annual

P. 283

Euphorbia cyanthophora

Annual Poinsettia, Fire-on-the-mountain, Painted Leaf

SIZE: Shrubby, from 1½ to 3 feet

Full sun

Light, poor to average, well-drained, evenly moist soil

Bears showy leaves and bracts that turn red at the stem tops like small poinsettias in summer

Warm-weather annual

P. 284

Euphorbia lathyris

Gopher Spurge, Mole Plant, Caper Spurge

SIZE: 1 to 4 feet

Full sun

Light, poor to average, well-drained, evenly moist soil

Leathery, gray- to blue-green leaves and 10- to 12-inch-wide umbels of yellow cyanthia in summer

Warm-weather annual

P. 284

Euphorbia marginata

Snow-on-the-mountain, Ghost Weed

SIZE: 1 to 3 feet

Full sun

Light, poor to average, well-drained, evenly moist soil

Grown for its white-edged leaves and bracts borne in loose clusters in summer and fall

Warm-weather annual

P. 284

▲ *Eustoma grandiflorum*
'Lisa Blue'

Prairie Gentian, Texas Bluebell

SIZE: 1 to 3 feet

Full sun

Average, moist, well-drained soil

Gray-green leaves and bell-shaped, satiny-textured flowers in spring and summer

Biennial or cool-weather annual

P. 285

▼ *Evolvulus glomeratus*
'Blue Daze'

SIZE: 1½ to 2 feet

Full sun

Poor to average, well-drained soil

Silky-hairy, silver-gray leaves and funnel- or bell-shaped, lilac-pink or blue flowers in summer

Tender perennial or warm-weather annual

P. 286

▲ *Exacum affine*

Persian Violet

SIZE: 5 to 12 inches

Full sun to partial shade

Rich, evenly moist, well-drained soil

Bears clusters of flowers with showy yellow stamens and lavender-blue, pink, or white petals in summer

P. 286

▼ *Felicia amelloides*

Blue Daisy

SIZE: Bushy, from 1 to 2 feet

Full sun

Light, poor to somewhat rich, very well drained yet evenly moist soil

Pale to deep blue daisylike flowers with yellow centers from summer to fall

Tender perennial or warm-weather annual

P. 287

Felicia bergeriana

Kingfisher Daisy

SIZE: 8 to 10 inches

Full sun

Light, poor to somewhat rich, very well drained yet evenly moist soil

Deep blue daisylike flowers with yellow to black centers in summer

Warm-weather annual

P. 287

Fuchsia × hybrida 'Lord Beaconsfield'

Common Fuchsia

SIZE: Shrubby, to 10 to 2 feet or more

Partial shade, or morning sun and afternoon shade

Rich, well-drained, evenly moist soil

Pendent, single, semidouble, or double, often bicolor flowers from summer to fall

Tender perennial or warm-weather annual

P. 288

Fuchsia magellanica

Hardy Fuchsia

SIZE: Shrubby, 2½ to 3 feet tall in the North, to 10 feet in frost-free climates

Partial shade, or morning sun and afternoon shade

Rich, well-drained, evenly moist soil

Dainty, red and purple-red flowers in summer

Tender perennial

P. 289

Gaillardia pulchella 'Red Plume'

Blanket Flower, Indian Blanket

SIZE: 1 to 1½ feet

Full sun

Average to rich, well-drained soil

Bears red, yellow, or red-and-yellow, daisylike flowers with purple-black centers from summer to fall

Warm-weather annual

P. 290

Gazania Hybrid 'Daybreak Mix'

SIZE: 8 to 12 inches

Full sun

Poor to average, light, very well drained soil

Showy daisylike flowers in hot colors, often marked with contrasting colors, from summer to fall

Tender perennial or warm-weather annual

P. 291

Gerbera jamesonii 'Advantage Mix'

Transvaal Daisy, Barberton Daisy

SIZE: 1 to 1½ feet

Full sun

Average to rich, evenly moist, well-drained soil

Bears single or semidouble daisylike flowers all summer in oranges, reds, yellows, and creams

Tender perennial or warm-weather annual

P. 292

Gilia capitata

Queen Anne's Thimble

SIZE: 1½ to 2 feet

Full sun

Average, well-drained soil; best in areas with cool summers or for spring bloom only

Feathery leaves and rounded clusters of small lilac-blue flowers in summer

Cool-weather annual

P. 293

Gilia tricolor

Bird's Eyes

SIZE: 1 to 1½ feet

Full sun

Average, well-drained soil; best in areas with cool summers or for spring bloom only

Bears lilac- to violet-blue flowers with orange or yellow centers and purple-blue spots from spring to late summer

Cool-weather annual

P. 293

Glaucium flavum

Yellow Horned Poppy

SIZE: 1 to 3 feet

Full sun

Poor to average, well-drained soil

Blue-green leaves topped by yellow to orange flowers in summer

Biennial or cool-weather annual

P. 294

Gomphrena globosa

Gomphrena, Globe Amaranth

SIZE: 1 to 2 feet

Full sun

Average, well-drained soil

Bears rounded flower heads in shades of pink, purple, or white from summer to fall

Warm-weather annual

P. 294

Gomphrena haageana 'Lavender Lady'

Gomphrena, Globe Amaranth

SIZE: 2 feet

Full sun

Average, well-drained soil

Rounded flower heads in shades of pale red to reddish orange, plus pale purple, from summer to fall

Warm-weather annual

P. 295

Gossypium hirsutum

Upland Cotton

SIZE: 2 to 5 feet

Full sun

Light, rich soil

Gray-green leaves, cream or pale yellow flowers, and fluffy cotton boles in mid- to late summer

Warm-weather annual

P. 295

Gypsophila elegans

Annual Baby's Breath

SIZE: 1 to 2 feet

Full sun or very light shade

Rich, well-drained, evenly moist soil

Produces masses of tiny flowers in white or pink in summer

Cool-weather annual

P. 296

Hedychium coccineum

Red Ginger Lily

SIZE: 6 to 10 feet

Full sun or partial shade

Rich, constantly moist, well-drained soil

Produces rounded trusses of 10-inch-long, red, pink, orange, or white flowers from late summer to fall

Tender perennial

P. 297

Helianthus annuus

Annual Sunflower, Common Sunflower

SIZE: 1 to 15 feet, depending on the cultivar

Full sun

Average, moist but well-drained soil

Showy, dark-centered single, semidouble, or double daisylike flowers in summer

Warm-weather annual

P. 298

Helichrysum italicum ssp. *serotinum*

Curry Plant

SIZE: Shrubby, to 1½ feet

Full sun

Poor to average, well-drained soil

Woolly, grayish white leaves with a rich curry-like fragrance and tiny golden flowers from summer to fall

Tender perennial or warm-weather annual

P. 299

Helichrysum petiolare 'Limelight'

Licorice Plant

SIZE: Shrubby, from 1½ to 2 feet, spreading to 5 feet

Full sun

Poor to average, well-drained soil

A foliage plant grown for its woolly, heart-shaped leaves

Tender perennial or warm-weather annual

P. 300

Heliotropium arborescens 'Marine'

Heliotrope, Cherry Pie

SIZE: Shrubby; dwarf types, to 1½ feet, standard types, to 4 feet

Full sun or partial shade

Rich, well-drained soil

Bears showy, usually fragrant, clusters of lavender, violet, or white flowers in summer

Tender perennial or warm-weather annual

P. 301

Hesperis matronalis

Dame's Rocket, Sweet Rocket

SIZE: 2 to 3 feet

Partial shade

Rich, evenly moist, well-drained soil

Loose clusters of fragrant flowers in white or pinkish purple from late spring to midsummer

Biennial

P. 302

Hibiscus rosa-sinensis 'Euterpe'

Chinese Hibiscus, Hawaiian Hibiscus

SIZE: Shrubby, from 5 to 10 feet

Full sun

Rich, well-drained soil

Bears showy, single, semidouble, or double flowers in many colors from summer to fall

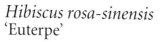

Tender perennial

P. 303

Hibiscus trionum

Flower-of-an-hour

SIZE: 1 to 2 feet

Full sun

Rich, well-drained soil

Bears an abundance of brown-centered yellow flowers from summer to early fall

Tender perennial or warm-weather annual

P. 303

Hordeum jubatum

Squirrel-tail Grass, Fox-tail Barley

SIZE: 2 feet

Full sun

Average, well-drained soil

Bears feathery, green flower spikes flushed with pale pink or purple from early to midsummer

Hardy perennial or cool-weather annual

P. 304

Humulus japonicus 'Variegatus'

Variegated Japanese Hops

SIZE: Vine, to 10 feet or more

Full sun or partial shade

Average to rich, evenly moist but well-drained soil

Bears lobed, maplelike leaves and small greenish flowers that appear from mid- to late summer

Cool-weather annual

P. 304

Hunnemannia fumariifolia

Mexican Tulip Poppy, Mexican Golden-cup

SIZE: 2 to 3 feet

Full sun

Average, well-drained soil

Ferny, blue-green leaves and golden yellow, glossy-petaled flowers from midsummer to frost

Tender perennial grown as a cool-weather annual

P. 305

▲ *Hypoestes phyllostachya* 'Pink Splash'

Polka-dot Plant, Freckle Face

SIZE: To 1 foot

Partial shade

Rich, evenly moist, well-drained soil

A foliage plant grown for its rounded leaves spotted with pink or white

Tender perennial or warm-weather annual

P. 306

▼ *Iberis amara*

Rocket Candytuft

SIZE: 6 to 18 inches

Full sun; partial shade in areas with hot summers

Poor to average, well-drained, evenly moist soil

Bears rounded clusters of mildly fragrant, white to lilac-white flowers in summer

Cool-weather annual

P. 306

Iberis umbellata

Globe Candytuft

SIZE: 6 to 12 inches

Full sun; partial shade in areas with hot summers

Poor to average, well-drained, evenly moist soil

Flattened clusters of fragrant flowers in shades of white, pink, lilac, purple, and red in summer

Cool-weather annual

P. 307

Impatiens balsamina 'Camellia Flowered Mix'

Garden Balsam

SIZE: 1 to 2½ feet

Partial to full shade

Rich, evenly moist, well-drained soil

Produces single or double flowers borne along the main stem from summer to early fall

Warm-weather annual

P. 308

Impatiens New Guinea Hybrids

New Guinea Impatiens

SIZE: 12 to 14 inches

Full sun to light shade

Rich, evenly moist, well-drained soil

Handsome green, bronze, or variegated leaves and flowers in many colors from summer to frost

Tender perennial or warm-weather annual

P. 308

Impatiens walleriana

Garden Impatiens, Busy Lizzie, Patience Plant

SIZE: ½ to 2 feet

Partial to full shade

Rich, evenly moist, well-drained soil

Green or bronze-flushed leaves and single or double flowers in many colors from summer to frost

Tender perennial or warm-weather annual

P. 309

Ipomoea alba

Moonflower

SIZE: Vine, to 15 feet

Full sun

Average, well-drained, evenly moist soil

Bears large, fragrant, white flowers that open at dusk from early or midsummer to frost

Warm-weather annual or tender perennial

P. 310

Ipomoea batatas 'Margarita'

Sweet Potato

SIZE: Vine, climbing or spreading to 10 feet or more

Full sun

Average, well-drained, evenly moist soil

A foliage plant grown for its rounded to heart-shaped leaves in chartreuse, purple-black, or variegated colors

Tender perennial or warm-weather annual

P. 310

Ipomoea lobata

Spanish Flag, Exotic Love

SIZE: Vine, from 6 to 15 feet

Full sun

Average, well-drained, evenly moist soil

Produces clusters of flowers with red buds that turn orange, yellow, then cream from early or midsummer to frost

Tender perennial or warm-weather annual

P. 310

Ipomoea × multifida

Cardinal Climber

SIZE: Vine, from 3 to 6 feet

Full sun

Average, well-drained, evenly moist soil

Deeply lobed leaves and crimson flowers in summer

Warm-weather annual

P. 311

Ipomoea nil 'Early Call'

Morning Glory

SIZE: Vine, to 15 feet

Full sun

Average, well-drained, evenly moist soil

Bears white-tubed flowers in shades of pale to deep blue, plus red, purple, or white from midsummer to fall

Warm-weather annual

P. 311

Ipomoea quamoclit

Cypress Vine, Star Glory

SIZE: Vine, from 6 to 20 feet

Full sun

Average, well-drained, evenly moist soil

Bears scarlet flowers in summer

Warm-weather annual

P. 311

Ipomoea tricolor 'Heavenly Blue'

Morning Glory

SIZE: Vine, from 10 to 12 feet

Full sun

Average, well-drained, evenly moist soil

Bears 3-inch-wide flowers with white throats in shades from pale blue to purple in summer

Warm-weather annual

P. 311

Ipomopsis aggregata

Skyrocket, Scarlet Gilia

SIZE: 2 feet

Full sun

Average, very well drained soil

Produces showy clusters of tubular to funnel-shaped flowers in red, pink, yellow, or nearly white in summer

Biennial or cool-weather annual

P. 312

Ipomopsis rubra ▸

Standing Cypress

SIZE: 3 to 6 feet

Full sun

Average, very well drained soil

Narrow panicles of solid red flowers or red flowers dotted with yellow in summer

Biennial or cool-weather annual

P. 313

▴ *Iresine herbstii* 'Aureoreticulata'

Painted Blood Leaf, Beefsteak Plant, Chicken Gizzard

SIZE: Bushy; from 5 to 6 feet in frost-free areas; to 1 foot in the North

Full sun

Rich, evenly moist, well-drained soil

A foliage plant grown for its rounded, waxy leaves that are variegated or have contrasting veins

Tender perennial or warm-weather annual

P. 313

Iresine lindenii

Blood Leaf

SIZE: To 3 feet in frost-free areas; shorter in the North

Full sun

Rich, evenly moist, well-drained soil

A foliage plant grown for its glossy, dark red leaves, leafstalks, and stems

Tender perennial or warm-weather annual

P. 314

Lablab purpureus

Hyacinth Bean, Lablab

SIZE: Vine, from 6 to 20 feet

Full sun

Average to rich, well-drained soil

Bears clusters of rose-purple flowers all summer followed by flat, glossy, maroon-purple pods

Tender perennial or warm-weather annual

P. 314

Lagenaria siceraria

Bottle Gourd, White-flowered Gourd, Calabash

SIZE: Vine, spreading or climbing to 30 feet

Full sun

Rich, well-drained soil

Heart-shaped leaves and large white flowers all summer followed by fruit in various shapes and sizes

Warm-weather annual

P. 316

Lagurus ovatus

Hare's Tail Grass

SIZE: Clump-forming, to 20 inches

Full sun

Light, poor to average soil that is very well drained

In summer, plants bear greenish white plumes tinted with purple that ripen to creamy tan

Warm-weather annual

P. 316

▲ *Lantana camara* 'Radiation'

Lantana

SIZE: Shrubby, from 3 to 6 feet

Full sun

Poor to average, well-drained soil

Produces rounded flower heads with tiny flowers in many colors from late spring to fall

Tender perennial or warm-weather annual

P. 318

▼ *Lantana montevidensis*

Weeping Lantana

SIZE: Shrubby, from ½ to 3 feet tall; spreading 2 to 4 feet

Full sun

Poor to average, well-drained soil

Small clusters of tiny rose-lilac flowers all summer

Tender perennial or warm-weather annual

P. 318

Lathyrus odoratus

Sweet Pea

SIZE: Bushy or climbing; compact types, to 2 feet; climbers, from 6 to 8 feet

Full sun to partial shade

Rich, well-drained soil; best in areas with cool summers

Bears flowers in lavender, rose-pink, purple-pink, white, and purple from summer to fall

Cool-weather annual

P. 319

Lavatera trimestris 'Silver Cup'

Lavatera, Tree Mallow

SIZE: 2 to 4 feet

Full sun

Average, well-drained soil

Bears funnel-shaped flowers in white and pale to reddish pink from early summer to fall

Cool-weather annual

P. 320

Layia platyglossa

Tidy Tips

SIZE: 1 to 1½ feet

Full sun or light shade

Poor to average, moist but well-drained soil; best in areas with cool summers or for spring bloom only

Produces daisylike flowers with golden centers and yellow petals tipped with white from summer to fall

Cool-weather annual

P. 320

Leonotis leonurus

Lion's Ear

SIZE: Shrubby, to 6 feet

Full sun or partial shade

Average, well-drained soil

Aromatic leaves and orange-red to scarlet flowers in fall

Tender perennial

P. 321

Leucanthemum paludosum

SIZE: 2 to 6 inches

Full sun

Average, well-drained, evenly moist soil

Bears masses of solitary daisylike flowers with white petals and yellow centers in summer

Cool-weather annual

P. 322

Limnanthes douglasii

Fried Eggs, Meadow Foam, Poached-egg Plant

SIZE: 6 inches

Full sun or partial shade

Rich, moist, well-drained soil

Masses of fragrant, golden yellow flowers with white-edged petals from summer to fall

Cool-weather annual

P. 323

Limonium sinuatum

Statice

SIZE: 1½ feet

Full sun

Average, well-drained soil

Showy clusters of flowers in many colors from summer to early fall

Warm-weather annual

P. 323

Linanthus grandiflorus

Mountain Phlox

SIZE: 1 to 2 feet

Full sun

Average, well-drained soil; best for areas with cool summers, or start for early-season bloom

Dense heads of flowers in shades of purplish pink, lavender, or white in spring and summer

Cool-weather annual

P. 324

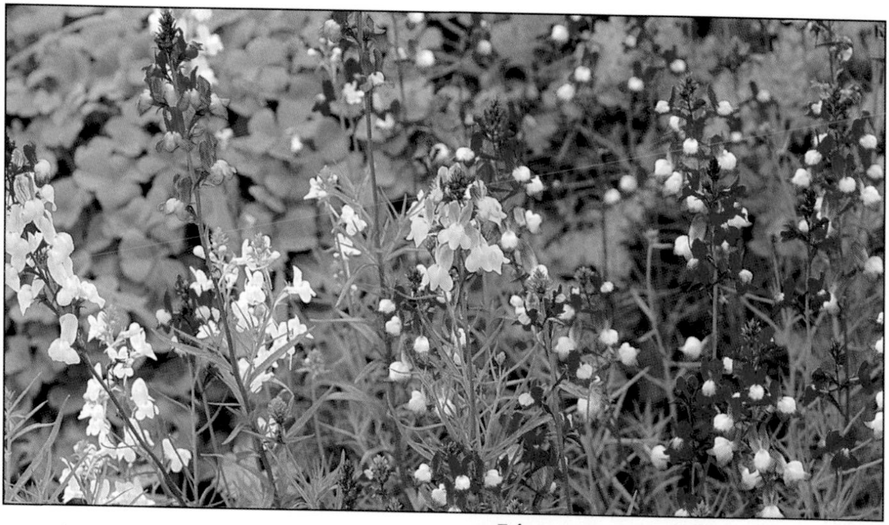

▲ *Linaria maroccana*

SIZE: ½ to 2 feet

Full sun

Average to rich, light, well-drained soil

Loose clusters of flowers in many colors in summer

Cool-weather annual

P. 325

▼ *Linum grandiflorum* 'Rubrum'

Flax

SIZE: 1½ to 3 feet

Full sun

Average to rich, light, well-drained soil; best for areas with cool summers, or start for early-season bloom

Saucer-shaped flowers in shades of lilac-blue, red, white, and pink in summer

Cool-weather annual

P. 326

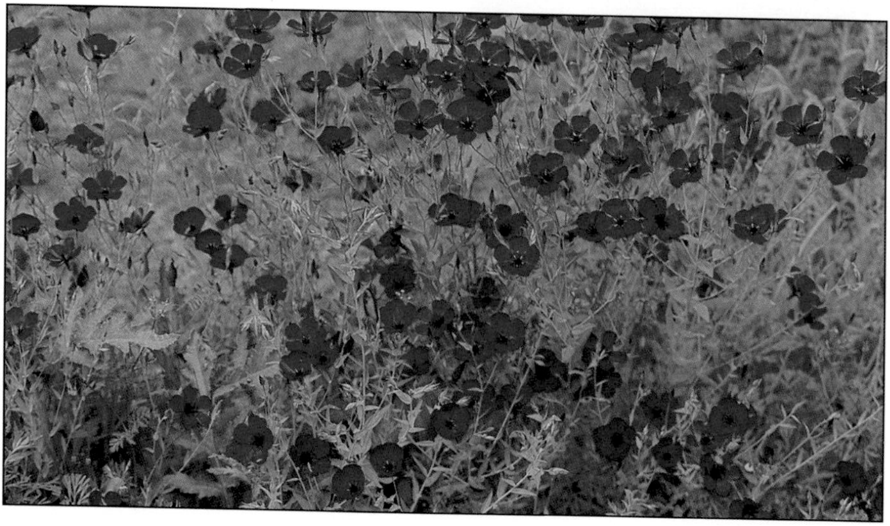

Lobelia erinus

Edging Lobelia

SIZE: 4 to 9 inches

Full sun to partial shade

Rich, evenly moist soil; afternoon shade in areas with hot summers

Small clusters of blue, violet, white, or pink flowers from early summer to frost

Warm-weather annual

P. 326

Lobelia erinus 'Bright Eyes'

Edging Lobelia

SIZE: 4 to 9 inches

Full sun to partial shade

Rich, evenly moist soil; afternoon shade in areas with hot summers

Small clusters of blue, violet, white, or pink flowers from early summer to frost

Warm-weather annual

P. 327

Lobularia maritima 'Rosie O'Day'

Sweet Alyssum

SIZE: Dwarf types, 2 to 4 inches; standard types, to 12 inches

Full sun or partial shade

Average, well-drained soil

Bears rounded rose-pink flower clusters from spring to fall; also comes in white and lilac

Cool-weather annual

P. 328

Lobularia maritima 'Snow Crystal

Sweet Alyssum

SIZE: Dwarf types, 2 to 4 inches; standard types, to 12 inches

Full sun or partial shade

Average, well-drained soil

Bears rounded clusters of tiny white flowers from spring to fall

Cool-weather annual

P. 328

Lonas annua

Yellow Ageratum, African Daisy

SIZE: 1 foot

Full sun

Average, well-drained soil

Rounded clusters of small, round, buttonlike flower heads

Warm-weather annual

P. 328

Lotus berthelotii

Lotus Vine, Parrot's Beak, Coral Gem

SIZE: 6 to 8 inches; spreading to several feet

Full sun

Average, well-drained soil

Silver-green, needlelike leaves and orange-red to scarlet flowers from spring to summer

Tender perennial or warm-weather annual

P. 329

Lunaria annua

Money Plant, Honesty

SIZE: ½ to 1 foot tall; to 3 feet in bloom

Full sun or partial shade

Rich, evenly moist, well-drained soil

Rose-purple or sometimes white flowers in summer followed by ornamental round seedpods

Biennial

P. 330

Lupinus texensis

Texas Bluebonnet

SIZE: 10 to 12 inches

Full sun

Average, well-drained soil

Dense racemes of blue to violet-blue flowers in summer

Cool-weather annual

P. 331

Lychnis coronaria

Rose Campion, Mullein Pink, Dusty Miller

SIZE: 2½ to 3 feet

Full sun or partial shade

Average, well-drained soil

Woolly, silver-gray leaves topped by clusters of small magenta-pink or white flowers in mid- to late summer

Biennial

P. 332

Machaeranthera tanacetifolia

Tahoka Daisy

SIZE: 1 to 2 feet

Full sun or light shade

Average to rich, well-drained soil; best in areas with cool summers

Bears abundant daisylike flowers with yellow centers and pale purple petals in summer

Biennial or cool-weather annual

P. 333

▲ *Malcomia maritima*

Virginia Stock

SIZE: ½ to 1½ feet

Full sun to light shade

Average to rich, well-drained soil; best in areas with cool summers

Bears loose spikes of fragrant, purplish pink, pink, lavender, red, or white flowers

Cool-weather annual

P. 334

▼ *Malope trifida*

Annual Mallow, Malope

SIZE: 2 to 3 feet

Full sun

Average, well-drained, evenly moist soil; best in areas with cool summers

Trumpet-shaped flowers in rose- and purple-red to magenta-pink and white from summer to fall

Cool-weather annual

P. 334

Mandevilla × amoena 'Alice DuPont'

SIZE: Vine, to 20 feet or more; shorter in the North

Full sun to light shade

Average to rich, moist but well-drained soil

Funnel-shaped, 3- to 4-inch-wide, rich pink flowers in summer

Tender perennial or warm-weather annual

P. 335

Matthiola incana

Common Stock, Gillyflower

SIZE: ½ to 3 feet

Full sun to light shade

Average to rich, well-drained soil; best in areas with cool summers

Erect clusters of spicy-scented, single or double flowers in shades of pink and white from late spring to summer

Tender perennial or cool-weather annual

P. 336

Matthiola longipetala ssp. *bicornis*

Night-scented Stock

SIZE: 1 to 1½ feet

Full sun to light shade

Average to rich, well-drained soil; best in areas with cool summers

Loose racemes of pink, mauve, or purple flowers that are fragrant at night in summer

Cool-weather annual

P. 336

Maurandya scandens

Chickabiddy, Creeping Gloxinia

SIZE: Vine, from 6 to 15 feet

Full sun

Average, moist but well-drained soil

Bears trumpet-shaped flowers with flaring violet, lavender, or pink lobes in summer

Tender perennial or warm-weather annual

P. 337

Melianthus major

Honey Bush

SIZE: Shrubby, from 6 to 10 feet

Full sun

Average to rich, well-drained, evenly moist soil

Featherlike, gray-green leaves and showy racemes of red-brown flowers from spring to midsummer

Tender perennial or warm-weather annual

P. 338

Mentzelia lindleyi

Blazing Star

SIZE: ½ to 2 feet

Full sun

Average, well-drained soil

Featherlike leaves and golden yellow flowers that are fragrant at night in summer

Cool-weather annual

P. 339

Michauxia tchihatchewii

SIZE: 5 to 7 feet

Full sun

Average, well-drained soil

Rosettes of toothed leaves yield stiff, branched racemes of white flowers in midsummer

Biennial

P. 340

Mimulus × hybridus

Hybrid Monkey Flowers

SIZE: 6 to 12 inches

Full sun to partial shade

Rich, moist to wet soil; best in areas with cool, wet summers

Bears tubular flowers with flared, often spotted, faces in orange-red, red, and yellow in summer

Tender perennial or cool-weather annual

P. 341

Mirabilis jalapa

Four-o'clock, Marvel of Peru

SIZE: 2 feet

Full sun to partial shade

Average, well-drained soil

Bears pink, red, magenta, yellow, or white flowers that open in the afternoon in summer

Warm-weather annual or tender perennial

P. 342

Moluccella laevis

Bells-of-Ireland, Shell Flower, Molucca Balm

SIZE: 2 to 3 feet

Full sun to light shade

Poor to average, well-drained soil

Bears erect stalks of tiny, fragrant, white flowers surrounded by showy, cup-shaped, green calyxes in summer

Cool-weather annual

P. 343

Myosotis sylvatica

Forget-me-not

SIZE: 5 to 12 inches

Full sun or light shade

Average, well-drained, moist soil

Bears clusters of tiny, saucer-shaped flowers in spring and early summer

Cool-weather annual or biennial

P. 344

Nemesia strumosa

SIZE: 6 to 12 inches

Full sun

Average to rich, well-drained, evenly moist soil; best in areas with mild summers

Racemes of brightly colored flowers that may be a solid color or bicolor in mid- to late summer

Cool-weather annual

P. 344

Nemophila maculata

Five-spot

SIZE: 6 to 12 inches

Full sun or partial shade; dappled shade in areas with hot, humid summers

Rich, moist, well-drained soil

Featherlike leaves with white flowers that have a purple spot at the tip of each petal in summer

Cool-weather annual

P. 345

Nemophila menziesii

Baby Blue Eyes

SIZE: 8 inches

Full sun or partial shade; dappled shade in areas with hot, humid summers

Rich, moist, well-drained soil

Featherlike leaves and blue flowers with lighter blue centers in summer

Cool-weather annual

P. 345

▲ *Nicandra physaloides*

Apple of Peru, Shoo Fly Plant

SIZE: 2 to 3 feet

Full sun or partial shade

Rich, moist, well-drained soil

Bears light purple-blue, bell-shaped flowers from summer to fall followed by inedible berries in lantern-shaped calyxes

Warm-weather annual

P. 346

▼ *Nicotiana alata* 'Nicki Bright'

Flowering Tobacco

SIZE: Compact forms, 1½ to 2 feet; some types reach 5 feet

Full sun or partial shade

Rich, evenly moist, well-drained soil

Bears 4-inch-long trumpets in summer; some cultivars, including Nicki Series, are fragrant

Warm-weather annual

P. 347

Nicotiana langsdorfii

SIZE: 5 feet

Full sun or partial shade

Rich, evenly moist, well-drained soil

Airy clusters of small, 2-inch-long, green flowers with tubular bases and bell-like faces in summer

Warm-weather annual

P. 347

Nicotiana sylvestris

SIZE: 3 to 5 feet

Full sun or partial shade

Rich, evenly moist, well-drained soil

Bears clusters of fragrant, white, 3½-inch-long trumpets in summer

Warm-weather annual

P. 348

▲ *Nierembergia caerulea* 'Purple Robe'

SIZE: 8 inches

Full sun

Rich, evenly moist, well-drained soil

Bears lavender-blue to violet, cup-shaped flowers with yellow centers in summer

Tender perennial or cool-weather annual

P. 348

▼ *Nierembergia repens*

White Cup

SIZE: 2 inches tall; spreading to 2 feet or more

Full sun; dappled afternoon shade in areas with hot summers

Dry, sandy soil

Bears white, 1- to 2-inch-wide, bell-shaped flowers with yellow centers in summer

Tender perennial or cool-weather annual

P. 348

Nigella damascena

Love-in-a-mist, Devil-in-a-bush

SIZE: 1½ to 2 feet

Full sun

Average, well-drained soil; they prefer cool weather

In summer, bears flowers in shades of purple, pink, and white, each surrounded by a ruffled collar of threadlike bracts

Cool-weather annual

P. 349

Nigella hispanica 'Curiosity'

Fennel Flower

SIZE: 1½ feet

Full sun

Average, well-drained soil; they prefer cool weather

Blue, faintly fragrant flowers with maroon-red stamens in summer

Cool-weather annual

P. 349

▲ *Nolana paradoxa* 'Blue Bird'

SIZE: 8 to 10 inches

Full sun

Average, well-drained soil; best in areas with cool summers

Bears purple-blue flowers with yellow throats and white eyes in summer

Cool-weather annual

P. 350

▼ *Ocimum basilicum*

Common or Sweet Basil

SIZE ½ to 2 feet

Full sun

Fairly rich, well-drained, evenly moist soil

Richly fragrant green or purple leaves and spikes of small white flowers that are usually removed as they appear in summer

Tender perennial or warm-weather annual

P. 351

Ocimum basilicum 'Cinnamon'

Cinnamon Basil

SIZE ½ to 2 feet

Full sun

Fairly rich, well-drained, evenly moist soil

Aromatic leaves and spikes of small white flowers that are usually removed as they appear in summer

Tender perennial or warm-weather annual

P. 351

Oenothera biennis var. *candscens*

Evening Primrose

SIZE: 3 to 5 feet

Full sun

Poor to average, well-drained soil

Carries fragrant, bowl-shaped flowers that open pale yellow and age to gold from summer to fall

Biennial or cool-weather annual

P. 352

Omphalodes linifolia

Venus's Navelwort

SIZE: 1 to 1½ feet

Full sun

Light, rich, well-drained soil

Bears airy racemes of white or pale blue flowers from spring to summer

Cool-weather annual

P. 353

Onopordum acanthium

Scotch Thistle, Cotton Thistle

SIZE: 3 to 9 feet

Full sun to light shade

Rich, evenly moist, well-drained soil

Produces a rosette of large, spiny, gray-green leaves topped by rose-purple or white flowers in summer

Biennial

P. 354

Origanum majorana

Sweet Marjoram, Knotted Marjoram

SIZE: 2 to 3 feet

Full sun

Poor to average, well-drained soil

Aromatic gray-green leaves and clusters of white to pink flowers from early to late summer

Warm-weather annual, biennial, or tender perennial

P. 355

Osteospermum Hybrid 'Burgundy Mound'

SIZE: Mounding, from ½ to 2 feet tall, spreading to 3 feet

Full sun

Average to poor, light, well-drained soil; not for areas with hot, humid, wet summers

Bears daisylike flowers in rich magenta-purple from spring to fall

Warm-weather annual or tender perennial

P. 355

▲ *Osteospermum ecklonis*

SIZE: Shrubby, from 2 to 5 feet tall; spreading to 4 feet

Full sun

Average to poor, light, well-drained soil; not recommended for areas with hot, humid, rainy summers

Bears showy, white, daisylike flowers with violet-blue centers; from spring to fall petals are violet-blue underneath

Tender perennial or warm-weather annual

P. 356

▼ *Osteospermum jucundum*

SIZE: Mounding, from ½ to 2 feet tall; spreading to 3 feet

Full sun

Average to poor, light, well-drained soil; not recommended for areas with hot, humid, rainy summers

Bears gray-green leaves and daisylike flowers in mauve to magenta-purple from spring to fall

Warm-weather annual or tender perennial

P. 356

Papaver commutatum

SIZE: 1½ feet

Full sun; afternoon shade in areas with hot summers

Average to rich, evenly moist, well-drained soil

Brilliant red, 3-inch-wide flowers with black spots at the base of each petal in summer

Cool-weather annual

P. 357

Papaver croceum

Iceland Poppy, Arctic Poppy

SIZE: 1 to 2 feet

Full sun; afternoon shade in areas with hot summers

Average to rich, evenly moist, well-drained soil

Bears showy, 3- to 5-inch-wide flowers in the full range of poppy colors in spring and early summer

Hardy perennial, biennial, or cool-weather annual

P. 357

Papaver rhoeas Shirley Series

Flanders Poppy, Corn Poppy, Field Poppy

SIZE: 2 to 3 feet

Full sun; afternoon shade in areas with hot summers

Average to rich, evenly moist, well-drained soil

Bears bowl-shaped, single or double flowers in brilliant red plus pastel shades in summer

Cool-weather annual

P. 357

Papaver somniferum

Opium Poppy, Bread Poppy

SIZE: 3 to 4 feet

Full sun; afternoon shade in areas with hot summers

Average to rich, evenly moist, well-drained soil

Blue-green leaves and showy flowers in pink, white, or red in summer

Cool-weather annual

P. 358

Pelargonium × hortorum 'Pink Parfait'

Zonal, Bedding, or Common Geranium

SIZE: 1 to 1½ feet

Full sun to light shade

Rich, well-drained soil

Rounded leaves and showy clusters of flowers in red, pink, white, or purple from early summer to frost

Tender perennial or warm-weather annual

P. 360

Pelargonium peltatum

Ivy Geranium

SIZE: 3 to 4 feet high and wide

Full sun to light shade

Rich, well-drained soil

Fleshy ivy-like leaves and clusters of single or double flowers in pink, lilac, or white from summer to frost

Tender perennial or warm-weather annual

P. 359

Pelargonium 'Peppermint'

Scented Geranium 'Peppermint'

SIZE: Shrubby, from 1½ to 2 feet or more

Full sun to light shade

Rich, well-drained soil

Richly aromatic leaves and small clusters of single, 1-inch-wide flowers in summer

Tender perennial or warm-weather annual

P. 360

Pennisetum setaceum 'Purpureum'

Fountain Grass

SIZE: 3 feet

Full sun

Average to rich, well-drained soil

Produces purple leaves and plumelike, 1-foot-long, pinkish or purplish flower heads in late summer and fall

Tender perennial or warm-weather annual

P. 361

Pennisetum villosum

Feathertop

SIZE: 2 feet

Full sun

Average to rich, well-drained soil

Bears plumy, cylindrical, green or white flowers that mature to purplish seed heads in summer

Tender perennial or warm-weather annual

P. 361

Penstemon × gloxinoides 'Sour Grapes'

Hybrid Penstemon

SIZE: 2 feet

Full sun to partial shade; afternoon shade where summers are hot

Rich, well-drained, evenly moist soil; best in areas with cool summers

Erect spikes of tubular, lavender-pink flowers from midsummer to fall

Annual, biennial, or tender perennial

P. 362

Penstemon Hybrid 'Garnet' ▸

Hybrid Penstemon

SIZE: 2 to 2½ feet

Full sun to partial shade; afternoon shade where summers are hot

Rich, well-drained, evenly moist soil; best in areas with cool summers

Erect spikes of tubular, wine red flowers from midsummer to fall

Annual, biennial, or tender perennial

P. 362

▾ *Pentas lanceolata*

Star Cluster, Star Flower, Egyptian Star Cluster

SIZE: Shrubby, to 6 feet in frost-free climates; from 1 to 2 feet in the North

Full sun

Rich, well-drained soil

Sshowy clusters of flowers in pink, magenta, purple-red, or white from spring to fall

Tender perennial

P. 363

Perilla frutescens

Beefsteak Plant, Chinese Basil, False Coleus

SIZE: 1 to 3 feet

Full sun to partial shade

Very rich, moist, well-drained soil

A foliage plant grown for its deeply toothed red-purple, bronzy, or green leaves; bears tiny white flowers in summer

Warm-weather annual

P. 364

Persicaria capitata

SIZE: 3 inches tall, spreading to 20 inches

Full sun or partial shade

Moist, average soil

Bears rounded leaves and pink flower heads of tiny, bell-shaped blooms in summer

Warm-weather annual or tender perennial

P. 365

Persicaria orientale

Prince's Feather, Princess Feather, Kiss-me-over-the-garden-gate

SIZE: 3 to 5 feet

Full sun or partial shade

Moist, average soil

Bears arching, branched spikes of tiny pink, rose-red, or white flowers from late summer to fall

Warm-weather annual

P. 365

Petroselinum crispum

Curled Parsley

SIZE: ½ to 2½ feet

Full sun

Rich, evenly moist, well-drained soil

A popular herb with handsome, dark green, finely cut, curled leaves

Cool-weather annual or biennial

P. 366

▲ *Petunia × hybrida*
'Prism Sunshine'

Grandiflora Hybrid Petunia

SIZE: 8 to 10 inches

Full sun or light shade

Average to rich, moist but well-drained soil

Bears large 3- to 4-inch-wide flowers on mounding plants from early summer to fall

Tender perennial or warm-weather annual

P. 367

▼ *Petunia × hybrida*
'Purple Pirouette'

Double-flowered Hybrid Petunia

SIZE: 10 to 12 inches

Full sun or light shade

Average to rich, moist but well-drained soil

Bears large, double, 3- to 4-inch-wide flowers on mounding plants from early summer to fall

Tender perennial or warm-weather annual

P. 367

Petunia integrifolia

SIZE: To 2 feet tall, spreading to 3 feet

Full sun or light shade

Average to rich, moist but well-drained soil

Bears small, magenta-pink flowers with dark centers from spring to frost

Tender perennial or warm-weather annual

P. 368

Petunia Surfinia Mix

SIZE: 8 inches tall; spreading to 2½ feet

Full sun or light shade

Average to rich, moist but well-drained soil

Flowers in purple-blue, pink, white, fuchsia, lavender-blue, and purple-red all summer long

Tender perennial or warm-weather annual

P. 368

Phacelia campanularia

California Bluebell

SIZE: 6 to 12 inches

Full sun

Well-drained soil; best for areas with cool summers

Sticky-hairy leaves and loose clusters of bell-shaped blooms in dark blue from late spring to summer

Cool-weather annual

P. 368

Phaseolus coccineus

Scarlet Runner Bean

SIZE: Vine, from 8 to 12 feet

Full sun

Average to rich, moist but well-drained soil

Loose clusters of scarlet flowers from early summer to frost followed by edible beans

Warm-weather annual or tender perennial

P. 369

Phlox drummondii

Annual Phlox, Drummond Phlox

SIZE: 4 to 18 inches

Full sun

Average to rich, moist, well-drained soil; best in areas with cool weather

Clusters of purple, lavender, salmon, pink, or red, single or double blooms in spring

Cool-weather annual

P. 370

Phormium tenax

New Zealand Flax

SIZE: Clumping, from 3 to 9 feet

Full sun

Rich, moist, well-drained soil

Handsome green leaves or variegated with bronze, green, rose-pink, or red; dark red flowers in summer

Tender perennial

P. 371

Phygelius aequalis

SIZE: 3 feet

Full sun; dappled afternoon shade in very hot climates

Rich, moist, well-drained soil

Bears showy, foot-long clusters of trumpet-shaped flowers in pink, red, or yellow in summer

Tender perennial

P. 372

Phygelius × *rectus* 'Moonraker'

SIZE: 3 to 5 feet

Full sun; dappled afternoon shade in very hot climates

Rich, moist, well-drained soil

Bears panicles of greenish yellow flowers in summer; other cultivars bear salmon-orange or pink blooms

Tender perennial

P. 372

Platystemon californicus

Cream Cups

SIZE: 4 to 12 inches

Full sun

Average, loose, well-drained soil

Bears 1-inch-wide, six-petaled, creamy yellow flowers in spring

Cool-weather annual

P. 373

Plectranthus argentatus

SIZE: Shrubby, 2 to 3 feet tall and wide

Dappled shade

Average to rich, well-drained soil

Bears ribbed, scallop-edged, gray-green leaves and spikes of bluish white flowers in summer

Tender perennial or warm-weather annual

P. 374

▲ *Plectranthus forsteri* 'Marginatus'

SIZE: 10 inches tall; spreading to 3 feet or more

Dappled shade

Average to rich, well-drained soil

Hairy, rounded, scallop-edged leaves and tiny, pale pink or white flowers in summer

Tender perennial or warm-weather annual

P. 374

▼ *Portulaca grandiflora*

Portulaca, Moss Rose, Rose Moss

SIZE: 4 to 8 inches

Full sun

Poor, well-drained soil

Fleshy, cylindrical leaves and single or double flowers in an array of bright colors in summer

Warm-weather annual

P. 375

Primula malacoides

Fairy Primrose

SIZE: 6 to 8 inches

Partial shade; tolerates full sun in areas with cool summers

Rich, evenly moist, well-drained soil

Bears tiers of single or double flowers in shades of lavender-purple, reddish pink, or white in spring

Tender perennial or cool-weather annual

P. 376

Primula obconica

Fairy Primrose, German Primrose

SIZE: 9 to 16 inches

Partial shade; tolerates full sun in areas with cool summers

Rich, evenly moist, well-drained soil

Bears tiers of flowers in shades of pink, red, lilac-blue, and white in spring

Tender perennial or cool-weather annual

P. 376

▲ *Proboscidea louisianica*

Unicorn Plant, Devil's Claw

SIZE: 1½ feet tall; spreading to 3 feet

Full sun to very light shade

Rich, well-drained soil

Bears softly hairy leaves and funnel-shaped, creamy white to purplish flowers in summer followed by ornamental seedpods

Warm-weather annual

P. 377

▼ *Psylliostachys suworowii*

Rattail Statice, Russian Statice

SIZE: 1 to 1½ feet

Full sun

Average, well-drained soil

Bears branched, cylindrical spikes of pink flowers from summer to early fall

Warm-weather annual

P. 378

Psylliostachys suworowii

Rattail Statice, Russian Statice

SIZE: 1 to 1½ feet

Full sun

Average, well-drained soil

Bears branched, cylindrical spikes of rose-pink flowers from summer to early fall

Warm-weather annual

P. 378

Rehmannia elata

Chinese Foxglove

SIZE: 3 to 5 feet

Full sun to dappled shade

Average to rich, evenly moist, well-drained soil; best in areas with cool summers

Bears tubular, rosy purple flowers with red-spotted throats from summer to fall

Biennial or tender perennial

P. 378

Reseda odorata

Common Mignonette

SIZE: 1 to 2 feet

Partial shade

Average, well-drained soil; prefers cool conditions

Rounded spikes of tiny, yellowish green, white, or reddish green flowers from summer to fall

Cool-weather annual

P. 379

Rhodanthe chlorocephala ssp. *rosea*

SIZE: 1 to 2 feet

Full sun

Poor to average, well-drained soil

Bears papery white or pink, yellow-centered daisies that close in cloudy weather in summer

Warm-weather annual

P. 380

Rhodochiton atrosanguineum

Purple Bell Vine

SIZE: To 10 feet in northern gardens; more in frost-free regions

Full sun

Rich, evenly moist, well-drained soil

Bears dark maroon-purple flowers with lighter mauve-pink calyxes from summer to fall

Tender perennial or warm-weather annual

P. 381

Ricinus communis 'Zanzibarensis'

Castor Bean

SIZE: Shrubby, to 6 to 10 feet or more

Full sun

Rich, well-drained soil

Large, lobed, green, red-purple, or bronze-red leaves; greenish yellow summer flowers and red-brown seed heads

Tender perennial or warm-weather annual

P. 382

▲ *Rosmarinus officinalis*

Rosemary

SIZE: Shrubby, to 5 or 6 feet tall and spreading as far

Full sun

Poor to average, evenly moist, well-drained soil

Fragrant gray-green foliage and clusters of small lavender-blue flowers in summer

Tender perennial

P. 383

▼ *Rudbeckia hirta*

Gloriosa Daisies, Black-eyed Susan

SIZE: 1 to 3 feet

Full sun to light shade

Average to rich soil

Bears single or semidouble flowers in rich red-browns, yellows, and rusty oranges from summer to early fall

Short-lived perennial, biennial, or cool-weather annual

P. 383

Salpiglossis sinuata 'Casino Mix'

Painted Tongue

SIZE: 1½ to 2 feet

Full sun

Average to rich, well-drained, evenly moist soil; best where summers are not excessively hot

Showy, five-lobed flowers from summer to fall in a rich array of colors

Cool-weather annual

P. 385

Salvia argentea

Silver Sage, Silver Salvia

SIZE: 2 to 3 feet

Full sun to partial shade; afternoon shade in areas with hot summers

Average to rich, well-drained, evenly moist soil

Grown primarily for its large, gray-green, silvery-hairy leaves; bears white to pinkish flowers in summer

Warm-weather annual or biennial

P. 386

Salvia coccinea 'Lady in Red'

SIZE: 1½ to 3 feet

Full sun to partial shade; afternoon shade in areas with hot summers

Average to rich, well-drained, evenly moist soil

Spikes of flowers with flaring lower lips in red, pink, or white from summer to fall

Warm-weather annual

P. 386

Salvia farinacea

Mealy-cup Sage

SIZE: 2 feet

Full sun to partial shade; afternoon shade in areas with hot summers

Average to rich, well-drained, evenly moist soil

Dense spikes of small, violet, violet-blue, or white flowers on purple stems from summer to fall

Warm-weather annual or tender perennial

P. 387

Salvia greggii

Gregg Sage, Autumn Sage

SIZE: Shrubby, from 1 to 2 feet

Full sun to partial shade; afternoon shade in areas with hot summers

Average to rich, well-drained, evenly moist soil

Bears showy spikes of red, purple, violet, pink, or yellow from late summer to frost

Warm-weather annual or tender perennial

P. 387

Salvia guaranitica

SIZE: Shrubby, to 5 feet

Full sun to partial shade; afternoon shade in areas with hot summers

Average to rich, well-drained, evenly moist soil

Bears deep blue, 2-inch-long flowers with purple-blue calyxes from late summer to fall

Tender perennial or warm-weather annual

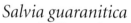

P. 387

Salvia leucantha

Mexican Bush Sage

SIZE: Shrubby, from 2 to 3½ feet

Full sun to partial shade; afternoon shade in areas with hot summers

Average to rich, well-drained, evenly moist soil

Gray-green leaves and dense spikes of white or purple flowers with showy purple calyxes in fall

Tender perennial or warm-weather annual

P. 387

Salvia splendens 'Flare'

Scarlet Sage

SIZE: 1 to 2 feet

Full sun to partial shade; afternoon shade in areas with hot summers

Average to rich, well-drained, evenly moist soil

Bears scarlet as well as mauve-purple, creamy white, and pink flowers with showy bracts from summer to fall

Warm-weather annual or tender perennial

P. 388

Salvia splendens 'Purple Salsa'

Scarlet Sage

SIZE: 1 to 2 feet

Full sun to partial shade; afternoon shade in areas with hot summers

Average to rich, well-drained, evenly moist soil

Bears dense, showy spikes of flowers in scarlet, mauve-purple, creamy white, and pink from summer to fall

Warm-weather annual or tender perennial

P. 388

Salvia uliginosa

Bog Sage

SIZE: Shrubby, from 4 to 6 feet

Full sun to partial shade; afternoon shade in areas with hot summers

Average to rich, well-drained, evenly moist soil

Bears handsome spikes of sky blue flowers from late summer to fall

Tender perennial or warm-weather annual

P. 388

Sanvitalia procumbens

Creeping Zinnia

SIZE: Mat-forming, from 6 to 8 inches tall; spreading to 2½ feet

Full sun

Average to rich, well-drained soil

Bears golden yellow, daisylike flowers with black centers from early summer to fall

Warm-weather annual

P. 389

Satureja hortensis

Summer Savory

SIZE: 10 inches

Full sun

Loose, average to rich, well-drained soil

Fragrant, peppery-tasting leaves and small spikes of white or pink flowers in summer

Cool-weather annual

P. 389

Scabiosa atropurpurea

Sweet Scabious, Pincushion Flower

SIZE: 2 to 3 feet

Full sun

Average, well-drained soil

Bears fragrant flower heads in shades of purple, lavender, white, pink, or purple-blue in summer

Warm-weather annual

P. 390

Scabiosa stellata

Star Flower

SIZE: 1½ feet

Full sun

Average, well-drained soil

Pale bluish white or pink flowers in summer followed by round, ornamental, 3-inch-wide seed heads

Warm-weather annual

P. 390

▲ *Scaevola aemula* 'Blue Wonder'

Fan Flower, Australian Blue Fan Flower, Fairy Fan Flower

SIZE: ½ to 2 feet; spreading from 4 to 5 feet

Full sun or dappled shade

Average, evenly moist, well-drained soil

Bears racemes of lilac- or purple-blue flowers in summer

Tender perennial or warm-weather annual

P. 391

▼ *Schizanthus pinnatus*

Butterfly Flower, Poor-man's Orchid

SIZE: ½ to 1½ feet

Full sun

Rich, evenly moist, well-drained soil; best in areas with cool summers

Tubular flowers with flaring lips in pinks, purples, reds, yellows, or white from spring to fall

Cool-weather annual

P. 392

Senecio cineraria 'Silver Queen'

Dusty Miller

SIZE: 1 to 2 feet

Full sun to very light shade

Average to rich, well-drained soil

A foliage plant grown for its deeply cut, woolly white leaves; bears small, mustard yellow flowers in summer

Cool-weather annual or tender perennial

P. 393

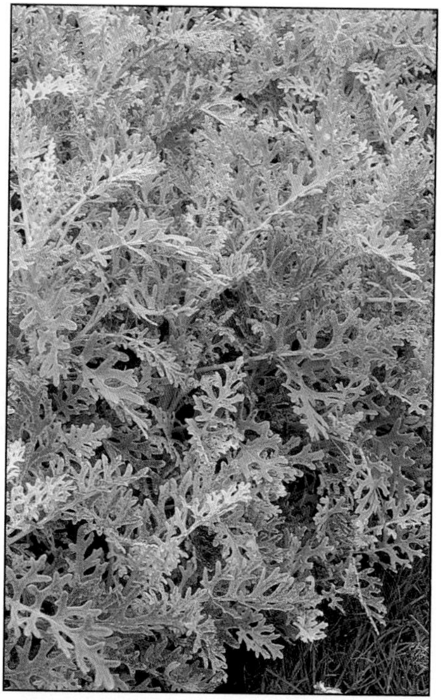

Senecio confusus

Orange Glow Vine

SIZE: Vine, to 20 feet in frost-free climates

Full sun to very light shade

Average to rich, well-drained soil

Produces clusters of fragrant, 2-inch-wide, orange flower heads that fade to red in summer

Tender perennial

P. 393

Setaria italica

Foxtail Millet

SIZE: 3 to 5 feet

Full sun to partial shade

Average to rich, well-drained soil

Ornamental grass with brownish to purplish, cylindrical flower heads in summer

Warm-weather annual

P. 394

Silene armeria

Sweet William Catchfly

SIZE: 1 foot

Full sun or partial shade

Average, well-drained soil

Gray-green leaves and showy clusters of magenta-pink, ½-inch-wide flowers in late summer

Cool-weather annual

P. 394

Silene coeli-rosa

Rose of Heaven

SIZE: 10 to 20 inches

Full sun or partial shade

Average, well-drained soil

Gray-green leaves and clusters of rose-pink flowers with white centers and notched petals in summer

Cool-weather annual

P. 395

Silybum marianum

Mary's Thistle, Our Lady's Thistle, Holy Thistle, Milk Thistle

SIZE: Foliage, from 6 to 8 inches; from 2 to 5 feet in bloom

Full sun

Poor to average, well-drained soil

Bears a handsome rosette of spiny leaves veined and mottled with white and purple-pink flower heads in summer

Cool-weather annual

P. 395

▲ *Solanum jasminoides*

Potato Vine

SIZE: Vine, to 20 feet in warm climates

Full sun

Average to rich, well-drained, evenly moist soil

Bears small clusters of fragrant, bluish white flowers from summer to fall

Tender perennial or warm-weather annual

P. 396

▼ *Solenopsis axillaris*

SIZE: 1 foot

Full sun

Average, well-drained soil

Fernlike leaves and starry, pale to deep lavender-blue flowers from early summer to fall

Tender perennial or warm-weather annual

P. 397

▲ *Solenostemon scutellarioides* 'Belengrath Pink'

Coleus, Flame Nettle, Painted Nettle

SIZE: Shrubby, from 1 to 3 feet

Partial shade to full sun; afternoon shade in areas with hot summers

Rich, well-drained, evenly moist soil

A foliage plant grown for its handsome leaves that come in many colors, shapes, and sizes

Tender perennial or warm-weather annual

P. 398

▼ *Solenostemon scutellarioides* 'Solar Sunrise'

Coleus, Flame Nettle, Painted Nettle

SIZE: Shrubby, from 1 to 3 feet

Partial shade to full sun; afternoon shade in areas with hot summers

Rich, well-drained, evenly moist soil

A foliage plant grown for its handsome leaves that come in many colors, shapes, and sizes

Tender perennial or warm-weather annual

P. 398

Strobilanthes dyeranus

Persian Shield

SIZE: Shrubby, to 4 feet in frost-free climates

Partial shade to full sun

Rich, well-drained, evenly moist soil

A foliage plant with dark green leaves marked with purple and overlaid with a silvery sheen

Tender perennial

P. 399

Tagetes erecta

African Marigold, American Marigold

SIZE: Compact cultivars, to 1½ feet tall; standard types, to 3 feet

Full sun; afternoon shade in areas with hot summers

Average, well-drained soil

Bears showy, carnation-like, double flowers in shades of yellow, gold, and orange from late spring to fall

Warm-weather annual

P. 400

Tagetes patula 'Tiger Eyes'

French Marigold

SIZE: 6 to 12 inches

Full sun; afternoon shade in areas with hot summers

Average, well-drained soil

Showy, single, semidouble, or crested flowers in yellows, oranges, or red-browns from late spring to fall

Warm-weather annual

P. 401

Tagetes tenuifolia Signet Group 'Lemon Gem'

Signet Marigold

SIZE: Mounding, from 9 to 12 inches

Full sun; afternoon shade in areas with hot summers

Average, well-drained soil

Bears dainty, single flowers in gold, lemon yellow, or orange from late spring to fall

Warm-weather annual

P. 401

▲ *Thunbergia alata*

Black-eyed Susan Vine

SIZE: Vine, to 8 feet

Full sun; partial afternoon shade in areas with hot summers

Rich, evenly moist, well-drained soil

Bears orange, orange-yellow, yellow, or creamy white flowers, usually with dark centers, from summer to fall

Tender perennial or warm-weather annual

P. 402

▼ *Thymophylla tenuiloba*

Dahlberg Daisy, Golden Fleece

SIZE: Mounding, from 6 to 12 inches

Full sun

Average, well-drained soil

Feathery leaves and starry, yellow, daisylike flowers from spring to summer

Cool-weather annual

P. 403

Tibouchina urvilleana

Glory Bush, Brazilian Spider Flower

SIZE: Shrubby, from 10 to 20 feet in frost-free regions; smaller in the North

Full sun or dappled shade

Rich, evenly moist soil

Bears satiny-textured, 2-inch-wide, violet-purple flowers from summer to fall

Tender perennial or warm-weather annual

P. 403

Tithonia rotundifolia

Mexican Sunflower

SIZE: 3 to 6 feet

Full sun

Poor to average, well-drained soil

Bears 3- to 4-inch-wide daisies in orange or orange-red from late summer to frost

Warm-weather annual

P. 404

▲ *Torenia fournieri* 'Summer Wave'

Wishbone Flower

SIZE: 8 inches to 1 foot

Partial shade

Rich, well-drained, evenly moist soil

Bears yellow-throated flowers in purple, violet, and white in summer

Warm-weather annual

P. 405

▼ *Trachelium caeruleum*

Blue Throatwort

SIZE: 3 to 4 feet

Full sun to partial shade; shade during the hottest part of the day is best

Average, very well drained, evenly moist soil

Bears dense, flattened clusters of starry, violet-blue, white, or lavender-mauve flowers in summer

Warm-weather annual or biennial

P. 406

Trachymene coerulea

Blue Lace Flower

SIZE: 2 feet

Full sun

Average, well-drained soil

Lacy, 2-inch-wide umbels of lightly fragrant, lavender-blue flowers in summer

Warm-weather annual or biennial

P. 406

Tradescantia pallida 'Purpurea'

Purple Heart

SIZE: 8 inches tall; trailing to several feet

Partial shade to full sun

Rich, moist soil

A foliage plant with rich violet-purple stems and leaves and clusters of small pink flowers in summer

Tender perennial

P. 407

▲ *Tropaeolum majus*
Alaska Series

Common Nasturtium, Indian Cress

SIZE: Bushy types, 1 to 12 inches; standard types, trailing or climbing from 2 to 8 feet

Full sun

Poor, well-drained soil; best in areas with relatively cool summers

Variegated leaves topped by flowers in reds, oranges, or yellows from summer to fall

Warm-weather annual

P. 409

▼ *Tropaeolum majus*
'Empress of India'

Common Nasturtium, Indian Cress

SIZE: Bushy types, 1 to 12 inches; standard types, trailing or climbing from 2 to 8 feet

Full sun

Poor, well-drained soil; best in areas with relatively cool summers

Rounded leaves and long-spurred flowers in reds, oranges, or yellows from summer to fall

Warm-weather annual

P. 409

Tropaeolum peregrinum

Canary Vine, Canary Creeper

SIZE: Climbing to 12 feet

Full sun

Well-drained, evenly moist soil of average fertility; best in areas with relatively cool summers

Lobed, gray-green leaves and yellow flowers with fringed petals from summer to fall

Tender perennial or warm-weather annual

P. 409

Tropaeolum polyphyllum

SIZE: 2 to 3 feet tall; trailing to 3 feet

Full sun

Well-drained, evenly moist soil of average fertility; best in areas with relatively cool summers

Deeply lobed, blue-green leaves and spurred yellow flowers over a long season in summer

Warm-weather annual or tender perennial

P. 409

Tropaeolum speciosum

Flame Flower, Flame Nasturtium

SIZE: Climbing, to 10 feet

Full sun; also grows in partial shade

Rich, well-drained, evenly moist soil; best in areas with relatively cool summers

Dark green leaves and brilliant scarlet flowers from summer to fall

Warm-weather annual or tender perennial

P. 410

Tulbaghia violacea

Society Garlic, Pink Agapanthus

SIZE: 1½ to 2 feet

Select a site in full sun and average to rich, well-drained soil

Gray-green leaves and small umbels of fragrant lilac flowers from midsummer to fall

Tender perennial

P. 410

▲ *Tweedia caerulea*

SIZE: Shrubby, from 2 to 3½ feet

Full sun

Average to rich, evenly moist, well-drained soil

Bears clusters of pinkish buds that open to sky blue flowers from summer to early fall

Warm-weather annual or tender perennial

P. 411

▼ *Ursinia anthemoides*

SIZE: 1 to 1½ feet

Full sun

Poor to average, light, very well drained soil; best in areas with cool summers or for spring bloom only

Aromatic, deeply cut leaves and showy yellow-orange daisies with purple centers in summer

Warm-weather annual

P. 412

Verbascum bombyciferum 'Arctic Summer'

Turkish Mullein

SIZE: 5 to 8 feet

Full sun

Poor to average, well-drained soil

Woolly white leaves and erect spikes of saucer-shaped, yellow flowers in summer

Biennial or short-lived perennial

P. 413

Verbena bonariensis

SIZE: Shrubby, from 3 to 6 feet

Full sun; dappled shade in areas with hot summers

Average, well-drained, evenly moist soil

Erect, branching stems with clusters of small purple flowers from midsummer to fall

Tender perennial or warm-weather annual

P. 414

Verbena × hybrida

Common Garden Verbena

SIZE: To 1½ feet; may be bushy or spreading

Full sun; dappled shade in areas with hot summers

Average, well-drained, evenly moist soil

Bears clusters of small flowers in purples, reds, and whit,e most with a white eye from summer to fall

Tender perennial or warm-weather annual

P. 414

Verbena rigida

Vervain

SIZE: 1½ to 2 feet

Full sun; dappled shade in areas with hot summers

Average, well-drained, evenly moist soil

Bears loose clusters of fragrant, purple or magenta flowers in summer

Tender perennial or warm-weather annual

P. 415

▲ *Verbena tenuisecta*

Moss Verbena, Cut-leaf Verbena

SIZE: ½ to 1½ feet

Full sun; dappled shade in areas with hot summers

Average, well-drained, evenly moist soil

Aromatic leaves topped by clusters of flowers in purple, mauve, and white from summer to fall

Warm-weather annual or tender perennial

P. 415

◂ *Vinca major* 'Variegata'

Greater Periwinkle

SIZE: 1½ feet; spreading indefinitely in frost-free areas

Full sun or partial shade

Any soil

Handsome variegated leaves and purple-blue flowers from spring to fall

Tender perennial or warm-weather annual

P. 416

▲ *Viola tricolor*

Johnny-jump-up, Hearts-ease

SIZE: 3 to 5 inches

Full sun or partial shade; afternoon shade is best in areas with hot summers

Rich, moist, well-drained soil

Bears dainty flowers marked with violet, purple, white, or yellow in a facelike pattern from early spring to fall

Cool-weather annual, biennial, or short-lived perennial

P. 417

▼ *Viola × wittrockiana*

Pansy

SIZE: 6 to 9 inches

Full sun or partial shade; afternoon shade is best in areas with hot summers

Rich, moist, well-drained soil

Bears showy, 2½- to 4-inch-wide flowers in many patterns and colors from early spring to summer

Cool-weather annual or biennial

P. 417

Viola × wittrockiana 'Melody Purple and White'

Pansy

SIZE: 6 to 9 inches

Full sun or partial shade; afternoon shade is best in areas with hot summers

Rich, moist, well-drained soil

Bears showy, 2½- to 4-inch-wide flowers in many patterns and colors from early spring to summer

Cool-weather annual or biennial

P. 417

Xeranthemum annuum

Immortelle

SIZE: 1 to 3 feet

Full sun

Poor to average, well-drained soil

Silvery leaves and single or double flower heads in shades of bright pink, purple, or white from summer to fall

Warm-weather annual

P. 418

Zea mays 'Variegata'

Variegated Corn

SIZE: 4 to 12 feet

Full sun

Rich, well-drained, evenly moist soil

A foliage plant with leaves striped in cream and white

Warm-weather annual

P. 419

Zinnia elegans 'Peppermint Stick'

Common Zinnia

SIZE: 2 feet

Single or double, 1½- to 5-inch-wide flowers from early summer to fall in many sizes and colors

Full sun

Average to rich, well-drained soil

Warm-weather annual

P. 419

Zinnia elegans 'Peter Pan Orange'

Common Zinnia

SIZE: ½ to 4 feet

Full sun

Average to rich, well-drained soil

Single or double, 1½- to 5-inch-wide flowers in many sizes and colors from early summer to fall

Warm-weather annual

P. 419

Zinnia haageana 'Chippendale'

Narrow-leaved Zinnia, Mexican Zinnia

SIZE: 1 to 2 feet

Full sun

Average to rich, well-drained soil

Disease-resistant plants with showy, daisylike flowers in golds, oranges, white, pinks, and orange-red in summer

Warm-weather annual

P. 420

▲ *Zinnia haageana* 'Gold Star'

Narrow-leaved Zinnia, Mexican Zinnia

SIZE: 1 to 2 feet

Full sun

Average to rich, well-drained soil

Disease-resistant plants with showy, daisylike flowers in golds, oranges, white, pinks, and orange-red in summer

Warm-weather annual

P. 420

▼ *Zinnia peruviana*

SIZE: 2 to 3 feet

Full sun

Average to rich, well-drained soil

Mildew-resistant leaves and daisylike flowers with dark centers and red or yellow petals in summer

Warm-weather annual

P. 420

Encyclopedia of Plants

Encyclopedia of Plants

Abelmoschus

ah-bel-MOS-kus. Mallow family, Malvaceae.

The members of this genus of 15 or so heat-loving annuals or tender perennials hail from the tropics of Asia. They bear five-petaled, hibiscus-like blooms singly in leaf axils or in racemelike clusters. *(Abelmoschus* species were all once classified in *Hibiscus.)* Two species of tender perennials, hardy to Zone 9, are commonly grown as annuals. Both have handsome, dark green, palmately lobed leaves that lend a tropical air to beds and borders and produce an abundance of flowers, each of which lasts only a day, from late summer to frost. Okra *(A. esculentus),* cultivated for its young seedpods, also is a well-known member of the genus.

HOW TO GROW

Full sun, warm temperatures, and rich, well-drained soil are ideal. Sow seeds indoors in individual peat pots 8 to 10 weeks before the last spring frost date, and germinate at 50° to 55°F. Transplant after the weather has settled in spring (indoor sowing is especially helpful north of Zone 6 and in any area where spring is cool and rainy). Seedlings resent transplanting, so handle them carefully. Or in areas with long growing seasons, sow outdoors after the last frost date. Plants take about 3 months to bloom from seeds. Feed with a balanced fertilizer in midsummer. Both species self-sow in mild climates.

A. manihot P. 32

a. MAN-ih-hot. Sunset Hibiscus. A shrubby plant reaching 5 to 6 feet in height by summer's end. Lush, 1- to 1½-foot-long leaves. Pale lemon yellow, 5- to 6-inch-wide flowers with burgundy centers. Tender perennial.

A. moschatus

P. 32

a. moe-SHAW-tus. Musk Mallow. Compact, bushy plants that stay between 1½ and 2 feet in northern gardens but reach 4 feet or more in warm climates. Leaves ranging from 2 to 3 inches to as much as a foot in length. Showy, 3-inch-wide flowers with white centers come in shades of pink, orange-red, and scarlet. Tender perennial.

Abutilon

ah-BEW-tih-lon. Mallow family, Malvaceae.

Closely related to hollyhocks and hibiscus, *Abutilon* contains about 150 species of tender shrubs, small trees, perennials, and annuals. These tropical natives, most hardy from Zone 8 or 9 south, are grown for their colorful, pendulous, bell- or cup-shaped flowers. The solitary 2- to 3-inch-long flowers appear continuously from spring to fall and have five petals, a calyx that in some forms is also colorful, and a hibiscus-like column of fertile parts at the center. The leaves are simple or lobed and maplelike—thus the common name flowering maple. Many hybrids and cultivars are available.

HOW TO GROW

Give abutilons full sun or partial shade and rich, well-drained soil. Where hardy, grow them outdoors as shrubs; in areas where they are marginally hardy, try a site against a south-facing wall for extra winter protection. In the North, grow them in containers and overwinter them indoors in a bright, cool (40° to 45°F) spot, or use as bedding plants replaced annually. Grow forms with pendulous or vinelike stems in baskets or train them to trellises. Upright types make handsome standards. Water deeply during dry weather and feed pot-grown plants a few times during the summer with a balanced fertilizer. Prune to shape plants in late winter or early spring: cut them back hard, if necessary. Pinch to encourage bushy growth. Since young plants bloom best—the older ones become woody—consider growing new ones from cuttings taken annually or every other year. Take cuttings in spring to propagate for garden use or in late summer to overwinter the plants. Sow seed in spring at about 60°F; use cuttings for hybrids and cultivars, which do not come true from seeds.

A. × *hybridum*

P. 33

a. × HI-brih-dum. Flowering Maple. A shrubby plant reaching 15 feet in height. Pendent, bell- to cup-shaped flowers in yellow, orange, red, or white. Ovate to lobed, maplelike leaves may be variegated. Cultivars include 'Souvenir de Bonn', with soft orange flowers and white-edged leaves; 'Moonchimes', with yellow flowers; and 'Huntington Pink', with rich pink blooms. Tender perennial.

A. megapotamicum P. 33

a. meg-ah-poe-TAM-ih-cum. Trailing Abutilon. A shrubby species with trailing or arching shoots reaching 6 feet in height and spread. Bright green, ovate leaves. Pendent flowers with red heart-shaped calyxes and yellow petals. 'Variegatum' has yellow-mottled leaves. Tender perennial.

A. pictum P. 34

a. PICK-tum. An erect to spreading shrubby species reaching 15 feet in height. Ovate to maplelike leaves. Yellow to orange flowers with red veins. 'Thompsoni' has pale orange flowers and yellow-mottled leaves. Tender perennial.

Acalypha

ack-ah-LIF-ah. Spurge family, Euphorbiaceae.

This genus contains about 450 species of tender shrubs with oval to ovate leaves and tiny, densely packed petalless flowers in fuzzy, pendent, catkinlike clusters. Flower clusters are either showy—somewhat resembling colorful pipe cleaners—or insignificant. Two species are grown as annuals or tender perennials for the tropical air they add to the summer garden.

HOW TO GROW

Give these tropicals heat, humidity, and full sun or partial shade, along with average to fertile, well-drained soil. Grow them as bedding plants mixed with other annuals or in containers. Coarse, well-drained soil is best for container culture. Water regularly during the season and feed at least monthly with a balanced fertilizer. Pinch stem tips to encourage branching and shapely, compact growth. Keep plants vigorous by taking cuttings every 2 to 4 years (they are not commonly grown from seeds), either in early spring or in late summer. Overwinter plants indoors in a fairly warm spot (a minimum of 55° to 60°F at night and up to 10 degrees warmer during the day) in containers or as late-summer cuttings. Prune hard, as necessary, in late winter or early spring.

A. hispida P. 34

a. HISS-pih-dah. Chenille Plant, Red-hot-cat's Tail. Shrubby plants reaching 6 feet or more with rich green, oval leaves. Showy, crimson to maroon-red, 1-inch-wide flower clusters from 10 to 20 inches long. Semi-trailing forms of this species are available, and these make handsome additions to hanging baskets. Tender perennial.

A. wilkesiana P. 35

a. will-kes-ee-AN-ah. Copperleaf, Joseph's Coat. A shrubby plant reaching 6 feet with variegated oval leaves variously marked with bronze, copper, red, white, and green. The 4- to 8-inch-long flower clusters are green or coppery and relatively insignificant. Tender perennial.

Agapanthus

ag-ah-PAN-thuss. Lily family, Liliaceae.

Although commonly called lilies-of-the-Nile, the 10 species of *Agapanthus* hail from southern Africa, not along the Nile. They are tender perennials, some evergreen, that produce thick, fleshy roots and bold clumps of strap-shaped leaves. Striking rounded umbels of trumpet-shaped, blue, blue-violet, or white flowers appear on erect stalks above the foliage in summer. The flowers are ideal for cutting and also attract hummingbirds.

HOW TO GROW

Agapanthus species are hardy perennials from at least Zone 9 south; some hybrids, especially deciduous ones, are hardy to Zone 6 with protection. Give them full sun and fertile, well-drained, evenly moist soil. Where they are not hardy, grow these striking plants in large containers or tubs either

Agapanthus hybrid

set on terraces or sunk to the rim in the soil. Or plant clumps in the ground and dig them each fall for overwintering. They bloom best when the roots are slightly crowded. Feed pot-grown plants monthly in early summer until flower buds appear. Water regularly when plants are growing and flowering actively, but gradually withhold water in fall and keep them nearly dry over winter. Overwinter them in a bright, cool (40° to 50°F) spot, and water sparingly until active growth resumes in spring. Propagate by dividing the clumps, removing offsets, or sowing seeds (germinate at 55° to 60°F). Seeds take 1 to 3 months to germinate and 2 to 3 years to grow into blooming-size plants. Repot or divide in late winter or early spring as necessary.

A. Hybrids P. 35

Species and hybrids ranging from 1 to 4 feet in height are available. 'Peter Pan' is a heavy-blooming dwarf cultivar that reaches 18 inches. 'Bressingham White' bears white flowers. 'Headbourne Hybrids' have pale blue to violet flowers and are reportedly hardy to Zone 6. Tender perennial.

Agastache

ag-ah-STACK-ee. Mint family, Lamiaceae.

Square stems, ovate aromatic leaves, and erect clusters of small, two-lipped flowers characterize the 20 or so species of giant hyssops, also called Mexican hyssops. All are perennials; a few are hardy and suitable for perennial plantings in Zones 4 and 5. Several species are hardy from Zone 7 south (to 6 with protection). All can be grown as annuals.

HOW TO GROW

Give giant hyssops full sun or very light shade and rich, well-drained soil for best results. Grow them in the ground where they are hardy, but container culture is a good option in areas where they are not. They are easy to grow from seeds sown indoors 8 to 10 weeks before the last spring frost date. Germination takes 2 to 4 weeks at 55° to 60°F. For quicker results, and to propagate many of the cultivars, take cuttings or divide plants in spring. To overwinter the plants indoors, take cuttings in late summer.

A. barberi P. 36

a. BAR-ber-eye. Bushy 2-foot plants with fragrant, oval leaves. Loose spikes of red-purple flowers from midsummer to fall. 'Tutti-Frutti', with raspberry red flowers, is a popular cultivar. Hardy from Zone 6 south, or grow as tender perennial or annual.

A. foeniculum P. 36

a. foe-NICK-you-lum. Anise Hyssop. Anise-scented, 3- to 5-foot plants. Spikes of blue flowers with violet bracts from midsummer to fall. Self-sows. Hardy from Zone 6 south, or grow as tender perennial or annual.

A. mexicana P. 37

a. mex-ih-CAN-ah. Mexican Giant Hyssop. Lemon-scented foliage on 2- to 3-foot plants. Spikes of rose-red flowers in mid- to late summer. Hardy from Zone 7 south, or grow as tender perennial or annual.

Ageratum

ah-jer-AY-tum. Aster family, Asteraceae.

One member of this group of 40 annuals, perennials, and shrubs from the warmer reaches of North and South America is a popular bedding plant. All bear rounded clusters of small, fluffy, buttonlike flowers.

HOW TO GROW

Ageratums thrive in full sun or light shade and rich, moist, well-drained soil. In areas with long, hot summers, partial shade is best. Sow seeds indoors 6 to 8 weeks before the last spring frost date. Seeds can be sown outdoors after frost once the soil is warm, but the seedlings are easily swamped by weeds. When sowing, just press the tiny seeds into the soil surface, as they need light to germinate. Germination takes about 2 weeks at 70° to 75°F. In areas with mild winters (Zone 9 south), plant in late summer for fall to early winter bloom. Water during dry weather. Use ageratums as edging plants, in mixed plantings, and as cut flowers. The flowers attract butterflies.

A. houstonianum P. 37

a. hous-tone-ee-AN-um. Ageratum, Floss Flower. Compact, mound-forming annual with oval leaves that have heart-shaped bases. Lavender-blue, lilac, white, or pink flowers. Many cultivars are available. Dwarf types, from 6 to 8 inches tall, are ideal for edging, including lavender 'Blue Danube' and the Swing and Hawaii Series plants, which come in laven-

white. Ovate to lobed, maplelike leaves may be variegated. Cultivars include 'Souvenir de Bonn', with soft orange flowers and white-edged leaves; 'Moonchimes', with yellow flowers; and 'Huntington Pink', with rich pink blooms. Tender perennial.

A. megapotamicum P. 33

a. meg-ah-poe-TAM-ih-cum. Trailing Abutilon. A shrubby species with trailing or arching shoots reaching 6 feet in height and spread. Bright green, ovate leaves. Pendent flowers with red heart-shaped calyxes and yellow petals. 'Variegatum' has yellow-mottled leaves. Tender perennial.

A. pictum P. 34

a. PICK-tum. An erect to spreading shrubby species reaching 15 feet in height. Ovate to maplelike leaves. Yellow to orange flowers with red veins. 'Thompsoni' has pale orange flowers and yellow-mottled leaves. Tender perennial.

Acalypha

ack-ah-LIF-ah. Spurge family, Euphorbiaceae.

This genus contains about 450 species of tender shrubs with oval to ovate leaves and tiny, densely packed petalless flowers in fuzzy, pendent, catkinlike clusters. Flower clusters are either showy—somewhat resembling colorful pipe cleaners—or insignificant. Two species are grown as annuals or tender perennials for the tropical air they add to the summer garden.

HOW TO GROW

Give these tropicals heat, humidity, and full sun or partial shade, along with average to fertile, well-drained soil. Grow them as bedding plants mixed with other annuals or in containers. Coarse, well-drained soil is best for container culture. Water regularly during the season and feed at least monthly with a balanced fertilizer. Pinch stem tips to encourage branching and shapely, compact growth. Keep plants vigorous by taking cuttings every 2 to 4 years (they are not commonly grown from seeds), either in early spring or in late summer. Overwinter plants indoors in a fairly warm spot (a minimum of 55° to 60°F at night and up to 10 degrees warmer during the day) in containers or as late-summer cuttings. Prune hard, as necessary, in late winter or early spring.

A. hispida P. 34

a. HISS-pih-dah. Chenille Plant, Red-hot-cat's Tail. Shrubby plants reaching 6 feet or more with rich green, oval leaves. Showy, crimson to maroon-red, 1-inch-wide flower clusters from 10 to 20 inches long. Semi-trailing forms of this species are available, and these make handsome additions to hanging baskets. Tender perennial.

A. wilkesiana P. 35

a. will-kes-ee-AN-ah. Copperleaf, Joseph's Coat. A shrubby plant reaching 6 feet with variegated oval leaves variously marked with bronze, copper, red, white, and green. The 4- to 8-inch-long flower clusters are green or coppery and relatively insignificant. Tender perennial.

Agapanthus

ag-ah-PAN-thuss. Lily family, Liliaceae.

Although commonly called lilies-of-the-Nile, the 10 species of *Agapanthus* hail from southern Africa, not along the Nile. They are tender perennials, some evergreen, that produce thick, fleshy roots and bold clumps of strap-shaped leaves. Striking rounded umbels of trumpet-shaped, blue, blue-violet, or white flowers appear on erect stalks above the foliage in summer. The flowers are ideal for cutting and also attract hummingbirds.

HOW TO GROW

Agapanthus species are hardy perennials from at least Zone 9 south; some hybrids, especially deciduous ones, are hardy to Zone 6 with protection. Give them full sun and fertile, well-drained, evenly moist soil. Where they are not hardy, grow these striking plants in large containers or tubs either

Agapanthus hybrid

der, pink, or white. 'Blue Horizon', to 18 inches, is a good cut flower and, along with midsize cultivars such as 'Blue Mink', to 12 inches, also well suited for mixed plantings. Warm-weather annual.

Agrostemma

ah-gro-STEM-mah. Pink family, Caryophyllaceae.

Agrostemma contains two to four species of annuals native to poor, dry soil. They have linear to lance-shaped leaves covered with white hairs and solitary, trumpet-shaped, five-petaled flowers. One species is commonly grown.

HOW TO GROW

Select a site in full sun and poor to average, well-drained soil. Sow seeds in early spring while light frost is still possible, several weeks before the last spring frost date, or in late summer or fall in drifts outdoors where the plants are to grow. Germination takes 2 to 3 weeks. Space closely—at 3 to 4 inches—to help plants support one another, or use pea stakes to keep them erect. Another option is interplanting with shrubs, sturdier annuals, or perennials. Deadheading prolongs bloom. Plants self-sow.

A. githago P. 38

a. geh-THA-go. Corn Cockle. Gray-green leaves on 2- to 3-foot plants. Showy, 2-inch-wide, magenta to cerise-pink flowers. 'Milas', also sold as 'Rose Queen', is most common. This species has poisonous seeds and is an agricultural weed in some areas. The blooms are attractive to bees and make fine cut flowers. Cool-weather annual.

Alcea

AL-see-ah. Mallow family, Malvaceae.

While there are about 60 species of biennials and short-lived perennials in *Alcea* (formerly *Althaea*), only a handful have found their way to gardens. Common hollyhock *(A. rosea)*, by far the most popular, is grown for its showy, erect bloom stalks covered with colorful, funnel-shaped flowers that rise above mounds of large, lobed leaves. The flowers attract both butterflies and hummingbirds.

HOW TO GROW

Full sun to light shade and average, well-drained soil suit most *Alcea* species. A site protected from wind is best to help minimize the need to stake. For the showiest display, as well as to minimize problems with the common fungal disease rust, grow these plants as biennials. Some cultivars can be grown as annuals, provided they are started indoors in late winter, 6 to 8 weeks before the last spring frost. To grow them as biennials or perennials, sow indoors or out. Indoors, sow in individual pots 6 to 8 weeks before plants are scheduled to go into the garden, which means midsummer sowing for plants that are to be moved to the garden in early fall; winter sowing to produce seedlings for spring planting. Outdoors, sow seeds in spring or summer up to 2 months before the first fall frost. Whatever method you choose, barely cover the seeds, as light aids germination, which takes about 2 weeks at 60° to 70°F. Once established, hollyhocks survive dry conditions quite well, but for top-notch performance, water deeply in dry weather. Plants growing in rich soil may need staking. To grow hollyhocks as biennials, pull up 2-year-old plants after they have flowered and replace them. Plants self-sow.

A. rosea PP. 38, 39

a. ROSE-ee-ah. Common Hollyhock. Erect stems of single or double, 2- to 4-inch-wide blooms in yellow, white, pink, and red. Most plants grow 4 to 5 feet tall or taller, but there are dwarf cultivars, such as 2- to 3-foot 'Majorette'. 'Powder Puffs' and 'Chatter's Double' are popular double-flowered forms. 'Nigra' has maroon-black blooms. Single hollyhocks such as 'Country Romance' are ideal for cottage gardens. Short-lived perennial grown as a biennial.

Alternanthera

all-ter-NAN-ther-ah. Amaranth family, Amaranthaceae.

Grown for their brightly colored leaves rather than their flowers, alternantheras are commonly known as Joseph's coat or copperleaf. The genus contains about 200 species of tender annuals and perennials native to the Central and South American tropics. They bear spikes of insignificant, petalless flowers and linear to rounded leaves.

HOW TO GROW

Give these plants moist, well-drained soil and partial shade to full sun; a site in full sun yields the best leaf color. Sow seeds indoors 8 to 10 weeks before the last spring frost date and germinate at 55° to 60°F. Seedlings exhibit variable leaf color, so select the best colors and discard the rest. Alternantheras are most often propagated by division or cuttings, and both of these techniques yield uniform-looking plants identical to their parents. Select the most brightly colored or best-looking plants and take cuttings or divide plants in spring; to overwinter plants indoors, take cuttings in late summer. Use Joseph's coat or copperleaf as edging plants or to add color to the front of beds and borders; they are traditionally used in carpet bedding displays and knot gardens. To keep plants uniform and neat looking, clip or shear them regularly. In frost-free regions, use year-round as bedding plants, edgings, or ground covers.

A. dentata

a. den-TAY-tah. Narrow, dark green, 3½-inch-long leaves on bushy, 1- to 1½-foot-tall plants. 'Rubiginosa' bears glossy, red to purple foliage. Tender perennial.

A. ficoidea

P. 39

a. fie-COY-dee-ah. Joseph's Coat, Parrot Leaf. This variable species bears lance- to spoon-shaped leaves in a variety of sizes and colors. Dwarf selection *A. ficoidea* var. *amoena* ranges from 4 to 8 inches tall with narrow to rounded leaves variously marked with blotches or veining in green, brown-purple, red, and orange. 'Versicolor', which reaches 1 foot, has spoon-shaped leaves marked with coppery brown, red, and maroon. Tender perennial.

Alyssum maritimum *see Lobularia maritima*

Amaranthus

am-ah-RAN-thus. Amaranth family, Amaranthaceae.

Amaranthus is a cosmopolitan genus containing 60 species of annuals or short-lived perennials found in wastelands and tilled fields in mild and tropical regions around the globe. While many species are weedy—pigweed *(A. retroflexus)* belongs here—several bring brilliant foliage and/or exotic-looking flower clusters to the garden. They bear alternate leaves and erect or pendent clusters of tiny, densely packed, petalless flowers followed by small, bladderlike fruits.

HOW TO GROW

Plant amaranths in full sun to partial shade and evenly moist, average soil. Foliage types produce larger but less brilliantly colored leaves in rich soil. Sow seeds indoors 6 to 8 weeks before the last frost. Germination takes about a week at 70° to 75°F. Wait until after the last spring frost date, once the weather has settled and the soil has warmed up, to transplant. Outdoor sowing delays bloom but is practical in areas with long growing seasons—roughly from Zone 6 south: sow seeds outdoors after the last frost where plants are to grow. Water during dry weather to prolong flowering. Amaranths lend an exotic, tropical air to beds and borders. The flowers and foliage are effective from midsummer to frost. Plants self-sow.

A. caudatus P. 40

a. caw-DAY-tus. Love-lies-bleeding, Tassel Flower. Pale green, ovate leaves on bushy, 3- to 5-foot plants. Showy, pendulous, rope- or tassel-like clusters of flowers at the tips of the stems and in the leaf axils. Some cultivars have red or reddish purple leaves. The seeds are edible, and this species is grown as a grain in portions of South America. The foliage also is edible and is used medicinally in some cultures. 'Love-Lies-Bleeding' bears blood red flower clusters up to 2 feet in length. 'Viridis' and 'Green Tails' bear yellow-green flowers. *A. cruentus*, commonly called prince's feather or purple amaranth, is a somewhat similar species with purplish green leaves and cylindrical flower clusters that are green blushed with red at first and ripen to red-brown, purple, or sometimes yellow. Warm-weather annual.

A. hypochondriacus P. 40

a. hi-poe-kon-dree-AY-kus. Prince's Feather. Formerly *A. hybridus* ssp. *hypochondriacus*. Bushy, 3- to 4-foot plants with oblong- to lance-shaped, purple-green leaves. Erect, plumelike flower clusters reaching 6 inches or more in length. 'Pygmy Torch' is a 1- to 1½-foot cultivar with maroon flowers. Warm-weather annual.

A. tricolor P. 41

a. TRI-kull-er. Joseph's Coat. Showy, ovate leaves in shades of green, purple, flaming scarlet, and rich maroon on 1½- to 4½-foot plants. Also called Chinese spinach because the young leaves are edible fresh or cooked. Depending on the cultivar, the leaves also may be marked with rose-pink, gold, yellow, or brown. Insignificant flowers. Cultivars include 'Flaming Fountains' with narrow scarlet and bronze leaves; 'Illumination' with bronze lower leaves and flaming red upper ones; and 'Aurora Yellow' with a topknot of yellow leaves. Warm-weather annual.

Amberboa

am-ber-bo-ah. Aster family, Asteraceae.

This genus of six species of annuals or biennials from the Mediterranean and central and western Asia contains one commonly grown annual, a beloved cottage garden plant and cut flower. All *Amberboa* species bear solitary flower heads with thistlelike centers surrounded by a fringe of showy petals, more properly called ray florets.

HOW TO GROW

A site in full sun with average, well-drained soil suits any of these species, which grow naturally in sandy or gravelly soils. Sow seeds indoors 6 to 8 weeks before the last frost and germinate at temperatures between 55° and 60°F. Or sow outdoors just before the last frost while temperatures are still cool. For continuous bloom, make successive sowings every few weeks throughout the summer. Support plants with pea stakes, and deadhead to prolong bloom. Plants self-sow.

A. moschata P. 41

a. moe-SHAH-tah. Sweet Sultan. Formerly *Centaurea moschata.* Two-foot plants with gray-green, entire leaves at the base of the plant and deeply cut ones higher up the stem. Fragrant, 2-inch-wide flowers in white, yellow, pink, and purple. Cool-weather annual.

Ammi

AM-me. Carrot family, Apiaceae.

The lacy, rounded flower heads and deeply cut, fernlike leaves of the 10 or so species of annuals and biennials in this genus are reminiscent of their close relative Queen-Anne's-lace *(Daucus carota).* Two species grown as annuals make fine cut flowers and additions to beds and borders.

HOW TO GROW

Plant in full sun or partial shade in average to rich, well-drained soil that is evenly moist. Sow seeds outdoors in early spring before the last spring frost date or in fall. Indoors, sow 6 to 8 weeks before the last frost date and transplant after the last frost. Support plants with pea stakes when they are about 4 inches tall.

A. majus **P. 42**

a. MAY-jus. Lace Flower, Bishop's Flower, White Dill. Rounded, 6-inch-wide umbels of tiny white flowers borne in summer atop 3-foot plants. Cool-weather annual.

A. visnaga **P. 42**

a. vis-NAY-gah. Similar to *A. majus* but with handsome chartreuse flowers. Cool-weather annual.

Ammobium

am-MOE-be-um. Aster family, Asteraceae.

The botanical name of this genus of Australian perennials says much about its cultivation: it is derived from the Greek words for "sand," *ammos*, and "to live," *bios*. The two or three species feature woolly white, lance-shaped leaves and branched stems with thin, flattened wings. All bear papery flowers, and one species in particular is grown for its daisylike blooms, which are excellent for drying.

HOW TO GROW

A site in full sun with light, well-drained, average soil is ideal. Plants also thrive in dry conditions and soil low in nutrients. Sow seeds indoors 6 to 8 weeks before the last spring frost date. Press the seeds into the surface of a sterile germinating mix amended with half clean, washed sand. Germination takes about a week at 55° to 60°F. Or sow outdoors several weeks before the last frost or in fall for bloom the following spring. Although plants are perennials, they are not commonly overwintered, since they are easy and fast from seeds. To dry the blooms, harvest just before they are fully open and hang in small bunches in a warm, dry place; stems may rot if tied in large bunches. Plants self-sow.

A. alatum **P. 43**

a. ah-LAY-tum. Pearly or Winged Everlasting. Woolly white leaves on 1½- to 3-foot plants with branched, winged stems. Daisylike, 1-inch-wide flower heads with orange or yellow centers surrounding papery white bracts. Tender perennial grown as a cool-weather annual.

Anagallis

an-ah-GAL-liss. Primrose family, Primulaceae.

Commonly called pimpernels, *Anagallis* species are annuals, biennials, and perennials native to the Mediterranean and western Europe. Two of the 20 species in the genus are grown as annuals for their dainty blooms. The plants are low-growing and have saucer- to shallowly bell-shaped flowers with five lobes, or "petals."

HOW TO GROW

A site with full sun and average, light to sandy, well-drained soil is ideal. Sow seeds outdoors after the last spring frost date. Or sow seeds indoors in individual pots 6 to 8 weeks before the last frost date and germinate at 60° to 65°F. Germination takes about 3 weeks. Transplant with care. Perennial species can be propagated by cuttings taken in spring or early summer. Use pimpernels as edging plants in beds and borders. They also make attractive indoor container plants in winter and spring.

A. arvensis

a. are-VEN-sis. Scarlet Pimpernel. A weedy species with ovate leaves and trailing stems that reaches about 6 inches in height. The orange-red, ½- to ¾-inch flowers close in cloudy or cool weather, thus the common name poor man's weatherglass. *A. arvensis* var. *caerulea* bears blue flowers. Cool-weather annual.

A. monellii

P. 43

a. mon-ELL-lee-eye. Blue Pimpernel. Ovate to lance-shaped leaves on 1- to 1½-foot plants. Deep blue, ½-inch-wide flowers. Flax-leaved pimpernel (*A. monellii* ssp. *linifolia*) has narrow, lance-shaped leaves. A tender perennial (hardy to Zone 7) grown as a warm-weather annual.

Anchusa

an-KOO-sah. Bugloss family, Boraginaceae.

Commonly grown for their rich blue or violet flowers, *Anchusa* species, or alkanets, are annuals, biennials, or perennials native to Europe, western Asia, and Africa. Of the 35 species in the genus, one is grown as an annual. Alkanets bear narrow, lance-shaped to elliptic leaves that are often covered with bristly hairs and clusters of small, tubular, forget-me-not–like flowers with spreading lobes.

HOW TO GROW

Give bugloss *(A. capensis)* full sun to very light shade and average to rich soil that is evenly moist but well drained. Sow seeds indoors 6 to 8 weeks before the last spring frost date and germinate at 55° to 60°F. Seedlings appear in 2 to 4 weeks. Or sow outdoors in early spring about 2 weeks before the last frost date. Rejuvenate plants after the first flush of bloom by cutting them back hard—to within 6 to 8 inches of the ground. Water regularly in dry weather. Plants resent heat and humidity and commonly stop blooming during the heat of summer. Plant bugloss in masses in beds and borders; compact selections make handsome additions to containers. Plants self-sow and can become weedy.

A. capensis **P. 44**

a. cah-PEN-sis. Bugloss, Summer Forget-me-not. Lance-shaped, 5-inch-long leaves on ½- to 1½-foot-tall plants. Sprays of tiny, ¼-inch, true blue flowers with white throats. Cultivars include 8-inch-tall 'Blue Angel' and 18-inch 'Blue Bird', both with deep, rich blue flowers. Biennial grown as a cool-weather annual.

Anethum

ah-NEE-thum. Carrot family, Apiaceae.

Anethum contains two species of aromatic annuals or biennials with feathery blue-green leaves and umbels of tiny yellow flowers. One species —dill *(A. graveolens)*—is a popular herb that makes a pretty addition to mixed plantings.

Anethum graveolens

HOW TO GROW

Full sun and fertile, well-drained soil that remains evenly moist are all dill requires to grow well. Sow seed outdoors beginning in early spring, and sow new crops every 3 to 4 weeks to ensure a continuous supply of foliage and flowers. From Zone 9 south, sow outdoors from late summer through winter. Indoors, start seeds 6 to 8 weeks before the last spring frost date and germinate at 60° to 70°F, which takes about 3 weeks. Transplant with care, as the seedlings resent being disturbed. Water regularly during dry weather to keep plants from going to seed. Plants self-sow.

A. graveolens P. 44

a. grav-ee-OH-lens. Dill. Feathery, aromatic leaves and lacy yellow flower clusters on 2-foot plants. 'Fernleaf' is an 18-inch-tall cultivar with long-lasting, bushy foliage. Cool-weather annual.

Anisodontea

an-eye-so-DON-tee-ah. Mallow family, Malvaceae.

The 19 species in the genus *Anisodontea* are woody-based perennials or shrubs with sprays of bowl-shaped, five-petaled flowers. Native to South Africa, they bear linear, ovate, or lobed leaves that are evergreen in tropical climates. One species is grown as a tender perennial.

HOW TO GROW

Give these mallow-family plants rich, well-drained soil. They tolerate full sun in areas with cool summers, but a spot with late-afternoon shade is best where summers are warm, because the plants tend to stop blooming during the heat of summer. Water regularly in spring and summer when the plants are growing actively, and feed monthly with a balanced fertilizer. Remove seed heads regularly to keep plants blooming. Sow seeds indoors in late winter and germinate at 55° to 65°F. Or propagate by cuttings taken in early summer. Grow *Anisodontea* species in mixed plantings or in containers, and overwinter them indoors either as container plants or as cuttings. Gradually withhold water in fall and keep plants on the dry side over winter.

A. × hypomandarum P. 45

a. hi-poe-man-DARE-um. Rose Mallow. A shrub or subshrub, ranging from 3 to 5 feet in height. Ovate, three-lobed leaves. Pale pink, 1- to 1¼-inch-wide flowers with darker purple veins, borne from spring to fall. Tender perennial.

Antirrhinum

an-tir-RHY-num. Figwort family, Scrophulariaceae.

Common snapdragons, with their two-lipped flowers that have delighted children for generations, are by far the best-known members of this genus of 30 to 40 species of annuals, perennials, and tender subshrubs. *Antirrhinum* species bear racemes of tubular, two-lipped flowers and linear to lance-shaped leaves. Members of the genus are native to Europe, North Africa, and North America.

HOW TO GROW

Give snapdragons full sun and soil that is rich in organic matter and very well drained. They are easy from seeds, and many cultivars are available that come true from seeds. Sow indoors 8 to 10 weeks before the last spring frost. Use vermiculite or a sterile seed-starting mix, and just press the tiny seeds into the surface of the medium, as light is required for germination. Water from below to avoid washing the seeds away and to prevent damping off, which can be a problem. Germination takes 2 to 3 weeks at 55° to 60°F. Seedlings grown in cool conditions—45° to 50°F at night—are sturdier than ones grown at higher temperatures. In Zones 7 to 9, try growing them as biennials by sowing seeds in summer. Plant summer-sown seedlings out in fall and mulch them deeply over winter with a loose mulch such as straw or salt hay; some cultivars overwinter better than others. Indoors or out, when seedlings are about 3 inches tall, pinch out the tips to encourage branching. Deadhead plants regularly to lengthen the bloom season (leave some flowers to set seed if you want the planting to self-sow, although self-sown plants may not resemble their parents). After the first flush of bloom, or when hot weather arrives, cut the plants back hard, water, and feed them lightly with a balanced fertilizer: they will respond with new growth. Snapdragons also can be propagated by cuttings taken in spring or fall. Medium and tall cultivars need staking; install pea stakes or other supports when plants are still relatively small. Use snapdragons in beds and borders as well as the cutting garden. Hummingbirds visit the flowers. Dwarf and trailing cultivars make eye-catching container plants.

A. majus P. 45

a. MAY-jus. Common Snapdragon. Shrubby plants ranging from 8 inches to 3 feet in height with glossy, lance-shaped leaves. Dense spikes of two-lipped flowers in all colors except true blue, including white, yellow, orange, maroon, pink, red, and fuchsia. Flowers can be a solid color or bicolor. Butterfly snapdragons have flowers with flared, open-faced flowers that are single or double. Cultivars in three height categories are available: tall, to 3 feet; intermediate, from 1 to 2 feet; and dwarf, from 8 to 12 inches. Dwarf cultivars include 5-inch-tall 'Floral Showers Mix', 6- to 8-inch 'Chimes Mix', 10-inch 'Tahiti Mix', and 8-inch 'Bells Mix'. 'Sonnet Mix' plants are semidwarf at 14 inches and tolerate windy sites. 'Rocket Mix' plants reach 3 feet and are excellent cut flowers. 'Madame Butterfly Mix' plants feature fully double blooms on 2- to 2½-foot plants. Tender perennial usually grown as a cool-weather annual.

Arctotis

ark-TOE-tiss. Aster family, Asteraceae.

Commonly called African daisies, the 50 or so species in this genus are annuals and tender perennials, hardy to Zone 9. These natives of South Africa grow naturally in dry conditions, producing rosettes of gray- to silvery green leaves that are entire or lobed. The brightly colored daisylike flowers, borne one per stem from midsummer to fall, close at night. The blooms tend to open during sunny or bright weather, and do not open fully on dark days, a characteristic that limits their usefulness as cut flowers. Modern cultivars generally stay open longer than species. Use African daisies as edging plants, in beds and borders, and as container plants. *Arctotis* species also are listed as × *Venidioarctotis* and *Venidium.*

HOW TO GROW

African daisies thrive in full sun and light, very well drained soil that remains evenly moist. Sow seeds indoors 6 to 8 weeks before the last spring frost date at 60° to 70°F; germination generally takes 1 to 2 weeks. Use a sterile seed-starting mix, and barely cover seeds with mix. Water from below, and do not overwater; keeping the soil on the dry side is best, since damping off can be a problem. To minimize root disturbance, transplant seedlings to individual pots as soon as they are large enough to handle. Or sow outdoors after the last frost date once the soil has warmed up a bit. They also can be propagated by cuttings taken in spring or fall;

cuttings are a good option for multiplying plants with outstanding colors. The plants do not grow well in very hot summer weather. Plants self-sow in warm climates.

A. fastuosa P. 46

a. fas-tue-OH-sah. Monarch of the Veldt. Formerly *Venidium fastuosum.* A 1- to 2-foot species with silver-white, 5-inch-long leaves that are deeply lobed. Orange, 4-inch, daisylike flowers with dark purple or black centers. Tender perennial grown as a warm-weather annual.

A. × *hybrida* P. 46

a. HI-brih-dah. Vigorous, 18- to 20-inch-tall plants with silver-green leaves that have wavy margins. Showy, 3- to 3½-inch daisylike flowers with dark centers and orange-yellow, orange, pink, white, or red rays, or petals, that may have dark markings on them. Tender perennial grown as a warm-weather annual.

A. venusta P. 47

a. veh-NUE-stah. Blue-eyed African Daisy. Formerly *A. stoechadifolia.* A 2-foot-tall plant with lobed, dark green leaves that are silvery beneath. White, 3-inch-wide, daisylike flowers with blue centers. Tender perennial grown as a warm-weather annual.

Argemone

are-GEH-MO-nee. Poppy family, Papaveraceae.

Prickly poppies are well named: they feature poppylike flowers and prickly leaves and seedpods. About 28 annuals and perennials, plus one shrub, belong to this genus of plants native to North and Central America. Blue-green or blue-gray leaves are borne on the somewhat coarse plants, which can be spreading or erect and have yellow or orange sap. Showy, paperlike flowers with four to six yellow, white, or mauve-pink petals appear from summer to fall.

HOW TO GROW

Sun and poor, well-drained soil are all prickly poppies require. They thrive in alkaline soil and sandy or gravelly conditions; rich soil yields foliage but few flowers. Sow seeds outdoors after the last spring frost date. Or sow indoors in individual pots 6 weeks before the last spring frost date at 55° to 60°F. Germination takes about 2 weeks. Transplant indoor-sown seedlings with care, as they resent being disturbed. Use prickly poppies in rock gardens or raised beds, and give them plenty of space to spread, show off their handsome foliage, and soak up the sun. They also can be used in mixed plantings and allowed to grow up through and fill in around nearby plants. Plants self-sow.

A. grandiflora P. 47

a. gran-dih-FLOOR-ah. An annual or short-lived tender perennial, hardy from Zone 8 south, that forms clumps reaching 5 feet, although plants usually stay around 2 feet in height. Bears showy, 4-inch-wide, white or yellow flowers, singly or in small clusters. Warm-weather annual.

A. mexicana P. 48

a. mex-ih-KAN-ah. Mexican Prickly Poppy. A sprawling 2- to 3-foot-tall species with spiny, blue-green leaves. Solitary, pale lemon to deep yellow flowers from midsummer to frost. 'White Lustre' bears white flowers. Warm-weather annual.

Argyranthemum

ar-geh-RAN-the-mum. Aster family, Asteraceae.

Sometimes sold as chrysanthemums, members of this genus bear daisy- or chrysanthemum-like blooms from midsummer to frost. The flowers are single or double and come in shades of pink, yellow, and white. The genus contains about 23 species of subshrubs native to the Canary Islands and Madeira, but the plants commonly in cultivation are cultivars, generally of hybrid origin. The plants are erect or spreading and have leaves that are coarsely lobed to very finely dissected. Use them in beds and borders, as well as containers. Most also are suitable for seaside gardens.

HOW TO GROW

A site in full sun with well-drained, moderately fertile soil is ideal. They are hardy only in completely frost-free areas—Zones 10 and 11. In areas where they are marginally hardy, try a site against a south-facing wall for extra winter protection, and protect plants with a loose winter mulch such as straw or salt hay; plants killed to the ground may regrow from the base. Propagate by cuttings (cultivars do not come true from seeds) taken either in spring for the garden or in late summer for overwintering indoors. Pinch rooted plants to encourage bushy growth. Water regularly when plants are actively growing, and feed regularly; pot-grown plants are best fed weekly or biweekly. Deadhead to prolong bloom. Overwinter plants in a spot that is bright and cool (45° to 50°F nights).

A. frutescens P. 48

a. fru-TESS-sens. Marguerite Daisy, Boston Daisy. Formerly *Chrysanthemum frutescens.* A shrubby species reaching about 2 feet tall and wide. Deeply cut leaves. The species bears ¾-inch, white, daisylike flowers with yellow centers, but many cultivars of hybrid origin are available. 'Comtesse Du Chambourd' bears single white flowers and gray-green leaves. 'Pink Australian' has double pink flowers. 'Jamaica Primrose' bears single, yellow, daisylike blooms. Tender perennial.

Artemisia

are-teh-ME-see-ah. Aster family, Asteraceae.

Artemisias are grown for their handsome, deeply cut leaves that come in shades of gray-green, silver, white, and green, rather than for their rather insignificant flower heads. Most, but not all, species feature aromatic leaves. The genus contains about 300 species of annuals, perennials, and shrubs, most of which are native to dry habitats in the Northern Hemisphere. The perennial species are probably best known by gardeners, but one species is an annual used as an herb and in herb crafts.

HOW TO GROW

Full sun and average to fertile soil that is well drained will satisfy annual artemisia. Sow seeds outdoors in spring or fall, or start them indoors 6 to 8 weeks before the last spring frost date. Pinch stem tips to encourage bushy growth. Plants self-sow and can become weedy. Use them as fillers in beds and borders or in the herb garden.

A. annua P. 49

a. AN-yew-ah. Sweet Wormwood, Annual Artemisia, Sweet Annie. Deeply cut, featherlike, green leaves with a sweet fragrance on fast-growing, well-branched plants ranging from 1 to 5 feet or more in height. Bears panicles of tiny yellow flowers. Flowers and foliage are used in herbal preparations, and the dried foliage is popular for use in wreaths because of its sweet fragrance. Hang cut branches in small bunches in a warm, dark, dry place to dry. Cool-weather annual.

Asarina *see Maurandella* and *Maurandya*

Asclepias

ah-SKLEE-pee-as. Milkweed family, Asclepiadaceae.

Milkweeds bear rounded clusters of small flowers with reflexed petals and five hoodlike lobes. The flowers are followed by seedpods filled with flat seeds, each attached to a tuft of silky hair. *Asclepias* contains 110 species of perennials, subshrubs, and shrubs distributed in North, Central, and South America as well as South Africa. Most milkweeds have milky sap and lance-shaped or ovate leaves. One species is commonly grown as a tender perennial.

HOW TO GROW

Select a site with full sun and average to fertile soil that is well drained. Sow seeds of tender species, including bloodflower *(A. curvassica),* in individual pots 8 to 10 weeks before the last spring frost date and germinate at 60° to 65°F. Transplant with care; all milkweeds have easily damaged taproots. Move tender species to the garden after the last spring frost date, once the soil has warmed up. Use bloodflower in mixed plantings and gardens designed to attract bees and butterflies. Milkweeds also make attractive cut flowers: sear the stems with a flame, and then plunge them into water before arranging.

A. curassavica P. 49

a. kur-as-SAV-ih-kah. Bloodflower. A tender subshrub, hardy from about Zone 9 south. Showy, rounded, 2- to 4-inch-wide clusters of 1-inch flowers. Individual flowers are red-orange and yellow. Seedpods are narrow and erect. Naturalized in southern zones and can become weedy there. Tender perennial or warm-weather annual.

Asparagus

as-PAIR-ah-gus. Lily family, Liliaceae.

Common asparagus *(Asparagus officinalis)* is a well-known vegetable crop, but this genus of about 300 species also contains plants grown as ornamentals for their attractive foliage. Members of the genus have scale- or needlelike leaves; their plumy "fronds" actually consist of flattened, leaflike or threadlike stems called cladophylls, which are carried on larger stems that arch or climb. Plants bear tiny white or pink flowers followed by red, orange, or purple berries. They also produce clumps of fleshy tuberous roots.

HOW TO GROW

Give *Asparagus* species light shade or full sun and rich, well-drained soil; a spot with afternoon shade is best where summers are hot. Where hardy (species grown for foliage generally are hardy only from Zone 10 south), grow them outdoors in mixed plantings or as edgings. In the North, grow them in containers and overwinter them indoors (in a bright, 40° to 45°F spot). Sink plants into the soil in mixed plantings (either in or out of pots), or use them in container displays. Soak seeds in water for 24 hours, then sow indoors in late winter and germinate at temperatures between 60° and 70°F. Germination takes 3 to 4 weeks. Starting with fresh seeds is important, as seeds are not long-lived. Or propagate by dividing the clumps in spring. Water deeply during dry weather; the fleshy roots give plants some drought protection. Feed pot-grown plants monthly during the summer with a balanced fertilizer.

A. densiflorus P. 50

a. den-sih-FLOR-us. Asparagus Fern. Tender evergreen perennial ranging from 2 to 3 feet in height with featherlike "leaves," actually branched stems. Clusters of tiny (under ¼ inch) white flowers are followed by ½-inch red berries. 'Myersii', also sold as 'Myers', commonly called foxtail fern, bears erect, rounded, densely branched plumes to about 2½ inches wide and 2 feet long. 'Sprengeri', sometimes called emerald feather, bears rambling stems with loose, airy "fronds" that arch and then droop at the tips. Tender perennial.

Asperula

as-per-OO-lah. Madder family, Rubiaceae.

About 100 species of annuals, perennials, and shrubs belong to the genus *Asperula*. Commonly called woodruff or sweet woodruff, all bear clusters of tiny funnel-shaped flowers with spreading lobes in spring or summer. The leaves of these low-growing plants are linear to lance-shaped. One species is a popular annual.

HOW TO GROW

Give annual woodruff *(A. orientalis)* light shade in rich, moist, well-drained soil. Sow seeds outdoors in early spring as soon as the soil can be worked. Or sow indoors in pots 8 to 10 weeks before the last spring frost, and chill the sown pots in the refrigerator for 2 weeks before moving them to a warmer (50°F) spot for germinating. Plant annual woodruff in drifts for best effect, and combine it with other shade-loving plants. Plants may die out when hot summer weather arrives. Annual woodruff makes a good cut flower. Plants self-sow in favorable locations.

A. orientalis P. 50

a. or-ee-en-TAL-iss. Annual Woodruff. Also listed as *A. azurea.* Upright annual to 1 foot tall with lance-shaped to obovate leaves. Rounded clusters of fragrant, ⅜-inch-long, funnel-shaped flowers that open blue and fade to lavender. Some plants have white flowers. Cool-weather annual.

Aster tanacetifolius *see Machaeranthera tanacetifolia*

Atriplex

ah-TRIP-lex. Goosefoot family, Chenopodiaceae.

Members of this genus, commonly called saltbushes or orach, have insignificant flowers and often gray or silver foliage. Of the 100 annuals, perennials, subshrubs, and shrubs in the genus *Atriplex,* one species has showy, edible foliage and is grown as a bedding or salad-garden plant.

HOW TO GROW

Give annual orach *(A. hortensis)* full sun and rich, well-drained, evenly moist soil. Plants also tolerate saline soil. Sow seeds outdoors 2 to 3 weeks before the last spring frost date. Germination takes about 2 weeks. Sow again in summer for a fall crop; south of Zone 6, try orach as a winter crop. Water regularly throughout the season, especially if you plan to add the leaves to salads, because drought leads to bolting, bitter taste, and tough texture. Remove flowers as they appear and pinch plants to keep them bushy. Plants self-sow.

A. hortensis P. 51

a. hoar-TEN-sis. Orach, Mountain Spinach, Sea Purslane. Spinachlike leaves on 1- to 4-foot plants. Clusters of green or red-brown flowers. Green-, red-, and yellow-leaved cultivars are available; green-leaved selections have the sweetest taste. Cool-weather annual.

Bacopa

bah-KOPE-ah. Figwort family, Scrophulariaceae.

While most of the 56 species in this genus are aquatic perennials commonly called water hyssops, one species suitable for well-drained garden soil is gaining widespread popularity. A tender perennial, commonly referred to simply as bacopa, it is a prostrate plant grown for its small white flowers, which are borne in profusion from early summer through fall. It is especially effective when allowed to cascade over the side of a container or window box.

HOW TO GROW

Give bacopa a spot in full sun to partial shade and rich, well-drained soil. Afternoon shade is beneficial in hot climates. Propagate by taking cuttings in spring or early summer, as the cultivars available in the trade do not come true from seeds. Water regularly during dry weather; dry soil causes flowers to drop. Feed with a balanced fertilizer a few times during the summer. While the plants are normally grown as annuals, they are perennials hardy from Zone 9 south and could be overwintered indoors.

Bacopa sp. P. 51

Variously listed as *Bacopa* sp., *Sutera cordata*, and *B. monnieri*. A spreading, well-branched plant with rounded, toothed leaves that reaches only 3 inches tall but spreads from 1 to 1½ feet. Plants produce an abundance of tubular, white, ¾-inch-long flowers with five flared lobes. Two cultivars, 'Snowflake' and 'Snowstorm', are available; 'Snowstorm' is said to be more disease- and heat-resistant than 'Snowflake'. Tender perennial.

Ballota

bah-LOT-ah. Mint family, Lamiaceae.

Like their relatives the mints (*Mentha* spp.), *Ballota* species bear aromatic foliage and whorls of two-lipped flowers. The 30 to 35 species in the genus are low-growing perennials or subshrubs native to the Mediterranean, Europe, and western Asia.

HOW TO GROW

Plant in full sun and poor, dry, well-drained soil. Most are hardy from Zone 7 south and are grown as tender perennials elsewhere. Grow plants from cuttings taken in spring or early summer. Or sow seeds indoors in late winter in a sterile, very well drained medium. Cover the seeds lightly and germinate at 70°F. Where they are not hardy, replace plants annually or overwinter them indoors in pots or by taking cuttings in summer. Use them as foliage plants to fill out garden beds and mixed plantings. They tend to shed leaves in summer, so aren't the best choices for containers on a patio.

B. pseudodictamnus P. 52

b. sue-doe-dick-TAM-nus. False Dittany. A mound-forming, 2-foot-tall subshrub with woolly white stems and fuzzy gray-green leaves. Whorls of tubular, two-lipped, ½-inch-long flowers in white or pinkish white. Tender perennial.

Bassia

BAH-see-ah. Goosefoot family, Chenopodiaceae.

Although they don't look much alike, *Bassia* species (formerly *Kochia* spp.) are related to beets. The genus contains about seven species with very narrow leaves and inconspicuous flowers. One species is grown for the feathery effect its foliage adds to the garden, as well as its fall color.

HOW TO GROW

Give burning bush *(Bassia scoparia)* full sun and rich, well-drained soil. Sow seeds outdoors after the last spring frost date. Or sow indoors 4 to 6 weeks before the last frost date and germinate at between 65° and 70°F. Do not cover the seeds, which need light to germinate. Use burning bush as an edging or low, temporary hedge. Plants self-sow and can become weedy, especially in warm climates.

B. scoparia forma *trichophylla* P. 52

b. sko-PAIR-ee-ah forma tri-koe-FILL-ah. Burning Bush, Summer Cypress. Formerly *Kochia scoparia* forma *trichophylla*. A fast-growing, shrublike annual ranging from 1 to 5 feet with narrow, lance-shaped leaves that turn scarlet in fall. Warm-weather annual.

Begonia

beh-GOAN-yah. Begonia family, Begoniaceae.

The vast *Begonia* clan contains some 1,300 species—annuals, perennials, shrubs, climbers, succulents, and epiphytes—native to tropical and subtropical regions worldwide. Begonias have fleshy leaves and stems and grow from rhizomes, fibrous roots, or tubers. Male and female flowers are borne separately, usually on the same plant. (Female flowers have a swollen winged seed capsule directly behind the petals; males don't.) The fleshy leaves vary in shape, size, and color. Rounded and wing-shaped foliage is common. North of Zone 10, most begonias are suitable only for house or greenhouse culture, but a few species are popular perennials grown as annuals or tender perennials.

HOW TO GROW

Give wax begonias *(B. semperflorens)* average to rich, well-drained soil. They tolerate sun to shade; partial shade is best, especially in southern zones, where they struggle with the heat. Keep the soil evenly moist, especially if plants are in full sun. Use wax begonias as edging plants or to add color to shade gardens. Start begonias from cuttings or seeds sown in early to midwinter. Scatter the dustlike seeds thinly on the surface of a moist, sterile seed-starting mix. Do not cover them with soil, but place a pane of glass or a piece of plastic wrap over the container to keep the medium moist. Germination occurs in 2 to 3 weeks; keep wax begonias at 70°F, other species at 60°F. Propagate from cuttings taken anytime, or divide the clumps. (Double-flowered cultivars must be grown from cuttings or division; they do not come true from seeds.) Use begonias in containers and hanging baskets, as well as in mixed plantings and as edgings. Overwinter plants by taking cuttings in late summer, digging entire plants, or bringing in containers. Keep them in a sunny spot at temperatures between 60° and 65°F.

B. semperflorens P. 53

b. sem-per-FLOR-ens. Wax Begonia. Fibrous-rooted, mounding, 8- to 12-inch-tall perennials with fleshy stems, fleshy green or bronze leaves, and abundant clusters of white, pink, red, or bicolor blooms. Many cultivars with single or double blooms are available. Tender perennial or warm-weather annual.

B. sutherlandii

b. suh-ther-LAN-dee-eye. Sutherland Begonia. A tuberous species reportedly hardy to Zone 7; ideal for containers, baskets, or rich garden beds. Pendent clusters of orange, 1-inch flowers produced all summer atop mounds of bright green, lance-shaped leaves. Plants can reach 1 to 2 feet. Overwinter indoors as houseplants, or let plants go dormant and keep them relatively dry and cool, as for conventional tuberous begonias. Tender perennial.

Bellis

BELL-iss. Aster family, Asteraceae.

Of the 15 species of perennials that belong to this genus, one is grown as an annual or biennial. *Bellis* species form rosettes of oval- to spoon-shaped leaves and bear solitary, daisylike flower heads in shades of pink, reddish pink, and white.

HOW TO GROW

Give English daisy *(B. perennis)* full sun or light shade and average to rich, well-drained soil. Plants perform best in areas with cool summers. Although perennial and hardy in Zones 4 to 8, they are usually dug and discarded after they bloom. (From Zone 9 south, they are grown as annuals for fall to winter or early-spring bloom.) Sow seeds indoors 8 to 10 weeks before the last spring frost at 50° to 55°F; germination takes 2 to 4 weeks. Outdoors from Zone 7 north, sow from midsummer to fall for bloom the following year; cover plants with a loose mulch such as straw or salt hay over winter. From Zone 8 south, sow in early spring several weeks before the last spring frost date or in fall. When sowing, just press the seeds into the soil surface, as light aids germination. Water regularly and deadhead plants to prevent self-sowing. Discard plants after they flower, or divide the clumps and raise the divisions in a seedbed, as you would seedlings, for bloom the following year.

B. perennis P. 53

b. per-EN-iss. English Daisy. Low-growing, 2- to 8-inch-tall stoloniferous perennial with obovate to spoon-shaped leaves. The species bears ½- to 1¼-inch-white to pinkish flowers with yellow centers but is seldom grown. Cultivars, which come true from seeds, have large single or double flowers ranging from 1 to 3 inches across in shades of pink, red, and white. Perennial grown as a biennial.

Beta

BAY-tah. Goosefoot family, Chenopodiaceae.

The best-known member of this genus of five or six biennials and perennials is a common resident of the vegetable garden — beets (*Beta vulgaris* Crassa Group). Native to Europe and the Mediterranean, *Beta* species bear glossy ovate to triangular-ovate leaves and fleshy stems. The flowers are insignificant. Swiss chard, which is closely related to beets, is grown as an edible or ornamental for its colorful leaves and stems. Use it to add lush, season-long foliage color to mixed plantings.

HOW TO GROW

Plant Swiss chard in full sun to light shade and rich, well-drained soil. A site with afternoon shade is best in the South. Sow seeds outdoors 1 to 2 weeks before the last spring frost date. Germination takes about a week. Or sow indoors in pots 6 to 8 weeks before the last frost. Each "seed" actually consists of several seeds, so thin plants to leave the strongest seedling or two per clump. Keep the soil evenly moist throughout the season to discourage bolting, or going to seed, along with tough stalks and bitter foliage. Feed monthly with a balanced fertilizer. Use Swiss chard in mixed plantings, containers, edible landscapes, and the vegetable garden.

B. vulgaris Cicla Group. P. 54

b. vul-GAIR-iss. Swiss Chard, Leaf Beet. Clump-forming, 18-inch-tall biennial with glossy, 9- to 12-inch-long leaves on erect, fleshy stems. Leaves may be green or red to red-purple, with veins and stems in contrasting colors. 'Bright Lights' bears green leaves with stems and veins in various colors including yellow, gold, pink, and white. 'Rhubarb' bears dark green leaves with crimson stalks and veins. Biennial grown as a cool-weather annual.

Bidens

BI-dens. Aster family, Asteraceae.

This widely distributed genus contains some 200 species of annuals, perennials, and shrubs with clusters of daisylike flowers. Commonly called tickseeds, stick-tights, or burr marigolds, they have simple or pinnate leaves and barbed seeds: the name *Bidens* is from the Latin *bis*, "two," and *dens*, "tooth." Most tend to be weedy plants native to grasslands and waste plants and suitable for wild gardens. One species is grown as an annual or tender perennial.

HOW TO GROW

Give *Bidens* species full sun and evenly moist, average to rich soil that is well drained. Sow seeds indoors 6 to 8 weeks before the last spring frost date and germinate at 55° to 65°F. Or sow outdoors after the last frost date. Or propagate from cuttings taken in spring or late summer to early fall to overwinter the plants indoors. Clumps also can be divided. Plants self-sow.

B. ferulifolia P. 54

b. fer-you-lih-FOE-lee-ah. Spreading, 12-inch-tall perennial hardy from Zone 8 south with lacy, deeply divided leaves. Bears golden yellow, 1¼- to 1½-inch-wide, daisylike flower heads from summer to fall. 'Golden Goddess' bears 2-inch-wide flowers. Tender perennial. Overwinter plants or grow as an annual. Cool-weather annual.

Borago

boar-AH-go. Borage family, Boraginaceae.

Native to rocky soils in the Mediterranean and Europe, *Borago* species are annuals and perennials with hairy stems and leaves topped by clusters of nodding, star-shaped flowers. Of the three species in the genus, one is commonly grown as an herb, salad plant, and ornamental.

HOW TO GROW

Full sun to partial shade and average, well-drained soil satisfy common borage *(Borago officinalis)*. Sow seeds outdoors in spring about a week before the last spring frost date. Or sow seeds in late summer or fall for germination the following spring. Do not cover the seeds, which need light to germinate. Use borage in mixed plantings and the herb garden, as well as in containers. Plants self-sow.

B. officinalis P. 55

b. oh-fih-shih-NAL-iss. Common Borage. A large, vigorous, 2-foot-tall annu-

Borago officinalis

al with lance-shaped to ovate, hairy, grayish green leaves. Clusters of 1-inch-wide, star-shaped flowers in summer in rich, true blue. There also are white- and pink-flowered forms. Cool-weather annual.

Bouvardia

boo-VAR-dee-ah. Madder family, Rubiaceae.

The genus *Bouvardia* comprises about 30 species of tender perennials and shrubs native to southern regions of North America to South America. They bear ovate to lance-shaped leaves and clusters of tube- to funnel-shaped flowers.

HOW TO GROW

Give *Bouvardia* species full sun and average to rich, well-drained soil that remains evenly moist; a spot with midday shade is best where summers are hot. In frost-free or nearly frost-free climates (roughly Zone 9 south), grow them outdoors as shrubs in mixed plantings; in areas where they are marginally hardy, try a site against a south-facing wall for extra winter protection. In the North, grow them in containers and overwinter them indoors (in a bright spot with temperatures between 50° and 55°F at night). In summer, sink plants—pot and all—into the soil in mixed plantings, or use them in container displays. Water regularly and feed every two weeks when plants are growing and flowering actively; gradually withhold water after they bloom and keep them nearly dry over winter. Prune plants to shape them and remove weak and crowded growth in late winter or early spring. Since young plants bloom best, replace them annually or every other year. Take stem cuttings in spring to propagate for garden use or in late summer to overwinter the plants; cuttings root best if given bottom heat. Or take root cuttings in midwinter. *Bouvardia* species are rarely grown from seeds, as cultivars do not come true.

B. ternifolia P. 55

b. tern-ih-FOE-lee-ah. Scarlet Trompetilla. A 2- to 3-foot shrub with lance-shaped leaves. Showy clusters of tubular scarlet flowers from late summer onward. Tender perennial.

Brachyscome

brah-key-SCO-me. Aster family, Asteraceae.

Natives of Australia, New Zealand, Tasmania, and New Guinea, *Brachyscome* (also spelled *Brachycome*) species bear mounds of daisylike flowers with yellow centers and purple, blue, or white petals, more accurately called ray florets. One annual in this genus of 60 to 70 species of annuals and perennials is commonly grown in gardens.

HOW TO GROW

Give Swan River daisy *(B. iberidifolia)* full sun and rich, well-drained soil. Brachyscomes do not perform well in areas with very hot, humid summers. Sow seeds outdoors after danger of frost has passed. Or sow seeds indoors 4 to 6 weeks before the last spring frost date and germinate at temperatures between 60° and 70°F. Water from below and keep the soil on the dry side to avoid damping off. Make successive sowings every 3 weeks for continued bloom. Support plants with twiggy brush. Use Swan River daisies in containers and along the front edges of mixed plantings.

B. iberidifolia P. 56

b. eye-ber-id-ih-FOE-lee-ah. Swan River Daisy. A densely branched, 1- to 1½-foot annual with deeply cut, gray-green, nearly fernlike leaves. Bears fragrant, 1½-inch-wide, daisylike flowers in purplish blue, white, and pink in summer. Splendour Series cultivars come in white, purple, and lilac-pink with black centers. 'Blue Star' reaches 1 foot and bears purple-blue flowers with pointed petals. Cool-weather annual.

Bracteantha

brack-tee-AN-tha. Aster family, Asteraceae.

Commonly called strawflowers or everlastings, *Bracteantha* species are perennials and annuals from the scrublands of Australia. Once classified in the genus *Helichrysum*, they bear hairy, lance-shaped to ovate leaves. Their daisylike flowers actually consist of all disk florets—they lack the "petals," or ray florets, of many aster-family plants. The showy "petals" in this case are papery, petal-like bracts in bright yellows, pinks, and white. One of the seven species in the genus is a popular annual and an exceptional dried flower.

HOW TO GROW

Give strawflowers full sun and average to dry, well-drained soil. They thrive in areas with long, hot summers. Sow seeds indoors 6 to 8 weeks before the last spring frost date and germinate at 65° to 70°F. Seedlings appear in 1 to 3 weeks. In the South, where summers are long, strawflowers can be sown outdoors in spring. Do not cover.seeds, which need light to germinate. Wait to transplant until after the last frost, once the soil has warmed up, and handle plants with care. Tall cultivars require staking. To dry the flowers, pick them before they are fully open, then hang them in small bunches in a warm, dark, dry place.

B. bracteata P. 56

b. brack-tee-AY-tah. Strawflower. Formerly *Helichrysum bracteatum.* An annual or short-lived perennial with lance-shaped, gray-green leaves and papery, 1- to 3-inch-wide flower heads in yellow, pink, red, and white. Dwarf types, including Bright Bikinis Series, reach only 1 foot in height; taller types range from 3 to 5 feet. Warm-weather annual.

Brassica

BRASS-ih-kah. Cabbage family, Brassicaceae.

In addition to a wealth of popular vegetable crops—including cabbage, broccoli, Brussels sprouts, mustard, bok choy, and kale—this genus of about 30 species contains ornamental forms of cabbage and kale grown for their showy, colorful leaves. *Brassica* species are annuals, biennials, perennials, or sometimes subshrubs with rounded or lobed leaves and sprays of four-leaved, cross-shaped flowers.

HOW TO GROW

Ornamental cabbage and kale thrive in full sun; rich, well-drained soil; and cool temperatures. They benefit from midday to afternoon shade in areas where they might be exposed to warm temperatures. Grow them for fall to winter color, since their foliage colors up best after temperatures turn cool (below 50°F) and the days short. Sow seeds in mid- to late summer either indoors in pots or in an outdoor seedbed. Do not cover seeds with soil. Germination takes a week at 65° to 70°F. Keep plants evenly moist. Try to keep them cool—ideally 65°F, slightly cooler at night—then transplant to the garden in late summer or early fall. Feed plants with a balanced fertilizer about 3 weeks after transplanting, and mulch to keep the soil cool. Use the earlier schedule—midsummer sowing and late-summer transplanting—in northern zones. In the South, where these plants can "bloom" all winter, sow in late summer for early-fall transplanting. Use ornamental cabbages and kales in beds with other cold-tolerant annuals, or plant them as edgings. They also make excellent container plants.

B. oleracea P. 57

b. ol-er-AY-cee-ah. Flowering Cabbage, Flowering Kale. Loose, 10- to 14-inch-tall rosettes of colorful, edible leaves in combinations of green and red, green and creamy white, blue-green and mauve-pink, or green and magenta or pink. Flowering cabbages (*B. oleracea* Acephala Group) have wavy-edged leaves, while kales (*B. oleracea* Capitata Group) tend to have leaves with fringed or ruffled edges. Biennial grown as an annual.

Briza

BREE-zah. Grass family, Poaceae.

While the best-known ornamental grasses are perennials, the genus *Briza* contains two species of attractive annuals. The 12 to 20 species of *Briza* all bear linear leaves and loose racemes or panicles of spikelets ("flowers") that hang from very fine stalks, and as a result quake and flutter in the slightest breeze.

HOW TO GROW

Give annual quaking grasses full sun to light shade and average to rich soil that is well drained. Sow seeds outdoors in fall or in spring after the last spring frost date. Or sow indoors in individual pots 6 to 8 weeks before the last frost and transplant with care. Keep plants evenly moist for best results. Use quaking grasses in mixed plantings, or grow them in rows in the cutting garden to produce stems for drying. To dry, cut stems when they are either green or have dried to brown. Hang them in a warm, dark place to dry, or stand a bunch in a vase.

B. maxima P. 57

b. MAX-ih-mah. Big Quaking Grass. A 1½- to 2-foot annual with loosely branched panicles of nodding, ovate, 1-inch-long spikelets. Flowers are heart-shaped, ½-inch-long spikelets that appear from late spring to late summer and turn from green to red-brown- or purple-flushed, ripening to straw-colored. Warm-weather annual.

B. minor

b. MY-nor. Little Quaking Grass. A 6-inch to 1½-foot annual with ovate, nodding, ¼-inch-long spikelets in loose panicles. Flowers are small ½-inch spikelets that appear from early summer to fall and ripen from green, often purple-tinged, to pale tan.

Browallia

bro-WAL-lee-ah. Nightshade family, Solanaceae.

The genus *Browallia* contains six species of annuals and tender perennials native to tropical South America and the West Indies. Commonly called browallias or bush violets, they have narrow, ovate to elliptic leaves and trumpet-shaped flowers with five broad lobes, or "petals." Flowers come in shades of purple, blue-violet, and white and will attract hummingbirds.

HOW TO GROW

Plant browallias in full sun or partial shade and rich, well-drained soil. Sow seeds indoors 8 to 10 weeks before the last spring frost date and germinate at 65° to 70°F. When sowing, just press the seeds into the soil surface, as light is required for germination. Seedlings appear in 1 to 3 weeks. Pinch plants several times to encourage branching. In areas with very long summers, it is possible to sow seeds outdoors where the plants are to grow.

B. americana

b. ah-mair-ih-CAN-ah. Browallia, Bush Violet. Formerly *B. elata.* A 1- to 2-foot annual with ovate, somewhat sticky leaves and 2-inch-wide flowers borne singly or in small clusters. Warm-weather annual.

B. speciosa P. 58

b. spee-cee-OH-sah. Browallia, Bush Violet, Sapphire Flower. A tender, woody-based perennial that can reach 5 feet in the tropics but ranges from 1 to 2 feet when grown in gardens. Ovate to elliptic leaves and 2-inch-wide flowers borne singly or in small clusters. Cultivars include Troll Series plants, which bear their flowers on rounded, compact, 10-inch plants. Tender perennial or warm-weather annual.

Brugmansia

brug-MAN-see-ah. Nightshade family, Solanaceae.

The five species of *Brugmansia* are tender shrubs or trees from South America. Once included in *Datura,* all bear large, pendent, trumpet-shaped flowers that usually have five pointed lobes that are curled back. Flowers are usually fragrant and are borne from late spring or early summer through fall, nearly year-round in frost-free areas. Leaves are oblong to ovate and either entire, toothed, or lobed. All parts of these plants are poisonous if ingested.

HOW TO GROW

Angel's trumpets thrive in full sun or very light shade and rich, well-drained soil. In frost-free areas—Zones 10 and 11—grow them outdoors as shrubs or specimen plants. Where they are not hardy, set these striking plants outdoors each spring, and dig them each fall for overwintering. They also grow in very large containers or tubs, but growing in the ground yields the most spectacular plants. Feed plants, especially pot-grown ones, every 2 to 3 weeks from spring to fall, and water regularly when plants are growing and flowering actively. Dig plants in early fall, before frost, keeping as much soil around the roots as possible. Store them in a bright, cool (40° to 50°F), frost-free place, and keep them nearly dry over winter. Plants may lose their leaves but will begin growing in spring, when temperatures warm up and watering is resumed. Prune plants as necessary in spring; they withstand hard pruning, to within several inches of the base of the plant. Repot container-grown specimens annually. Propagate *Brugmansia* species by seeds sown in winter or early spring and germinated at 60° to 70°F. Or take softwood or heel cuttings in summer; bottom heat speeds rooting.

B. arborea

P. 58

b. are-BORE-ee-ah. Common Angel's Trumpet. Also listed as *B. versicolor* and *Datura arborea.* A 6- to 12-foot shrub or tree with fragrant, white, 6-inch-long flowers. Tender perennial.

B. × candida

b. × can-DEE-dah. Angel's Trumpets. Formerly *Datura ×. candida.* A 10- to 15-foot shrub or tree with 6- to 12-inch-long trumpets that are fragrant at night. Flowers come in white, pale yellow, or sometimes pink. Double-flowered forms include 'Double White' and 'Plena'. Tender perennial.

B. sanguinea

P. 59

b. san-GWIN-ee-ah. Red Angel's Trumpet. Also listed as *B. rosei* and *Datura sanguinea.* A 10- to 30-foot shrub or tree with 6- to 10-inch-long, orange-red flowers that are not fragrant. Tender perennial.

B. suaveolens

P. 59

b. sua-vee-OH-lens. Angel's Trumpets. Formerly *Datura suaveolens.* A 10- to 15-foot shrub or tree with 8-inch-long flowers that come in white, yellow, or pink and are fragrant at night. Tender perennial.

Bupleurum

bup-LOOR-um. Carrot family, Apiaceae.

Related to carrots and dill, *Bupleurum* species bear rounded umbels of tiny, star-shaped flowers that are frequently surrounded by leafy bracts. The genus contains about 100 species of annuals, perennials, and shrubs with simple leaves that have parallel veins.

HOW TO GROW

Full sun and average to poor soil satisfy *Bupleurum* species. They tolerate exposed sites as well as dry or rocky soil and are suitable for seaside gardens. The flowers are good for cutting. Sow seeds indoors 6 to 8 weeks before the last spring frost date in individual pots. Transplant with care after the last frost. Or sow outdoors a few weeks before the last frost. Plants self-sow.

B. fruticosum

b. fru-tih-COSE-um. Shrubby Hare's Ear. A tender 4- to 6-foot-tall shrub, hardy from Zone 7 south, with glossy, blue-green leaves. Rounded, 1½-inch-wide umbels of starry yellow flowers from midsummer to fall. Tender perennial or cool-weather annual.

B. rotundifolium P. 60

b. roe-tun-dih-FOE-lee-um. Thorow Wax, Thorough Wax. A shrubby 1½- to 2-foot-tall annual or short-lived perennial hardy from Zones 4 to 8. Produces 1¼-inch-wide umbels of yellow-green flowers in summer. The common names refer to the ovate leaves, which appear to surround the stems: "thorow" and "thorough" are Middle English spellings from the Old English "thuruh," meaning "from end to end" or "through." Cool-weather annual.

Calceolaria

kal-see-oh-LAIR-ee-ah. Figwort family, Scrophulariaceae.

The showy, pouched or slipperlike flowers of *Calceolaria* species—*calceolus* is Latin for "slipper"—have given rise to a variety of common names, including pouch flower, slipper flower, slipperwort, and pocketbook plant. The genus contains some 300 annuals, biennials, perennials, and shrubs native to Central and South America. Flowers are borne singly or in clusters and have two lips like their relatives the snapdragons. The lower lip is pouched or inflated and is larger than the upper one, which may or may not be inflated.

HOW TO GROW

Choose a site with full sun to partial shade and light, loose, average to rich soil that is well drained yet remains evenly moist. These plants need cool, moist conditions and usually fail in hot, humid climates. The species listed here are usually grown for spring or early-summer color as biennials (sown in fall) or as annuals (sown in spring). Do not cover the seeds with soil, as they need light to germinate. Germination takes a week at 70° to 75°F. Damping off is a common problem, so sow in a sterile seed-starting mix and water from below, keeping the medium barely moist, never dry or wet. For best results, grow the seedlings at cool (50° to 55°F) temperatures. Stake plants with brushy twigs. Once buds appear, water freely. Use these plants in beds with rich soil and in containers.

C. Herbeohybrida Group P. 60

c. herb-ee-oh-HI-brih-dah. Pouch Flower, Slipper Flower, Slipperwort, Pocketbook Plant. Also listed as *C. hybrida.* Bushy, ½- to 1½-foot hybrids with ovate, softly hairy leaves. Clusters of pouched, 2- to 3-inch-wide flowers come in yellow, orange, red, and bicolor and are often marked with purple or other contrasting colors. Cultivars of the Anytime Series take 4 months to flower from seeds and reach 8 inches. Biennial.

C. integrifolia

c. in-teh-grih-FOE-lee-ah. Formerly *C. rugosa.* A somewhat shrubby perennial, hardy from Zone 8 south, that can reach 4 feet but is normally 1 to 1½ feet tall in gardens. Bears narrow, gray-green, toothed leaves and large clusters of 1-inch-wide yellow flowers in summer. Tender perennial or cool-weather annual.

Calendula

cah-LEN-du-lah. Aster family, Asteraceae.

Commonly called pot marigolds, *Calendula* species are annuals or woody-based perennials with single or double daisylike flowers and aromatic leaves. The flowers have petals, more properly called ray florets, in shades of yellow or orange, with centers (disk florets) in yellow, orange, purple, or brown. The genus contains some 20 to 30 species native to the Mediterranean and North Africa, one of which is a popular annual.

HOW TO GROW

Full sun or light shade and average, well-drained soil is ideal. Plants tolerate poor, relatively dry soil and are best in areas with cool summers. Sow seeds outdoors several weeks before the last spring frost date. Or sow indoors 6 to 8 weeks before the last frost date at 45° to 50°F at night and no more than 55° to 60°F during the day; seedlings grown at warmer temperatures tend to be floppy and weak. Sow in a sterile seed-starting medium, and water from below to prevent damping off, which can be a problem. When sowing, cover the seeds with soil, as darkness is required for germination. Germination takes up to 2 weeks. Also sow seeds in midsummer for fall bloom. In mild climates (Zone 8 and warmer), sow in late summer for winter and early-spring bloom. If plants begin dying out due to summer heat, cut them back hard, and they will resume growth when cooler weather returns. Use pot marigolds in beds and borders, in containers, and in the herb garden. The flowers attract butterflies and have edible petals. add them fresh to salads, or use them as a substitute for saffron and to add color to cakes and other desserts. The flowers are ideal for cutting.

C. officinalis P. 61

c. off-fish-in-NAL-iss. Pot Marigold. A fast-growing, 1- to 2½-foot species with lance- to spoon-shaped leaves and single or double daisylike flowers in shades of yellow, orange, apricot, and cream. Many cultivars are available including Bon Bon Series, 1-foot dwarf selections, and Prince Series, ideal for cutting at 2 to 2½ feet tall. Cool-weather annual.

Calibrachoa *see Petunia*

Callistephus

cal-ISS-teh-fus. Aster family, Asteraceae.

One species, a popular annual native to China, belongs to this genus: *Callistephus chinensis,* commonly called China aster. It has ovate to ovate-triangular leaves, sometimes coarsely toothed, and daisylike flowers from midsummer to fall. Many cultivars are available with both single and double flowers; the species is seldom grown.

HOW TO GROW

China asters thrive in a site with full sun or partial shade and rich, well-drained, evenly moist soil that is neutral or alkaline. Sow seeds indoors 6 to 8 weeks before the last spring frost date in individual pots. Germination takes 1 to 2 weeks at 65° to 70°F. Transplant with care. Or sow outdoors after the last frost date. For best results, choose disease-resistant cultivars and rotate planting locations annually to avoid problems with soilborne diseases. Space plants generously to ensure good air circulation: they resent hot climates, crowding, poor air circulation, and reflected heat. Stake taller selections. Plant new seeds every 2 weeks for continued bloom, or grow early, midseason, and late cultivars. Water regularly during dry weather, and deadhead to prolong bloom. Use China asters in beds and borders, in containers, and as cut flowers.

C. chinensis PP. 61, 62

c. chi-NEN-sis. China Aster, Annual Aster. A bushy, fast-growing annual with single or double, 3- to 5-inch flowers in shades of violet, lavender, purple, pink, red, white, and yellow. Cultivars in different heights are available: Taller ones, from 1½ to 3 feet tall, are best for cut flowers and include 'Powder Puff Mix' and 'Fireworks Mix'. Use shorter cultivars, including 8-inch-tall Comet Series plants, near the front of plantings and in pots. Cool-weather annual.

Calocephalus

cal-oh-SEFF-ah-lus. Aster family, Asteraceae.

The 18 species of annuals, perennials, and small shrubs that belong to *Calocephalus* all are native to rocky coastal areas in Australia. Most have leaves that are white and feltlike or woolly, as well as silvery white flower heads. One species is grown for its attractive foliage.

HOW TO GROW

Give cushionbush *(C. brownii)* a site in full sun and sandy, well-drained soil. In warm, dry, frost-free areas (Zone 9 south) grow them outdoors year-round as small shrubs. In the North, grow them in containers and overwinter them indoors (in a bright, 40° to 45°F spot), or grow as bedding plants replaced annually. They are generally started from cuttings rather than seeds. Take cuttings from late summer to fall to overwinter plants, and root them in very well drained potting soil at around 50°F. Pinch to encourage bushy growth. Move plants to the garden several weeks after the last spring frost date, once night temperatures do not dip below 50°F. Use cushionbush as an edging plant, or add it to containers or mixed plantings. It is suitable for seaside gardens.

C. brownii

P. 62

c. BROW-nee-eye. Cushionbush. Formerly *Leucophyta browni.* A 1-foot-tall shrub with wiry branches, woolly white linear leaves, and silvery ½-inch flower heads. Tender perennial.

Calonyction aculeatum *see Ipomoea alba*

Campanula

cam-PAN-you-lah. Bellflower family, Campanulaceae.

The bellflower clan is a large one, comprising some 300 species of annuals, biennials, and perennials beloved by gardeners for their dainty flowers in shades of blue, lilac, violet, and white. The genus name translates as "little bell"—*campana* is Latin for "bell"—but in addition to bell-shaped, flowers can be star-, cup-, or saucer-shaped. They have five "petals," or lobes, and are usually borne in clusters. One species, Canterbury bells *(Campanula medium)* is a popular biennial, while two other species can be grown as tender perennials.

HOW TO GROW

A site with full sun to partial shade and rich, well-drained, evenly moist soil is ideal. The bellflowers listed here are best for areas with cool sum-

Campanula medium

mers and relatively low humidity. In areas with warm summers, give them partial shade, especially during the hottest part of the day. Sow seeds of *C. isophylla* and *C. pyramidalis* indoors 10 to 12 weeks before the last spring frost date at 50° to 55°F. Germination takes 3 to 4 weeks. With all bellflowers, just press the tiny seeds into the soil surface, as light is necessary for germination. To grow *C. medium* as an annual, sow indoors 6 to 8 weeks before the last frost date. To grow it as a biennial, sow outdoors in late spring or early summer in pots or in a holding bed in a protected site. Water, weed, and thin seedlings as necessary, and protect them over winter with a coarse mulch such as evergreen boughs or salt hay in Zones 5 to 7. Move plants to the garden in early spring the following year. Replace plants annually. Taller types may require staking. To overwinter *C. isophylla,* move plants to an airy, cool spot (45° to 50°F nights, slightly warmer during the day); repot in spring, and propagate by taking cuttings from shoots at the base of the plant. *C. pyramidalis* is best grown from seed and can be overwintered like *C. isophylla,* but is usually treated as a biennial. Use Canterbury bells in beds and borders, or try it in containers. *C. isophylla* and *C. pyramidalis* are ideal for pots and hanging baskets but also look great in mixed plantings.

C. isophylla

P. 63

c. eye-so-PHIL-ah. Italian Bellflower, Star of Bethlehem, Falling Stars. A trailing, 6- to 8-inch perennial, hardy in Zone 7 or 8, with heart-shaped leaves. Loose clusters of saucer-shaped, 1½-inch flowers in pale blue or white in midsummer. Tender perennial or biennial.

C. medium

P. 63

c. ME-dee-um. Canterbury Bells. A slow-growing, 1½- to 3-foot biennial, hardy in Zones 5 to 8, with lance-shaped to elliptic leaves. Showy racemes of bell-shaped, single or double, 1½- to 2-inch-long flowers in purple, lavender, white, or pink from late spring to midsummer. Biennial.

C. pyramidalis

P. 64

c. peer-ah-mid-AL-iss. Chimney Bellflower. A short-lived perennial, hardy in Zones 6 to 8, grows to 10 feet in height with toothed, ovate- to lance-shaped leaves. Showy, erect clusters of fragrant, cup-shaped, pale lilac-blue or white flowers from late spring to summer. Biennial.

Canna

CAN-ah. Canna family, Cannaceae.

Grown for their enormous leaves and showy hot-colored flowers in shades of yellow, red-orange, red, and hot pink, cannas are native to Asia and the tropics of North and South America. There are about 50 species of rhizomatous perennials in the genus, but gardeners primarily grow cultivars, which add a dramatic, tropical flair to gardens. Hummingbirds visit canna flowers.

HOW TO GROW

Cannas thrive in full sun and well-drained, evenly moist soil rich in organic matter. Wet soil rots the fleshy rhizomes. From Zone 8 south, grow cannas outdoors year-round. In the North, either replace them annually or overwinter the rhizomes indoors. Cannas can be started from seeds, but purchasing rhizomes is faster and the only way to get most of the improved cultivars. Rhizomes should have one or two pointed growing tips and be thick, fleshy, and firm with no soft spots. From Zone 7 south, plant the rhizomes outdoors, in soil amended with organic matter, after the last spring frost date. In the North, pot up the rhizomes indoors with the growing tips just under the soil surface. Keep them warm (75°F) and barely moist until they begin to grow, then move them to a sunny spot, keep them evenly moist, and fertilize weekly. Transplant to the garden after the last frost date, once the soil has warmed to about 65°F. Mulch, water regularly, and feed monthly in summer. Deadhead to keep the plants neat-looking and encourage rebloom. To overwinter, dig them after a light frost and cut back the tops. Store the rhizomes in barely damp vermiculite, peat, or sand in a cool (40° to 50°F), dry place. Sprin-

Canna × *generalis* hybrid

kle the soil with water occasionally during winter to keep the roots from shriveling. In spring, cut the rhizomes into pieces with two growing points each and start them as you would new rhizomes. (Do not divide the rhizomes in fall before storage, because the cut surfaces tend to rot over winter.) To start from seeds, sow in midwinter. Nick the hard seed coats with a file, and soak the seeds in warm water for 48 hours. Then place the seeds in a plastic bag filled with moist peat moss, and set it in a warm (75°F) place. Inspect the bag every few days, and pot up seedlings as they appear. Seed-grown plants will produce rhizomes that can be overwintered in subsequent years. Use cannas with annuals and perennials in beds and borders, in mass plantings, along foundations or shrub borders, and in tubs or large containers.

C. × *generalis* PP. 64, 65

c. x gen-er-AL-iss. Bold 5- to 6-foot-tall perennials with 1- to 2-foot-long leaves that can be green or variegated. Showy 1-foot-tall clusters of 3- to 5-inch flowers bloom from midsummer to frost. Many cultivars with solid green leaves and flowers in shades of red, orange, yellow, pink, or bicolor are available. Types grown for foliage as well as flowers include 'Pretoria' (also called 'Bengal Tiger'), with orange-yellow blooms and yellow-striped leaves; 'Roi Humbert' or 'Red King Humbert', with bronze-purple leaves and red flowers; and 'Durban', with red flowers and leaves striped with orange, yellow, and red. Dwarf cultivars include 2-foot-tall 'Tropical Rose', with rose-pink flowers, and 2½- to 3-foot-tall Pfitzer Series cultivars, both of which can be grown from seeds. Tender perennial or warm-weather annual.

Capsicum

CAP-sih-come. Nightshade family, Solanaceae.

All too often relegated to the vegetable garden without a second thought, peppers (*Capsicum* spp.) are handsome plants that deserve wider use. The genus contains about 10 species of annuals and perennials native to the tropics of the Americas. They have small white or purple, star- or bell-shaped flowers and shiny chambered fruits in a variety of sizes and shapes that can hang down or point up. Fruits usually start out green but ripen to yellow, red, purple, orange, or chocolate brown. Commonly cultivated forms all fall into one species, *C. annuum.*

HOW TO GROW

Give peppers full sun and average to rich soil that is well drained and evenly moist. Sow seeds indoors 6 to 10 weeks before the last spring frost date; seeds germinate in 1 to 2 weeks if the soil temperature is kept at about 85°F. Grow seedlings at 65° to 70°F, and transplant after the last frost date, once the soil has warmed to 60°F and the weather has settled. Stake taller types to keep them upright. Use them in mixed plantings, as edgings, and in containers.

C. annuum

P. 65

C. AN-nu-um. Chili peppers, sweet peppers, and ornamental peppers all fall here. Annuals or short-lived perennials, they have lance-shaped to ovate leaves. Both sweet and hot peppers are attractive plants, but cultivars developed specifically for ornamental use are generally best for bedding displays because their fruit (the most colorful part of the plant) isn't harvested. Ornamental types bear edible, but very hot, fruit that is held upright on the plants. Many feature showy, variegated foliage as well. Cultivars include 'Holiday Cheer', 'Poinsettia', 'Starburst', 'Thai Hot Ornamental', 'Trifetti', 'Marbles', and 'Pretty in Purple'. Warm-weather annual or perennial or winter annual (in Zones 10 and 11).

Cardiospermum

car-dee-oh-SPER-mum. Soapberry family, Sapindaceae.

The 14 species of *Cardiospermum* are perennial, woody-stemmed vines native to the tropics of Africa, India, and the Americas. Commonly called balloon vine or heart seed—*Cardiospermum* is from the Greek *kardia*, "heart," and *sperma*, "seed"—they bear fernlike leaves, insignificant four-petaled flowers, and inflated, ornamental seedpods.

HOW TO GROW

Give these tender plants full sun and rich, well-drained, evenly moist soil. They need a trellis upon which to climb. Sow seeds indoors 6 to 8 weeks before the last spring frost date. Germination takes 3 to 4 weeks at 65° to 70°F. In areas with long growing seasons, they can be sown outdoors after the last frost date. Water regularly in dry weather. Butterflies will visit the flowers.

C. halicacabum **P. 66**

c. hal-ih-kah-KAYH-bum. Balloon Vine, Love-in-a-puff. A tender, vining, 10- to 12-foot-tall perennial with fernlike, 6- to 8-inch-long leaves. Greenish white, ¼-inch flowers are followed by rounded, ¾- to 1¼-inch-wide seedpods that start out green and ripen to brown. Warm-weather annual.

Carthamus

car-THAM-us. Aster family, Asteraceae.

Spiny-leaved annuals and perennials native to the Mediterranean and western Asia, *Carthamus* species bear deeply divided leaves and thistlelike flower heads in yellow, red, orange, pink, or violet. One species, which has been grown for centuries as the source of yellow and red dye as well as for its edible seeds, the source of safflower oil, makes an unusual addition to the annual garden.

HOW TO GROW

Carthamus species thrive in full sun and light, dry, poor soil. Plants will not grow well in areas with wet, humid summers. Sow seeds indoors in individual pots 6 to 8 weeks before the last spring frost date at 50° to 60°F. Germination takes 2 to 3 weeks. Transplant with care. Or sow outdoors a few weeks before the last frost while the soil is still cool. Or sow in fall. Grow safflower *(C. tinctorius)* in the herb garden and informal mixed plantings. It also makes a fine dried flower: cut the blooms when they are just open, and hang them in a warm, dry spot.

C. tinctorius **P. 66**

c. tink-TOR-ee-us. Safflower, False Saffron. Spiny, gray-green leaves on 1- to 2-foot plants. Loose clusters of thistlelike flower heads are surrounded by stiff green bracts and with a showy cluster of orange or yellow ray florets at the center. Cool-weather annual.

Catharanthus

cath-ah-RAN-thus. Dogbane family, Apocynaceae.

This genus contains eight species of annuals and perennials from the island of Madagascar, off the coast of Africa. All bear simple leaves and five-petaled flowers carried singly or in clusters. One species is a popular bedding plant.

HOW TO GROW

Choose a site in full sun to partial shade and average to rich, well-drained, evenly moist soil. Plants thrive in heat and humidity, and thus are good choices for southern gardens. They require a long growing season to bloom best. Sow seeds indoors in winter, 3 to 4 months before the last spring frost date, at 65° to 75°F. Cover seeds, as darkness aids germination, which takes 2 to 3 weeks. Pinch seedlings to encourage branching, and transplant after the weather is warm and settled. Plants also can be propagated by cuttings taken in spring or early summer. Consider overwintering a plant or two indoors for use as stock plants in spring.

C. roseus

P. 67

c. ROE-see-us. Rose Periwinkle, Madagascar Periwinkle. Formerly *Vinca rosea.* A woody-based, 1- to 2-foot perennial hardy only from Zone 10 south, with oblong to ovate leaves. Bears flat-faced, trumpet-shaped flowers with five "petals," or lobes, from summer to frost. Flowers come in pale to hot pink, red, or white, commonly with a contrasting eye. Many cultivars are available, including Pretty and Pacifica Series, both of which are compact 12- to 14-inch plants. Tender perennial or warm-weather annual.

Celosia

seh-LOW-see-ah. Amaranth family, Amaranthaceae.

The best-known *Celosia* species are tender perennials grown as annuals, but this genus of 50 to 60 species also contains shrubs and climbers. All are from the tropics or subtropics, and most have simple, entire leaves. Although the individual flowers are small and chaffy, they are carried in large, showy, plumelike or crested inflorescences. The name *Celosia* is from the Greek *keleos,* for "burnt," and refers to the fiery colors of the flowers and their often flamelike shape.

HOW TO GROW

Give celosias full sun or very light shade and rich, well-drained soil that remains evenly moist. They thrive in hot, humid weather. Sow seeds indoors 6 to 8 weeks before the last spring frost. Cover the seeds with soil, as darkness aids germination, which takes 2 to 3 weeks at 65° to 70°F. Sowing in individual pots is best, because it minimizes transplant shock. For best results, seedlings need to grow unchecked: exposure to cold temperatures, damage to roots during transplanting, and periods of too-dry soil all lead to stunted plants with inferior, undersized blooms. Transplant about 2 weeks after the last spring frost date, once temperatures remain above 40°F at night. Water regularly throughout the season. Tall cultivars may need staking. Use celosias in beds and borders as well as cutting gardens. They also can be used in containers. Use the flowers fresh or dried. To dry them, harvest just as they fully open, strip off the leaves, and hang in small bunches in a warm, dry place.

C. argentea PP. 67, 68

c. are-JEN-tee-ah. Cockscomb. Formerly *C. cristata.* Two forms of this tender perennial are popular: Cristata Group cultivars bear rounded, crested flower heads that resemble enormous rooster combs or even cauliflowers, while Plumosa Group cultivars have erect, featherlike plumes. Both groups come in oranges, reds, yellows, and creams. Height is an important consideration when picking cultivars because it affects placement. Tall cultivars also are best for cutting and drying. Cristata-type cultivars include 6- to 8-inch 'Jewel Box Mix' and 2½- to 3-foot-tall 'Big Chief Mix'. Plumosa Group cultivars include the 8-inch Kimono Series, 20-inch 'Apricot Brandy', 2-foot Century Series, and 3-foot Sparkler Series. Warm-weather annual.

C. spicata P. 68

c. spy-KAY-tah. Wheat Celosia. Annuals with lance-shaped leaves on 2-foot plants and erect, wheatlike flower heads in silver-cream and pink. Flamingo Series cultivars are most widely available. Warm-weather annual.

Centaurea

sen-TOR-ee-ah. Aster family, Asteraceae.

There are about 450 species of annuals, biennials, perennials, and subshrubs in *Centaurea.* Commonly called cornflowers or knapweeds, they bear deeply cut, fernlike leaves and rounded, thistlelike flower heads with scaly, conelike bases. Each inflorescence consists of individual florets with deeply lobed petals that give the blooms a ragged appearance, and the heads have scaly, conelike bases. Flowers come in deep rich blue, mauve, hot pink, white, pale pink, and yellow.

HOW TO GROW

Give cornflowers full sun and average to rich, well-drained soil that is evenly moist. Too-rich soil yields plants with plenty of foliage but few flowers. Sow annual cornflowers, except *Centaurea cineraria,* outdoors on or just before the last spring frost date. In all but the coldest zones, try sowing seeds of annuals outdoors in fall for spring bloom. Indoors, sow in individual pots 6 to 8 weeks before the last frost date and chill the sown pots at 40°F for a week before moving them to a warmer (65° to 70°F) spot for germinating. Sow *C. cineraria* indoors 10 to 12 weeks before the last frost date. Transplant with care. Indoors or out, cover the seeds with soil, as darkness is required for germination. To extend the bloom period, sow new seeds every 2 to 3 weeks in spring and early summer. *C. cineraria* can be propagated by cuttings in late summer or early fall for overwintering indoors. Although all cornflowers tolerate dry soil, for best results water during dry weather. Deadheading encourages new flowers to form, but most cornflowers will self-sow, so let some flowers mature. Tall types may need staking. Use cornflowers in garden beds and borders. They also make fine cut flowers and can be dried. For cutting or drying, harvest when the flowers have expanded fully. *C. cineraria* also is an excellent container plant. Butterflies are attracted to the flowers.

C. americana P. 69

C. ah-mair-ih-CAY-ah. Basket Flower. An annual native to North America with lance-shaped leaves on 3- to 5-foot plants. Bears 4- to 6-inch-wide flower heads in shades of pink, rosy lilac, or white in summer. Cool-weather annual.

C. cineraria P. 69

C. sin-er-AIR-ee-ah. Dusty Miller. Formerly *C. gymnocarpa.* A tender, 8- to 24-inch-tall perennial or subshrub, hardy from Zone 7 south, grown for its woolly, white fernlike foliage. Remove its clusters of small, mustard yellow flowers. Tender perennial or cool-weather annual.

C. cyanus P. 70

C. sigh-AN-us. Bachelor's Buttons, Blue Bottle. An annual with lance-shaped leaves on ½- to 2½-foot plants. Bears 1- to 1½-inch-wide flowers in dark blue, mauve, pink, rosy red, or white from spring to early summer. Cool-weather annual.

C. moschata *see Amberboa moschata*

Ceratotheca

ceh-rat-oh-THEE-cah. Pedalium family, Pedaliaceae.

The five species of *Ceratotheca* are little-known relatives of sesame *(Sesamum indicum),* which also belongs to the Pedalium family. They are annuals or biennials native to Africa and carry ovate leaves and spikes of two-lipped, foxglove-like flowers, borne from late summer to fall.

HOW TO GROW

A site protected from wind in full sun or light shade with rich, moist soil is ideal. *Ceratotheca* species are best for areas with long growing seasons. Sow seeds indoors 10 to 12 weeks before the last spring frost date and germinate at 70° to 75°F. Transplant after the last frost date once the weather is warm and settled. Stake plants to keep them erect, and water regularly.

C. triloba P. 70

c. tri-LOW-bah. South African Foxglove. A 4- to 6-foot-tall annual with heart-shaped to triangular, round-toothed leaves and hairy stems. Two-lipped, 3-inch-long, lilac flowers that are often striped with purple appear from midsummer to frost. Warm-weather annual.

Cerinthe

ceh-RIN-thee. Borage family, Boraginaceae.

The genus *Cerinthe* includes 10 species of annuals, biennials, and perennials native to Europe. The plants have glaucous leaves and clusters of tubular, nectar-rich flowers surrounded by showy bracts.

HOW TO GROW

Full sun and average, well-drained soil are ideal. Plants grow best in areas with cool, moist summers and suffer in hot weather. Sow seeds indoors 8 to 10 weeks before the last spring frost date, or sow outdoors after the last frost date. Use *Cerinthe* species in mixed plantings.

C. major P. 71

c. MAY-jor. Honeywort. A 1- to 2-foot annual with gray-green leaves that have hairs around the edges. Clusters of yellow, ½- to ¾-inch-long flowers that have maroon edges or bands. The flowers are surrounded by purple bracts. Cool-weather annual.

Cherianthus cheiri see *Erysimum cheiri*

Chrysanthemum

Although *Chrysanthemum* once contained between 100 and 200 species, in recent years botanists have reclassified most of the plants that once belonged here. Today the genus contains about 20 species of annuals and perennials with aromatic, deeply lobed or fernlike leaves, including two annuals native to the Mediterranean grown for their showy, daisylike flowers.

HOW TO GROW

Choose a site in full sun with average to rich, well-drained soil. Except in areas with cool summers, both annual chrysanthemums described here are plants for spring or fall bloom, because they tend to die out when hot weather arrives. Sow seeds outdoors in early spring as soon as the soil can be worked. Or sow indoors 8 to 10 weeks before the last spring frost date. Sow new crops at 3-week intervals through late spring for continued bloom. Begin sowing again in midsummer for fall flowers. Pinch plants to encourage branching, stake as necessary, water if the weather is dry, and remove faded flowers promptly to lengthen bloom season. Pull up plants when hot weather arrives, and replace with warm-season annuals.

C. carinatum

P. 71

c. kar-in-AY-tum. Painted Daisy, Tricolor Chrysanthemum. Formerly *C. tricolor*. A fast-growing, well-branched, 2- to 3-foot annual with fernlike leaves and 2½-inch daisylike blooms in shades of red, orange, yellow, maroon, and white. Cool-weather annual.

Chrysanthemum sp.

C. coronarium **P. 72**

c. kore-oh-NAIR-ee-um. Crown Daisy, Garland Chrysanthemum. A 2½- to 4-foot annual with deeply cut, fernlike leaves. Plants bear yellow, single or double, 1- to 2-inch flowers. The cultivar 'Primrose Gem' bears pale yellow flowers with golden eyes. Cool-weather annual.

C. frutescens see Argyranthemum frutescens
C. paludosum see Leucanthemum paludosum

Cirsium

SIR-see-um. Aster family, Asteraceae.

While the genus *Cirsium* can count pernicious weeds among its 200 species of biennials and perennials—Canada thistle *(C. arvense)* and bull thistle *(C. vulgare)* belong here—it also has at least one species to offer gardeners who love annuals: *C. japonicum.* All members of the genus have spiny, often handsome, leaves and rounded heads of purple, red, pink, yellow, or white flowers that somewhat resemble shaving brushes.

HOW TO GROW

C. japonicum thrives in full sun and poor, average, or rich soil that is moist but well drained. In areas with mild winters, try sowing seeds in late summer to grow it as a biennial. The plants will produce a rosette of leaves in fall and bloom the following year. Elsewhere, sow seeds outdoors about 2 weeks before the last spring frost date. Plants require little care, but deadheading limits their tendency to self-sow. They generally self-sow only in moderation, and unlike weedy thistles, the seedlings are easy to pull up. Use *C. japonicum* in mixed beds, herb gardens, or meadowlike plantings.

C. japonicum **P. 72**

c. jah-PON-ih-kum. Plumed Thistle. A 3- to 6-foot biennial or short-lived perennial with deeply cut, thistlelike leaves that are soft to the touch, not spiny. Rounded, brushlike, rose- to lilac-pink flower heads in late summer and fall. Cool-weather annual.

Clarkia

CLARK-ee-ah. Evening primrose family, Onagraceae.

Known by an array of common names—including godetia, farewell-to-spring, Rocky Mountain garland, red ribbons, and fairy fans—*Clarkia* species are native to western North America and South America. Formerly known as *Godetia,* the genus *Clarkia* was named for Captain William Clark, of the Lewis and Clark Expedition, and contains 36 species of annuals with slender stems and oval, linear, or elliptic leaves. They are grown for their clusters of funnel-shaped flowers, which have a satiny or crepe-paper texture. Flowers have four petals, but double-flowered forms also are available.

HOW TO GROW

A site with full sun and average, moist but well-drained soil is ideal. Too-rich soil yields plants with plenty of foliage but few flowers. These plants resent heat and humidity, but a site with light shade, especially in the afternoon, may help them cope in areas with warm summers. In most areas, sow seeds outdoors on or before the last spring frost date. Sow a few weeks before the last frost date in areas with warm summers. From Zone 8 south, sow seeds in fall for late winter bloom. To lengthen the bloom season, sow new crops of seeds at 2-week intervals until late spring. Or sow indoors 6 to 8 weeks before the last frost in individual pots, and transplant with care. When sowing, just press the seeds into the soil surface, as light is required for germination. Stake with twiggy brush. Use these plants in mixed plantings and combined with other spring-blooming annuals. They make excellent cut flowers and also can be grown in containers.

C. amoena P. 73

c. am-oh-EE-nah. Farewell-to-spring, Satin Flower. Formerly *Godetia amoena.* A 2- to 2½-foot plant with lance-shaped leaves. Clusters of single or double, 2-inch-wide flowers in shades of lavender to lavender- and rose-pink in summer. Cool-weather annual.

C. unguiculata P. 73

c. un-guih-cue-LAY-tah. Farewell-to-Spring. Formerly *C. elegans.* A 1- to 3-foot annual with lance-shaped, elliptic, or ovate leaves. Solitary ½- to 2-inch-wide, single or double flowers in shades from lavender- to rose-pink or salmon pink as well as red, red-purple, and white in summer. Cool-weather annual.

Cleome

klee-OH-me. Caper family, Capparidaceae.

The genus *Cleome* includes approximately 150 species of annuals and shrubs distributed in tropical and subtropical regions throughout the world. Most bear palmate leaves with three to seven leaflets, and all have four-petaled asymmetrical flowers that have a spidery appearance, thus the common name spider flower. Blooms come in pinkish purple, pink, white, or yellowish to greenish and are carried in erect racemes that elongate as new flowers open throughout the summer. One species is a popular annual that adds height and airy color to mixed borders. It attracts hummingbirds and butterflies and also makes a stunning cut flower.

HOW TO GROW

A site in full sun with light, rich, well-drained soil is ideal. Sow seeds indoors 6 to 8 weeks before the last spring frost date and germinate at about 65°F. After seedlings emerge, grow them at 70° to 75°F. Some gardeners sow the seeds and then refrigerate the pots for 2 weeks before moving them to a warmer spot. Or sow outdoors after the last frost date, once nighttime temperatures remain above 40°F. Although established plants tolerate dry soil, for best results water regularly during dry weather. Plants self-sow, and seedlings can become a nuisance in warm climates. Deadheading is a tedious task, but it will curtail this tendency.

C. hasslerana

P. 74

c. hass-ler-AH-nah. Spider Flower. Sometimes listed as *C. spinosa* or *C. pungens.* A strong-scented annual with palmate leaves that ranges from 3 to 5 or more feet tall. Pink, purple, or white, 1¼-inch-wide flowers are carried in large racemes in summer. Several cultivars selected for color are avail-

Cleome hasslerana

able, including Queen Series cultivars and white-flowered 'Helen Campbell'. Warm-weather annual.

Clianthus

clee-AN-thus. Pea family, Fabaceae.

Two tender species, commonly referred to as glory peas, belong to this genus. One, an annual or short-lived perennial, is native to Australia, while the other, a shrub, to New Zealand. Both are climbing or trailing plants with pinnate, or featherlike, leaves with 15 or more leaflets and clusters of extremely showy flowers that have been described as resembling lobsters' claws or parrots' beaks. The pea-like flowers have upturned standards, or petals, and long, curved keels (also petals) that point downward. The botanical name *Clianthus* is from the Greek *kleios,* "glory," and *anthos,* "flower."

HOW TO GROW

Full sun and a warm spot with light, sandy, very well drained soil are essential. Sow seeds indoors and germinate at 55° to 65°F. Grow plants on the dry side: this is especially important with *C. formosus,* which resents overwatering. (Seedlings of this species are commonly grafted onto *Colutea arborescens* rootstocks, because plants grafted in this manner are less susceptible to overwatering.) *Clianthus puniceus,* a tender shrub hardy from about Zone 7 south, can be grown from cuttings taken in summer. In areas where it is marginally hardy, try a site against a south-facing wall for extra winter protection, make sure the soil drains perfectly, and protect plants with loose mulch over winter. Plants killed to the ground will resprout in spring as long as the roots survive. In the North, grow them in containers and overwinter them indoors in a bright, 40° to 45°F spot.

C. formosus P. 74

c. for-MOE-sus. Glory Pea, Desert Pea. An annual or short-lived perennial that can reach 4 feet on a trellis or other support. Clusters of showy, 2- to 3-inch crimson blooms with purple-black centers appear in summer. Warm-weather annual.

C. puniceus

c. pew-NEE-cee-us. Parrot's Bill, Parrot's Beak. A tender shrub that can reach 6 feet. Bears clusters of 3-inch-long red flowers from spring to early summer. Tender perennial.

Cobaea

COE-bee-ah. Phlox family, Polemoniaceae.

Native from Mexico to South America, the 20 species of *Cobaea* are tender, woody or herbaceous climbers. They have pinnate leaves and produce showy, bell-shaped flowers with five lobes.

HOW TO GROW

A site in full sun with average soil is ideal. Plants require a trellis or other support to climb and need regular watering throughout the growing season. In areas with hot summers, a spot with afternoon shade is best. Sow seeds indoors 8 to 10 weeks before the last spring frost date. (From Zone 9 south, it is possible to sow seeds outdoors where the plants are to grow.) To minimize problems with rot, use a sterile seed-starting mix and set the seeds long edge down, with the upper edge right at the soil surface. Seeds take from 10 to 30 days to germinate at temperatures of 60° to 70°F. Move plants to the garden after the last frost, when temperatures remain above 40°. Pinch seedlings to encourage branching. You also can propagate plants by taking cuttings in summer for overwintering indoors.

C. scandens P. 75

c. SCAN-dens. Cup-and-saucer Vine, Cathedral Bells. A vigorous tendril climber that can reach 40 feet or more where hardy (from Zone 10 south) but is considerably shorter in the North. Pinnate leaves with four leaflets and fragrant, 2-inch-long, bell-shaped flowers, each with a ruffled green cup (the calyx) at its base. Flowers open greenish white and age to purple. 'Alba' bears flowers that stay greenish white. Tender perennial or warm-weather annual.

Coix

COY-ex. Grass family, Poaceae.

Coix contains five or six species of annuals and perennials native to tropical Asia. All are tall grasses with narrow, lance-shaped leaves that produce separate clusters of male and female flowers. The female flower clusters are decorated with hard, hollow teardrop-shaped "beads" or "tears," which are actually modified leaf sheaths called utricles that protect the female flowers and seeds. The utricles are used to make necklaces, rosaries, and other decorations.

HOW TO GROW

A site with full sun or light shade and rich, well-drained soil is ideal. Sow seeds indoors 6 to 8 weeks before the last frost. Soak seeds overnight in warm water before sowing, and sow in individual pots. Germination takes 2 to 4 weeks at 60° to 70°F. Transplant after the last spring frost date, once temperatures remain above 45° or 50°F. In areas with long growing seasons, from Zone 8 or 9 south, try sowing seeds outdoors where the plants are to grow. Water during dry weather. Plants self-sow.

C. lacryma-jobi P. 75

c. lah-CRY-mah JOE-bee. Job's Tears. A 1½- to 3-foot annual with 2-foot-long leaves and jointed stems. Male and female flowers appear in fall. The "tears" on the female spikes are initially green and ripen into hard, shiny, oval to teardrop-shaped, ½-inch-long beads in shades of creamy white, gray, and purplish. Warm-weather annual.

Coleus *see Solenostemon*

Collinsia

col-LIN-see-ah. Figwort family, Scrophulariaceae.

Most of the 25 species of *Collinsia* are native to the western United States. These relatives of snapdragons (*Antirrhinum* spp.) and foxgloves (*Digitalis* spp.) have ovate to oblong leaves and two-lipped flowers with five lobes, two on the top lip, three on the bottom one. Flowers, which are commonly bicolored, come in shades of pink, white, blue, lavender-blue, or pinkish purple and are borne in whorls or singly.

HOW TO GROW

Partial shade, especially during the heat of the day, and rich, moist, well-drained soil are best. The plants do not do well in areas with hot, humid summers. Sow seeds outdoors a few weeks before the last spring frost date, when light frost is still possible. Make repeated sowings at 2-week intervals to prolong bloom season. *C. verna* is best in light shade; sow it in fall for spring bloom. Plants tend to sprawl; stake with twiggy brush if you want them to stay more erect. Water during dry weather to prolong bloom. Use *Collinsia* species in mixed plantings and wildflower gardens. They also make excellent cut flowers.

C. bicolor

P. 76

C. BI-col-or. Chinese Houses. Formerly *C. heterophylla.* A weak-stemmed, 2-foot annual carrying clusters of flowers with white upper lips and rose-purple lower ones. Cool-weather annual.

C. verna

C. VER-nah. Blue-eyed Mary. A ½- to 2-foot annual native to rich woods in the East and Upper Midwest. Bears clustered or solitary ½-inch-long flowers with white upper lips and blue lower ones. Cool-weather annual.

Consolida

con-SOE-lih-dah. Buttercup family, Ranunculaceae.

Commonly called larkspurs and once included in the genus *Delphinium,* the 40 species of *Consolida* are annuals from southeastern Europe and the Mediterranean to central Asia. They bear feathery, deeply cut leaves and spikelike clusters of spurred flowers. One species is a popular annual.

HOW TO GROW

Larkspurs prefer full sun to very light shade and average to rich, well-drained soil. In areas with cool summers, they bloom through much of the growing season, but in the South they provide spring and early-summer bloom, then die out in summer heat and humidity. Sow seeds outdoors in fall or in spring, beginning as soon as the soil can be worked to about 2 weeks before the last spring frost date. Repeated sowings at 3-week intervals lengthen the bloom season. Barely cover the seeds with soil, as darkness is required for germination. Outdoor sowing is generally best, but if you want earlier bloom, try sowing indoors in individual pots 8 to 10 weeks before the last frost date. Set the sown pots in the refrigerator for 2 weeks before moving them to a warmer (50° to 55°F) spot for germination, which takes 2 to 3 weeks. Transplant with care. Stake tall cultivars with twiggy brush, or let them lean on their neighbors. Water during dry weather. Deadhead to prolong bloom, but let some flowers set seeds, because plants self-sow. Use larkspur in mixed beds and borders and in cottage gardens. The flowers, which attract hummingbirds, are excellent for cutting and/or drying; tall cultivars are best for these uses. For fresh use, cut just as the lowest blooms on the stalk open. To dry, harvest before the entire spike has opened and hang in bundles in a warm, dry, dark place.

C. ajacis P. 76

c. ah-JAY-kis. Larkspur, Annual Delphinium. Formerly *C. ambigua.* Ferny, palmate leaves on 1- to 4-foot plants. Bears branched or unbranched ½- to 2-foot-long flower spikes packed with 1½-inch-wide flowers in shades of blue, violet, lavender, white, and pink. Imperial Series plants are 2 to 3 feet tall and available in separate colors. Dwarf Rocket and Dwarf Hyacinth Series plants range from 1 to 2 feet tall. Cool-weather annual.

Convolvulus

con-VOL-view-lus. Morning-glory family, Convolvulaceae.

About 250 species of annuals, perennials, subshrubs, and shrubs belong to this widely distributed genus, which contains beloved garden annuals as well as notorious weeds—field bindweed *(Convolvulus arvensis)* belongs here. These popular garden plants are from the Mediterranean and North Africa. Plants are erect or have trailing or climbing stems with entire, often heart- or arrow-shaped, leaves. The funnel-shaped flowers are borne singly or in clusters.

HOW TO GROW

A warm, protected site in full sun and poor to average or moderately fertile soil is best. Sow seeds indoors in individual pots 6 to 8 weeks before the last spring frost date at 70° to 80°F. In mild areas with long growing seasons (roughly Zone 8 south), gardeners have two growing options: either sow the seeds outdoors after the last frost date once temperatures remain above 50°F; or, sow seeds in fall for early bloom the following spring. Before sowing, nick the hard seed coats with a file or soak seeds in warm water for 24 hours. Germination takes 1 to 2 weeks at 55° to 65°F. Perennials and shrubs also can be propagated by cuttings taken in late spring or early summer.

C. cneorum P. 77

c. nee-OR-um. Silverbush. Lance-shaped, silver-green leaves on mounding 2-foot-tall, 3-foot-wide shrubs, hardy from Zone 8 south. Clusters of white, 1½-inch-wide flowers with yellow centers in spring and summer. Tender perennial.

C. sabatius P. 77

c. sah-BAY-tee-us. A trailing, 6-inch-tall perennial, hardy from Zone 8 south, with ovate leaves and lavender-blue, funnel-shaped, ½- to 1-inch-wide flowers from summer to early fall. Tender perennial.

C. tricolor

P. 78

c. TRI-cuh-lor. Dwarf Morning Glory. A 1- to 1½-foot-tall annual or short-lived perennial, hardy from Zone 9 south, with ovate to lance-shaped leaves. Solitary, 1½-inch-wide trumpets in rich blue with yellow-and-white throats appear in summer. Blooms last only a day and close in cloudy weather. Warm-weather annual.

Coreopsis

core-ee-OP-sis. Aster family, Asteraceae.

Between 80 and 100 species of annuals and perennials native to North and Central America belong to the genus *Coreopsis*. All bear daisylike, single or double flowers, generally in shades of gold, yellow, or yellow-orange. Leaves are simple and entire or cut in either a featherlike or palm-like fashion. Both the common name tickseed and the botanical name *Coreopsis* refer to the black seeds that follow the flowers—*Coreopsis* is from the Greek *koris*, "bug," and *opsis*, "resemblance."

HOW TO GROW

Choose a site with full sun and average to rich, well-drained soil. Plants tolerate drought and also sites with some morning shade as long as they receive afternoon sun. For annual species (such as *C. tinctoria*), sow seeds indoors 6 to 8 weeks before the last spring frost date or sow outdoors after the last frost date. Successive sowings every few weeks will extend bloom season. To grow *C. grandiflora* as an annual, sow indoors 8 to 10 weeks before the last frost. When sowing, just press the seeds into the soil surface, as light aids germination. Regular deadheading will lengthen the bloom season. Either cut off individual blooms or cut back the entire plant by about one-third. Plants self-sow, so let some flowers set seeds. *C. grandiflora* also can be propagated by division in early spring or early fall, or by cuttings taken in spring from the base of the plant or in summer from stem tips. Use tickseeds in beds and borders as well as meadow plantings. Their flowers attract butterflies and also are great cut flowers.

C. grandiflora

P. 78

c. gran-dih-FLOOR-ah. Large-leaved Coreopsis. A clump-forming, 1- to 3-foot perennial, hardy in Zones 3 or 4 to 9. Single, semidouble, or double, 1- to 2½-inch flowers in shades of yellow to yellow-orange from spring to late summer if plants are deadheaded regularly. The cultivar 'Early Sunrise' blooms well the first year from seeds. Hardy perennial or warm-weather annual.

C. tinctoria

P. 79

C. tink-TOAR-ee-ah. Calliopsis, Plains Coreopsis. An erect, 1- to 4-foot annual with solitary, yellow, 1- to 2-inch-wide daisylike flowers. The species bears bright yellow flowers with maroon centers, but cultivars with petals striped or marked with maroon, dark red, or purple-brown also are available. Warm-weather annual.

Coriandrum

cor-ee-AN-drum. Carrot family, Apiaceae.

Two aromatic-leaved annuals native to the Mediterranean belong to this genus. Both bear deeply divided ferny leaves and lacy-looking compound umbels of tiny white or pinkish to purplish blooms. One species, *Coriandrum sativum,* is known as cilantro when grown for its foliage and coriander for its seeds. Its lacy leaves also make an attractive filler for beds and borders as well as containers.

HOW TO GROW

Full sun or partial shade and average to rich, well-drained soil are ideal. In areas where summers are hot, select a site that receives shade during the hottest part of the day. Sow seeds outdoors after the last spring frost date. When sowing, cover the seeds with soil, as darkness aids germination. Seedlings take about 2 weeks to appear. Sow new crops of seeds every 3 weeks from spring through summer for a continual supply of leaves. In flower gardens, plants are most effective when grown in drifts of at least three to five plants. Plants self-sow.

C. sativum

P. 79

C. sah-TIE-vum. Cilantro, Coriander. Aromatic, shiny, green leaves that resemble flat-leaved parsley on 1- to 2-foot plants. Lacy, ½-inch-wide umbels of tiny white or pale purple flowers. Cool-weather annual.

Cosmos

COZ-mose. Aster family, Asteraceae.

Cosmos contains about 25 species of annuals and perennials native to the southern United States and Central America. All bear daisylike flowers, and most have deeply divided, almost featherlike leaves. The botanical name *Cosmos* refers to the attractive flowers of these easy-to-grow plants; it is taken from the Greek *kosmos,* meaning "ornament."

HOW TO GROW

Choose a planting site with full sun and poor to average, evenly moist, well-drained soil. Too-rich soil yields floppy plants and few flowers. Sow seeds outdoors after danger of frost has passed. Or, for earlier bloom, sow seeds indoors 4 to 6 weeks before the last spring frost date. If sowing indoors, place pots in the refrigerator for 2 weeks after sowing, then germinate between 70° and 75°F. Stake taller types with twiggy brush, or space plants closely so they will support each other. Deadheading lengthens the bloom season. Annuals self-sow. Tender perennial *C. atrosanguineus* is hardy from Zone 7 south. North of that, dig the roots after a light fall frost, and store them in barely damp vermiculite, peat, or sand in a cool (40° to 50°F), dry place, as you would dahlias. Cosmos come in several heights, and all make outstanding fillers for the middle or back of a perennial bed or border. All attract butterflies and make outstanding cut flowers.

C. atrosanguineus P. 80

c. ah-tro-san-GWIN-ee-us. Chocolate Cosmos, Black Cosmos. Formerly *Bidens atrosanguinea.* A 2½-foot-tall, tuberous-rooted perennial. Cup-shaped, 1¾-inch, daisylike flowers have maroon petals, dark red-brown centers, and a slight chocolate fragrance. Tender perennial or warm-weather annual.

C. bipinnatus P. 80

c. bi-pin-NAY-tus. Cosmos. A 1- to 5-foot annual bearing showy, daisylike, yellow-centered flowers with petals in shades of pink, maroon, crimson, and white. Cultivars with various flower forms and heights are available. 'Seashell Mix' cultivars have rolled petals resembling round shells and reach 3 feet; 'Sonata Mix' and 'Versailles Mix' plants are dwarf, ranging from 1½ to 2 feet. Warm-weather annual.

C. sulphureus P. 81

c. sulf-UR-ee-us. Cosmos. A 1- to 6-foot annual with single or double, 1½- to 2½-inch-wide, daisylike flowers in shades of yellow, orange, and orange-red. The Klondike and Ladybird Series are dwarf types, reaching only 14 to 18 inches. Warm-weather annual.

Craspedia

crass-PEE-dee-ah. Aster family, Asteraceae.

Craspedia contains about eight species of annuals and tender perennials; all bear rounded, buttonlike flower heads and are native to Australia, New Zealand, and Tasmania. Their blooms consist of disk florets, but no petal-like ray florets, and the flowers are carried on unbranched stalks above a dense rosette of leaves.

HOW TO GROW

A site in full sun and average, well-drained soil is ideal. Sow seeds indoors 8 to 10 weeks before the last spring frost date at 55° to 65°F. Water plants regularly when they are actively growing; if possible, avoid wetting the rosette of foliage. In areas with very mild winters, tender perennial species can be overwintered outdoors; gritty, perfectly drained soil is essential to success, because plants resent wet soil in winter. Use these plants in mixed plantings and for dried arrangements. To dry the blooms, harvest as soon as they are fully open, and hang them in bunches in a warm, dry, dark place.

C. globosa

P. 81

c. glow-BOW-sah. Bachelor's Buttons, Drumsticks. A tender perennial, hardy from Zone 9 south, with a low rosette of strap-shaped, woolly white leaves and stiff, unbranched flower stems reaching 2 to 3 feet. Rounded, 1¼-inch-wide, mustard yellow flower heads appear in summer. Tender perennial or warm-weather annual.

Crepis

KREY-puss. Aster family, Asteraceae.

Commonly called hawk's beards, *Crepis* species are milky-juiced annuals and perennials native to dry, rocky soils in the Northern Hemisphere. About 200 species belong to the genus. All bear flattened, dandelion-like flower heads, usually in shades of yellow or orange, and flattened rosettes of leaves that can be entire or deeply divided. One species native to Italy and Greece is grown as an annual.

HOW TO GROW

Crepis species require full sun and poor to average, well-drained soil. They generally will not grow well in areas with very hot, humid, wet summers. Sow seeds outdoors in early spring, a few weeks before the last spring frost date. Or sow indoors in individual pots 4 to 6 weeks before the last frost date. From Zone 5 south, try sowing seeds outdoors in fall for earlier bloom the following spring. Plants self-sow.

C. rubra

P. 82

c. RUE-brah. Hawk's Beard, Hawkweed. A 1- to 1½-foot annual or short-lived perennial, hardy from Zone 5 south, with a rosette of lance-shaped leaves. Showy, 1- to 1½-inch flowers in pinkish red from spring to summer. Cool-weather annual.

Cucurbita

cue-CURB-ih-tah. Gourd family, Cucurbitaceae.

Better known as residents of vegetable gardens, pumpkins and squashes can be useful in ornamental plantings as well. They bear attractive, lobed leaves that can exceed 8 inches across and trumpet-shaped, 5- to 6-inch-wide, yellow-orange flowers. The genus contains about 27 species, but most gardeners select these plants by looking at cultivar descriptions only. Pie-type pumpkins generally are classified as *Cucurbita moschata*, while carving pumpkins usually are *C. pepo*.

HOW TO GROW

Full sun; rich, well-drained soil; and plenty of space will satisfy pumpkins: standard-size pumpkins can spread 15 feet, while mini-pumpkins can spread 8 feet, and semibush types spread about 5 feet. Sow seeds indoors no more than 3 weeks before the last spring frost date in individual pots. Germination takes about 1 week if the soil is kept warm, about 75°F. Seeds will not germinate at all if the soil is below 60°F. Transplant with care after the last frost date, once the weather has settled and the soil has warmed up. In areas with long growing seasons, sow seeds outdoors after the soil has reached 60°F. The earliest pumpkin cultivars, including minis, require about 95 days to set and ripen fruit. Use pumpkins as fast, temporary, inexpensive ground covers in new gardens and under shrubs; just don't let them engulf shrubs. (They also will cover eyesores such as stumps.) Mini types make effective climbers for fences or trellises, and both their flowers and fruit are attractive.

C. pepo

P. 82

c. PEY-po. Pumpkins. Mini-type pumpkins bear handsome, full-size leaves and flowers. When allowed to scramble over the ground, they reach about 10 inches in height. 'Jack Be Little' bears ribbed, 3- to 4-inch, orange fruit, about 12 per plant; the fruit is edible and sweet-fleshed. 'Baby Boo' bears similar but white-skinned fruit. 'We-B-Little' is a semibush-type plant that bears about 8 unribbed, 3- to 3½-inch, orange fruits per plant. Warm-weather annual.

Cuphea

COO-fee-ah. Lythrum family, Lythraceae.

Some 250 annuals, short-lived perennials, and shrubs native to North, Central, and South America belong to the genus *Cuphea*. All bear tubular flowers either singly or in clusters; most have ovate to lance-shaped leaves and are covered with sticky hairs.

HOW TO GROW

A site in full sun or light shade with average to fertile, well-drained soil satisfies these plants. Sow seeds indoors 10 to 12 weeks before the last spring frost date. Just press the seeds into the soil surface, as light is required for germination, which takes 1 to 2 weeks at 70°F. Once seedlings appear, reduce the temperature to about 60°F. Most of the commonly grown species are tender perennials or tender shrubs, hardy from Zone 10 south. Propagate them by cuttings taken in late spring or by division. In the North, grow them in containers and overwinter them indoors (in a bright, 60° to 65°F spot), or treat them as bedding plants replaced annually. Use *Cuphea* species as edgings or in beds combined with other annuals. They also make attractive container plants, and hummingbirds visit the flowers.

C. hyssopifolia P. 83

c. hiss-up-ih-FOE-lee-ah. Mexican Heather, Hawaiian Heather, Elfin Herb. A bushy, tender, 1- to 2-foot shrub with narrow, lance-shaped leaves. Small clusters of pale pinkish purple, pink, or white, ½-inch-long flowers from summer to fall. Tender perennial or warm-weather annual.

C. ignea P. 83

c. IG-nee-ah. Cigar Flower, Firecracker Plant. Formerly *C. platycentra*. A tender, 1- to 2½-foot shrub or subshrub with lance-shaped to oblong leaves. Showy, tubular, ¾- to 1¼-inch-long flowers with red to red-orange calyxes (not true petals) appear singly in the leaf axils from early summer to fall. Each bloom has a white edge and two dark purple petals at the tip, making them resemble a lit cigarette. Tender perennial or warm-weather annual.

C. × *purpurea*

c. × pur-PUR-ee-ah. A tender 1- to 2-foot subshrub with lance-shaped or ovate leaves. Clusters of pink to red, 1¼-inch-long flowers appear from early summer to fall. Tender perennial or warm-weather annual.

Cynoglossum

sin-oh-GLOSS-um. Borage family, Boraginaceae.

Cynoglossum contains about 55 species of annuals, biennials, and short-lived perennials. All are characterized by rough, hairy stems and leaves, and sprays of small flowers that resemble forget-me-nots (*Myosotis* spp.). The tubular to funnel-shaped blooms come in rich, true blue, as well as purple, pink, and white.

HOW TO GROW

A site with full sun to partial shade and average, moist but well-drained soil is ideal. Too-rich soil yields lots of foliage but weak plants and few flowers. Sow seeds indoors 6 to 8 weeks before the last spring frost date. Or sow outdoors several weeks before the last spring frost date. From Zone 5 south, Chinese forget-me-not *(Cynoglossum amabile)* can be sown in fall and grown as a biennial. Germination takes 1 to 2 weeks at 65° to 75°F; be sure to cover the seeds with soil, as darkness is required for germination. Add these plants to beds and borders and semiwild gardens. Plants self-sow.

C. amabile

P. 84

c. ah-MAH-bil-ee. Chinese Forget-me-not. A 1½- to 2-foot biennial producing clumps of hairy, lance-shaped, gray-green leaves. Terminal cymes of ¼- to ½-inch flowers in blue or sometimes pink or white in mid- to late summer. 'Blue Showers' bears rich blue flowers; 'Mystery Rose' has soft lilac-pink ones. Biennial or cool-weather annual.

Dahlia

DAHL-ee-ah. Aster family, Asteraceae.

Dahlia contains some 30 species of tuberous-rooted, tender perennials from Central and South America, but gardeners are much more familiar with the hybrids of these popular plants. There are literally thousands to choose from, with showy flowers in an array of shapes and sizes, from enormous doubles 10 inches or more wide to petite daisylike singles. Dahlias bloom from midsummer to frost, and flowers, which attract hummingbirds, come in all colors except true blue. The plants have fleshy, pinnate leaves that are green or sometimes bronze or maroon.

HOW TO GROW

Give dahlias a site in full sun and rich, well-drained, evenly moist soil. Plants benefit from good air circulation but need protection from wind. They tolerate a site with only a half-day of sun but bloom less; in areas with very hot summers, shade during the hottest part of the day is beneficial. Grow dahlias as perennials from Zone 8 south. In the North, grow them as tender perennials overwintered indoors or as annuals. Most gardeners start dahlias from tubers, which is the only way to acquire most of the improved cultivars. Starting from seed offers the advantage of lots of plants for very little money; sow seeds indoors 4 to 6 weeks before the last spring frost date. To start from tubers, select thick, firm, fleshy tubers that each have a piece of stem attached: the eyes, or growing buds, are on the main stem, not on the tuber itself. Set tubers outdoors no more than 2 weeks before the last frost date (delay planting if the weather has been cold or wet), planting in a 6-inch-deep trench with the eyes, or buds, pointed up and about 2 inches below the soil surface (4 inches in hot climates). For a head start in areas with short seasons, pot up tubers indoors 4 to 6 weeks before the last frost date, with the buds just above the soil surface, and keep in a warm (60° to 75°F), bright spot. Keep the soil barely moist until sprouts appear in 2 to 4 weeks. Move them to the garden after the last spring frost date, and plant them with the tops of the tubers at the soil surface. Dahlias begin flowering about 2 to 2½ months after planting.

For cultivars that will exceed 3 feet in height, install stakes *before* planting. For full-size plants, 6- to 7-foot stakes driven 1½ feet into the ground should suffice. Set the tubers with the eye nearest the stake. When planting individual tubers, pinch off all but two shoots; when planting small clumps of tubers, pinch off all but four to eight. Pinch shoots again when they have two to three sets of leaves to encourage branching and bushy growth. When stems reach 2 feet, begin loosely tying full-size dahlias to their stakes with strips of cloth or nylon stockings. Mulch in early summer and water regularly. Feed plants first after thinning stems, again when buds first appear, and a third time about a month later. Deadheading encourages new flowers to form. To pick dahlias for arrangements, cut them when the flowers are nearly open but still firm in the center.

To overwinter the roots, cut the stalks back to about 6 inches after frost, and dig them up. Shake off the excess soil, and turn the clumps upside down for a few hours to dry. (Attach labels to the clumps as you dig them.) Store them in a well-ventilated, relatively dry, cool (36° to 45°F) spot in boxes of barely moist vermiculite or sand, in paper bags or wrapped in newspaper, or in plastic bags punched with plenty of air holes. High humidity causes rot. Storing the clumps whole is best, but if you divide in fall, dust cuts with sulfur before storage. Inspect monthly for signs of rotting. Trim off rotted spots and dust the cuts with sulfur. Barely mist the tubers if they begin to shrivel.

D. Hybrids P. 84

Dahlias come in a wealth of sizes, shapes, and heights. Enthusiasts recognize 16 different flower shapes, including cactus, water lily, ball, anemone, collarette, and single dahlias. Size categories range from Giant (or AA) blooms, which exceed 10 inches, to miniatures, which are 2 inches or less across. For dahlias that produce the most blooms per plant, stick to cultivars with flowers under 6 inches across. If you prefer low-growing plants, look for the words "dwarf" or "bedding" in the description. These will generally range from 1 to 1½ feet tall. (With dahlias the term "miniature" refers to the flowers only, and miniatures are as large as other standard-size plants.) Standard-size plants range from 3½ to 6 feet. 'Bambino Mixed' and 'Coltness' hybrids are dwarf plants that can be started from seeds. Seed mixes for full-size plants also are available. 'Bishop of Landaff' bears orange-red flowers with maroon foliage. Tender perennial or warm-weather annual.

Datura

dah-TOUR-ah. Nightshade family, Solanaceae.

Commonly called thorn-apples or angel's trumpets, *Datura* species are closely related to *Brugmansia* species, which once were classified here. Both bear showy, trumpet-shaped blooms, but those of daturas point up, rather than hang down. Most bear undivided leaves with smooth or wavy-toothed edges and fragrant flowers followed by thorny or spiny seed capsules. The genus contains eight species of annuals and short-lived perennials native to tropical, subtropical, and warm-temperate areas in the Americas. The foliage has an unpleasant scent when bruised, and all parts of the plants are poisonous if eaten. While jimsonweed *(D. stramonium)* is a fairly common North America weed, gardeners grow one species, *D. wrightii,* for its fragrant flowers.

HOW TO GROW

Give *Datura* species full sun and average, well-drained soil. Sow seeds indoors 8 to 10 weeks before the last spring frost date. Germination takes about 2 weeks at 60°F. Transplant with care, as the plants resent having their roots disturbed. In areas with long growing seasons, roughly Zone 9 south, seeds can be sown where the plants are to grow. Plants sprawl, but gracefully, so give them plenty of room. Or give them supports such as small tepees or twiggy brush to encourage them to stand taller. Use them in perennial gardens, shrub borders, or large containers. They are best when used near a terrace or other spot where their nighttime fragrance can be appreciated.

D. wrightii

P. 85

d. WRIGHT-ee-eye. Angel's Trumpet. Also listed as *D. metel, D. meteloides,* and *D. inoxa* ssp. *quinquecuspida.* A 3- to 5-foot annual with felted, wavy-toothed leaves. Showy, 5- to 6-inch-long, 6- to 8-inch-wide trumpets in white, white tinged with purple, or pale lilac. Each flower lasts only one night. 'Evening Fragrance' bears very fragrant white flowers touched with pale lavender. 'Cornucopaea' bears double purple trumpets and purple leaves. Warm-weather annual.

D. sanguinea see Brugmansia sanguinea
D. suaveolens see Brugmansia suaveolens

Dianthus

die-AN-thuss. Pink family, Caryophyllaceae.

Commonly called pinks, *Dianthus* species are beloved by gardeners for their dainty, often spicy-scented flowers and basically undemanding nature. The genus contains some 300 species of annuals, biennials, perennials, and subshrubs. The plants are generally low-growing and mound-shaped, and they feature attractive, blue- or gray-green, lance-shaped to grasslike leaves. Blooms come in all shades of pink, plus white, maroon, and ruby red. The common name pinks comes not from the color of the flowers, but from the fringed or ragged edges of the petals, which look as

Dianthus barbatus

if they were trimmed with pinking shears. Many pinks sport blooms in two or more shades, often with contrasting eyes or other markings. Flowers may be single, semidouble, or fully double.

HOW TO GROW

Give pinks full sun and dry to evenly moist soil that is well drained. Alkaline to neutral pH is best, but plants tolerate slightly acid soil (to pH 6.5). Pinks prefer cool weather; they aren't generally grown south of Zone 9. In areas with hot summers, a site with partial shade during the hottest part of the day provides beneficial heat protection. Test your soil's pH and adjust it before planting: an annual dose of wood ashes helps keep pH in the right range. Sow seeds indoors 8 to 10 weeks before the last spring frost date at 60° to 70°F. Germination takes 1 to 3 weeks. Transplant with care. Or sow outdoors a few weeks before the last frost date or, where plants are hardy, in fall for germination the following spring.

To grow sweet William *(Dianthus barbatus)* as a biennial, sow seeds in late spring or early summer in a nursery bed; transplant to where the plants are to bloom in early fall or the following spring. Take a large ball of soil with each plant, and move them with care. Discard plants after they bloom either the first or the second time. (Propagate double-flowered forms by cuttings.) Don't mulch pinks with organic mulches such as shredded bark, because they tend to keep the soil too damp. Deadheading prolongs bloom. Perennial species (even those grown as annuals) can be propagated by cuttings taken in summer from nonflowering shoot tips: remove the lowest leaves, root in coarse sand or a 50-50 mix of vermiculite or perlite and coarse sand, and keep the medium barely moist. Use pinks as edging plants for beds and borders, along pathways, and in raised beds. Butterflies visit the blooms, which also make terrific cut flowers. Plants self-sow.

D. armeria

d. are-MEER-ee-ah. Deptford Pink. A rosette-forming, 16-inch-tall annual or biennial, hardy from Zone 4 south, with hairy green leaves. Showy, 3- to 6-inch-wide clusters of ½-inch, rosy pink flowers in summer. Cool-weather annual.

D. barbatus P. 85

d. bar-BAY-tuss. Sweet William. A short-lived, 1- to 2-foot-tall perennial, hardy in Zones 3 to 9, with glossy, broad, lance-shaped leaves. Showy, 3- to 5-inch-wide, flat-topped clusters of flowers from late spring into early summer. Modern cultivars are usually not fragrant. Flowers come in shades of pale pink to maroon and white; many are bicolors. Where happy, plants self-sow prolifically. To encourage plants to perform as perennials, remove flowers as they fade and divide every 2 to 3 years. Dwarf types, including 6-inch-tall Roundabout Series as well as 6-inch 'Wee Willie', are best used as edging plants; taller types are suitable for mid-border and as cut flowers. Hybrid strains such as Ideal Series plants *(D. barbatus × D. chinensis)* exhibit more heat tolerance and earlier bloom than the species, but are less hardy than *D. barbatus*. Hardy, short-lived perennial or biennial.

D. caryophyllus P. 86

d. care-ee-oh-FILL-us. Wild Carnation. A tender perennial, hardy from Zone 7 south, with flattened, narrow leaves on stiff, 2½- to 3-foot stems. Small clusters of fragrant, 2-inch-wide flowers in summer. This species is the predecessor of the florist's carnation, so be sure to select a cultivar developed for the garden rather than the greenhouse, such as 2- to 3-foot 'Floristan Red' or dwarf, 1-foot-tall Knight Series. Cool-weather annual.

D. chinensis P. 86

d. chi-NEN-sis. China Pink. A 6- to 12-inch biennial or perennial, hardy from Zone 7 south, with lance-shaped leaves. Scentless flowers with fringed petals in 3-inch-wide clusters from midsummer to fall. Blooms come in a wide variety of colors and patterns. Parfait and Carpet Series plants, both to about 6 inches, are popular. Cool-weather annual.

Diascia

die-AH-see-ah. Figwort family, Scrophulariaceae.

Diascia contains about 50 species of annuals and perennials native to South Africa. Commonly called twinspurs, and related to such well-known plants as snapdragons (*Antirrhinum* spp.), these plants have either erect or sprawling stems and racemes of tubular flowers with five lobes, or "petals." The bottom lobe is flared and larger than the rest, while the two upper ones have backward-pointing spurs, or sacs (*Diascia* is from the Greek *dis*, "two," and *askos*, "sac"), which are marked by translucent yellow or maroon patches known as windows.

HOW TO GROW

A site with full sun and rich, well-drained, evenly moist soil is ideal. Twinspurs do not grow or flower well in areas with hot summers. Sow seeds indoors 8 to 10 weeks before the last spring frost date. Germination takes about 2 weeks at 60° to 65°F; grow seedlings slightly cooler, at 55° to 60°F. Pinch plants when they are about 2½ inches tall to encourage bushy growth. Or sow seeds outdoors in spring a few weeks before the last frost date. Deadheading encourages repeat bloom. Water regularly during dry weather. After the first flush of bloom, cut plants back to about 3 inches to encourage new flowers. In areas with long enough seasons, cut back a third time for another round of flowers. Propagate perennials for the garden or for overwintering (in a sunny, 55° to 60°F spot) by cuttings taken in spring or summer or by dividing plants in spring. Or simply pot up plants for overwintering. Use twinspurs in mixed beds and borders, as edging plants, in containers, and even in rock gardens.

D. barberae P. 87

d. BAR-ber-eye. Twinspur. A low, mat-forming tender perennial, hardy in Zones 8 and 9, with heart-shaped leaves reaching about 10 inches and spreading to 20 inches. Loose, erect racemes of ½- to ¾-inch pink flowers from summer to fall. 'Blackthorn Apricot' bears apricot-pink blooms. 'Ruby Field' bears salmon pink blooms. Tender perennial or cool-weather annual.

D. rigescens

d. rih-GESS-cens. A tender perennial, hardy in Zones 7 to 9, that reaches 1 foot and spreads to 2 feet. Bears heart-shaped leaves and dense racemes of ¾-inch-wide flowers in shades of pink. Tender perennial or cool-weather annual.

Didiscus coeruleus *see Trachymene coerulea*

Digitalis

dih-jih-TAL-iss. Figwort family, Scrophulariaceae.

The best-known member of this genus of about 22 species of biennials and short-lived perennials, common foxglove *(Digitalis purpurea)* is a beloved old-fashioned garden plant. It and other members of the genus bear erect spikes of tubular to funnel-shaped flowers above a rosette of large, broad, lance-shaped leaves. Flowers come in shades of pink as well as white and creamy yellow. The botanical name *Digitalis* is from the Latin word for "finger," *digitus,* and refers to the fingerlike shape of the flowers. *Digitalis* species are native from Europe and northwestern Africa to central Asia. All parts of these plants are poisonous.

HOW TO GROW

Give foxgloves full sun or partial shade and rich, evenly moist, well-drained soil. In areas with hot summers (Zone 7 south), a spot that receives afternoon shade is beneficial. Although common foxglove can be grown as an annual, for the most dramatic show grow it as a biennial. Sow seeds outdoors in late spring or summer up to 2 months before the first fall frost in a prepared seedbed, a nursery bed, or pots set in a protected location. Transplant seedlings to the garden in early fall or the following spring. Or sow indoors in individual pots 6 to 8 weeks before plants are scheduled to go into the garden—generally in late spring so the plants will be ready to move to the garden in early fall. When sowing, just press the seeds into the soil surface. Germination takes 1 to 2 weeks at 60° to 70°F. To grow common foxglove as an annual, start seeds indoors in midwinter, about 10 weeks before the last spring frost date. Handle the plants carefully when transplanting, keep them evenly moist until they

Digitalis purpurea

are established, and pull them up once they've flowered. Or leave flowers to set seeds, because plants self-sow. Foxgloves also can be propagated by division: dig the clumps in early spring or fall, discard the main rosette that has already bloomed, and replant the rosettes around it. Use foxgloves in drifts at the back of borders or near the center of beds planted with other annuals, perennials, shrubs, and roses. Their flowers attract hummingbirds.

D. ferruginea

P. 88

d. fer-rue-GIN-ee-ah. Rusty Foxglove. A 4-foot species hardy in Zones 4 to 7. Spikes of 1½-inch-long, golden brown flowers in summer. Biennial or short-lived perennial.

D. purpurea

P. 88

d. pur-PUR-ee-ah. Common Foxglove. A biennial or short-lived perennial ranging from 2 to 6 feet in height and hardy in Zones 4 through 8. Showy spikes of 2- to 2½-inch-long flowers in rose-purple, white, pink, and creamy yellow. Blooms commonly are spotted with purple inside. 'Foxy' is a 2- to 3-foot-tall cultivar that will bloom the first year from seed and can be grown as an annual. 'Excelsior Hybrids' reach 5 feet and come in a range of pastel shades. Cool-weather annual, biennial, or short-lived perennial.

Dimorphotheca

die-more-foe-TEE-cah. Aster family, Asteraceae.

Native to dry, generally sandy areas in South and tropical Africa, *Dimorphotheca* species are shrubby tender perennials closely related to another genus of African plants, *Osteospermum*, whose members once were classified here. Plants in both genera share the common names Cape marigold, African daisy, and star of the veldt. The seven species of *Dimorphotheca* bear aromatic leaves and solitary, daisylike flowers borne atop leafless stems from midsummer to fall. Unlike most other aster-family plants, both the disk florets (the "eye") and the ray florets (the "petals") are fertile.

HOW TO GROW

Full sun and average to poor soil that is light and well drained are ideal. Plants thrive in heat, tolerate dry soil, and perform best in areas with long growing seasons; they do not do as well in areas with hot, humid, rainy summers. In the Southeast, try starting plants indoors early, so they reach blooming size well before heat and humidity set in for the summer. Sow seeds indoors 6 to 8 weeks before the last spring frost date. Germination takes about 2 weeks at 60° to 65°F. Or, from Zone 9 south, sow seeds outdoors where the plants are to grow. Either way, barely cover the seeds with soil, and try to avoid wetting the foliage when watering to prevent fungal diseases. Deadheading prolongs bloom. Use cape marigolds in containers or add them to mixed plantings in beds and borders. They do not make good cut flowers, since the flowers close during cloudy weather and at night.

D. pluvialis P. 89

d. plu-vee-AL-iss. Rain Daisy, Weather Prophet. A 1- to 1½-foot annual with toothed or deeply cut, aromatic leaves. White, 2½-inch, daisylike flowers with a ring of purple around a darker eye. The backs of the petals, which close before rain, also are purple. Warm-weather annual.

D. sinuata P. 89

d. sin-you-AH-tah. Star of the Veldt. A 1-foot annual with toothed, lance-shaped, aromatic leaves. Bears 1½-inch daisylike flowers with purple-brown centers and white, yellow, orange, or pink petals. Warm-weather annual.

Dolichos lablab *see Lablab purpureus*

Dorotheanthus

dor-oh-the-AN-thuss. Carpetweed family, Aizoaceae.

Succulent-leaved annuals from South Africa, *Dorotheanthus* species are grown for their showy flowers that resemble daisies. About 10 species belong to this genus, all once included in *Mesembryanthemum*. They bear fleshy, linear or spoon-shaped leaves covered with crystal-like lumps called papillae. While the flowers resemble daisies—they have petals surrounding a darker eye—each bloom is actually a single flower. (True daisies and other Aster-family plants bear heads that consist of many individual flowers.)

HOW TO GROW

Choose a site with full sun and poor to average, very well drained soil. Poor, sandy soil that is on the dry side is best, although plants will grow in richer soil as long as it is well drained. Sow seeds indoors 8 to 10 weeks before the last spring frost date. Or sow outdoors after the last frost. Either way, just press the seeds into the soil surface. Deadhead to prolong bloom. Sowing new seeds every few weeks also extends the bloom season. Use these plants as temporary ground covers, as edgings, on slopes, and in rock gardens.

D. bellidiformis P. 90

d. bell-ih-dih-FOR-miss. Livingstone Daisy. Formerly *Mesembryanthemum criniflorum.* A 6-inch-tall annual that spreads to 1 foot with fleshy, obovate to spoon-shaped leaves. Showy, solitary, 1½-inch-wide flowers in pink, purple, orange, red, cream, or yellow, sometimes with two-tone petals that create a contrasting eye zone. Warm-weather annual.

Dracocephalum

dray-coe-CEFF-ah-lum. Mint family, Lamiaceae.

This genus contains about 50 species of annuals, perennials, and small shrubs mostly native to Eurasia, as well as North Africa and the northern United States. The plants have square stems—they are related to mints (*Mentha* spp.)—and have entire, toothed, or lobed leaves that are often aromatic. Both the common name dragon's head and the botanical name *Dracocephalum* refer to the tubular, two-lipped flowers, which are borne in whorls around the stems: *Dracocephalum* is from the Greek *drakon,* "dragon," and *kephale,* "head."

HOW TO GROW

Give these plants full sun to light shade and average to rich, well-drained soil. (Light shade is beneficial during the hottest part of the day.) Sow seeds outdoors around the last spring frost date. Or sow indoors 6 to 8 weeks before the last frost. Pinch seedlings when they are about a month old to encourage branching. Use these plants to fill spaces in beds and borders as well as in wild gardens.

D. moldavicum P. 90

d. mol-DAV-ih-come. Moldavian Balm, Dragon's Head. A 1- to 2-foot annual with aromatic leaves native from Europe to Siberia and naturalized in

North America. Bears narrow, spikelike racemes of violet-blue or white, 1-inch-long flowers in summer. Warm-weather annual.

Dyssodia tenuiloba *see Thymophylla tenuiloba*

Eccremocarpus

eck-crey-moe-CAR-puss. Bignonia family, Bignoniaceae.

The five species of *Eccremocarpus* are exotic, fast-growing, herbaceous or woody climbers native to Chile and Peru. They bear leaves divided in a fernlike fashion (bipinnate), each ending in a tendril. Showy clusters of tubular, hot-colored flowers, which attract hummingbirds, appear throughout the growing season. The botanical name refers to the seedpods that follow the flowers: *Eccremocarpus* is from the Greek *ekkremes*, "pendent" or "hanging," and *carpus*, "fruit." One species is grown as a tender perennial.

HOW TO GROW

A site in full sun and fertile, well-drained soil, preferably on the sandy side, is ideal. Plants require a trellis or other support upon which to climb. They will clamber over brushy twigs and through and over shrubs, and the flowers attract hummingbirds. From Zone 10 south, grow Chilean glory vine *(E. scaber)* as a perennial; since plants can be killed to the ground and will resprout from the roots, they may survive the winter a bit farther north if protected by a mound of loose soil over the roots. Sow seeds indoors 8 to 10 weeks or more before the last frost and germinate at 55° to 65°F. Move them to the garden a few weeks after the last spring frost date, once the weather is warm and settled. Propagate the plants by cuttings taken in spring or summer, which can be used to overwinter the plants indoors.

E. scaber P. 91

e. SKAY-ber. Chilean Glory Vine. A fast-growing climber that can reach 10 to 15 feet in warm climates but stays somewhat shorter in the North. Clusters of tubular, 1-inch-long flowers in shades of orange-red, orange, red, pink, or yellow. Tender perennial or warm-weather annual.

Echium

ECK-ee-um. Borage family, Boraginaceae.

Native primarily to the Mediterranean and the Canary Islands, *Echium* species are annuals, biennials, perennials, and shrubs. The 40 species in the genus feature a range of common names, including tower-of-jewels, pride of Madeira, blue devil, and viper's bugloss. The plants produce a rosette of generally narrow leaves that are silvery and hairy or bristly. The rosette is topped by spikes or panicles of funnel- or bell-shaped flowers in shades of violet-blue, purple, white, yellow, or red.

HOW TO GROW

Give these plants full sun and poor to average soil that is well drained. They grow and bloom best in poorer soils that stay on the dry side; rich soil yields rank growth and plants that fail to flower or produce inferior blooms. They also are best in mild, dry climates, such as coastal California. Sow seeds indoors 8 to 10 weeks before the last spring frost date at 60° to 65°F. Germination takes 1 to 3 weeks. Transplant with care, and do not try to move established plants. Or sow seeds outdoors after the last frost date. All are biennials or tender perennials hardy from about Zone 9 south; in areas where they are not hardy, grow them in containers and overwinter them indoors. Where plants are hardy, seeds can be sown in fall for bloom the following year. Plants self-sow, sometimes excessively.

E. candicans P. 91

e. CAN-dih-cans. Pride of Madeira. A 5- to 8-foot, woody-based biennial with silvery-hairy leaves and dense, cylindrical, 1-foot-long panicles of bluish purple or white flowers in spring and summer. Biennial.

Echium sp.

E. pininana

e. pin-ee-NAY-nah. Tower-of-jewels, Pride of Tenerife. A 6- to 12-foot biennial or short-lived perennial with a woody base and silvery-hairy leaves up to 3 feet long and a foot wide. Bears dense, cylindrical panicles of purple-blue, ½-inch-long flowers; panicles can range from 5 to 10 or more feet long, and plants die after flowering. Biennial.

E. vulgare P. 92

e. vul-GAH-ree. Viper's Bugloss. A 2-to 3-foot biennial with linear to lance-shaped leaves covered with stiff white hairs. Bears dense clusters of violet-blue flowers in late summer. Naturalized in North America. Cool-weather annual.

E. wildpretii

e. wild-PRET-ee-eye. Formerly *E. bourgaenanum.* A woody-based, 4- to 6-foot biennial or short-lived perennial with silvery-hairy, lance-shaped leaves. Rounded panicles, up to 3 feet long, of small violet or red flowers. Biennial.

Emilia

eh-MIL-ee-ah. Aster family, Asteraceae.

Flora's paintbrush and tassel flower are two of the common names that have been applied to members of this genus of 24 species of annuals from India, tropical Africa, and Polynesia. They bear tassel- or ball-like heads of brightly colored flowers on wiry stems. The blooms consist of all disk florets—they lack the "petals," or ray florets, of many aster-family plants.

HOW TO GROW

Full sun and average, well-drained soil will suffice for these plants. Sow seeds outdoors 2 to 3 weeks before the last spring frost date, or from Zone 8 south, in fall. Or sow indoors 6 to 8 weeks before the last frost. Transplant with care. Either way, barely cover the seeds with soil, as darkness aids germination. Regular deadheading increases bloom. Plants self-sow.

E. coccinea P. 92

e. cox-SIN-ee-ah. Flora's Paintbrush. Formerly *E. flammea, E. javanica.* A 1½- to 2-foot annual with a rosette of ovate, toothed leaves. Produces loose clusters of ½-inch red to red-orange flowers in summer. Cool-weather annual.

Eryngium

eh-RIN-gee-um. Carrot family, Apiaceae.

Commonly called sea hollies, the 230 species of *Eryngium* are annuals, biennials, and perennials native to dry, sandy or rocky soils—primarily in the Mediterranean. Unlikely looking relatives of carrots and Queen-Anne's-lace *(Daucus carota)*, they bear leathery, often deeply divided, spiny-margined leaves that are oval or heart- or sword-shaped. Their tiny flowers are borne in rounded conelike umbels with showy, stiff, spiny bracts at the base. Foliage comes in shades of steely blue-gray, gray-green, or silver-green, while flowers are metallic purple-blue or blue-gray.

HOW TO GROW

Give these plants full sun and average, well-drained soil. They tolerate heat, drought, and poor soil, but giant sea holly *(E. giganteum)* also thrives in rich, evenly moist, well-drained soil. Since the seeds go dormant quickly, sea hollies can be hard to grow from seed. Sow fresh seeds outdoors in fall or in spring several weeks before the last spring frost date. Or sow indoors in pots and place the pots in the refrigerator for 4 to 6 weeks. Then germinate at about 65°F. Seedlings will germinate irregularly; transplant them as they appear. They are taprooted, so transplant promptly and carefully. Once you have established plants in your garden, they will self-sow. Sea hollies make excellent cut and dried flowers. For drying, pick just before the blooms have fully expanded, and hang them in a warm, dry, dark place.

E. giganteum P. 93

e. jy-GAN-tee-um. Giant Sea Holly, Miss Willmott's Ghost. A 3-foot-tall biennial or short-lived perennial with a rosette of heart-shaped, spiny leaves. Branched stems of 2½-inch-long, steel blue flowers surrounded by 2½-inch-long, spiny, silvery bracts. Biennial or cool-weather annual.

Erysimum

er-RIS-ih-mum. Mustard family, Brassicaceae.

Grown for their dense clusters of four-petaled flowers, *Erysimum* species are native to well-drained, mostly alkaline soils in Europe, northern Africa, Asia, and North America. About 80 species of well-branched annuals, biennials, and perennials belong to the genus. Commonly called wallflowers, they bear narrow, sometimes toothed, leaves and feature flowers in shades of yellow, orange, red, and lilac- to mauve-pink. Common wallflower *(E. cheiri)* is best known and is grown as either a biennial or cool-weather annual.

HOW TO GROW

Give common wallflower full sun to partial shade and poor, average, or somewhat rich soil that is well drained. The plants prefer cool temperatures and need to be replaced once hot weather arrives. To grow it as a biennial, sow seeds outdoors in a nursery bed or pots set in a sheltered spot from early to midsummer, then transplant seedlings in midfall to the spots where they will bloom. Or sow indoors in spring 8 to 10 weeks before the last spring frost date. Damping off is a common problem, so sow in a sterile seed-starting mix, and water from below. Pull up the plants when they have finished blooming. Use wallflowers with other annuals in bedding displays, in containers, and as cut flowers.

E. cheiri **P. 93**

e. CHEE-er-eye. Common Wallflower. Formerly *Cherianthus cheiri.* An evergreen, short-lived perennial ranging from 6 to 30 inches in height. Bears dense racemes of fragrant, 1-inch-wide flowers in spring. Many cultivars are available in shades of rich yellow, scarlet, orange-red, pale pink, and lemon yellow. 'Prince Formula Mix' and 'Tom Thumb Mix' are dwarf strains, from 6 to 9 inches tall; Bedder Series plants reach 1 foot. Cool-weather annual.

Eschscholzia

eh-SCHOLT-zee-ah. Poppy family, Papaveraceae.

Wildflowers native to western North America, the 8 to 10 species of *Eschscholzia* are annuals and perennials with finely divided, fernlike leaves and cup-shaped, poppylike flowers. One species, commonly called California poppy, is a popular annual.

HOW TO GROW

Give eschscholzias full sun and poor to average, well-drained soil. Plants grow well in sandy soil; rich soil yields abundant foliage but few flowers. Sow seeds outdoors after the last spring frost date or in fall where winters are mild — roughly Zone 6 south. Or sow indoors 2 to 3 weeks before the

Eschscholzia californica

last frost date in individual pots. Germination takes 1 to 3 weeks at 60° to 65°F. Transplant with care: direct sowing is generally best to prevent root damage. Deadheading increases flower production, but leave some flowers to encourage self-sowing. Use California poppies in mixed plantings, containers, and rock gardens. They make attractive but short-lived cut flowers.

E. californica **P. 94**

e. cal-ih-FORN-ih-kah. California Poppy. A well-branched, mat-forming, 8- to 12-inch annual or short-lived perennial with blue-green, fernlike leaves. Showy, 3-inch-wide, four-petaled flowers in orange, yellow, or red that close when the weather is cloudy. Thai Silk Series plants bear single or semidouble flowers with ruffled petals in shades of red, pink, yellow, and orange. 'Mission Bells Mix' features semidouble flowers ranging from cream to orange. Cool-weather annual.

Euphorbia

you-FORB-ee-ah. Spurge family, Euphorbiaceae.

An enormous and varied genus, *Euphorbia* contains some 2,000 species of annuals, biennials, perennials, subshrubs, and trees, as well as exotic-looking succulents. Poinsettias *(E. pulcherrima)* and crown-of-thorns *(E. milii)* are well-known houseplants that belong here; several species are easy, popular annuals. All euphorbias have milky sap and very small flowers that are clustered together in an arrangement called a cyantheum, in which a single female flower is surrounded by several male flowers. The showy "flowers" of these plants are actually colorful petal-like bracts (modified leaves) borne beneath the true flowers.

HOW TO GROW

Full sun and poor to average, well-drained soil that is evenly moist and light in texture will suffice for euphorbias grown as annuals. Sow seeds indoors 6 to 8 weeks before the last frost. Germination takes 2 to 4 weeks at 70° to 75°F. Transplant after the weather has settled and temperatures remain above 50°F. In areas with long, hot summers—roughly Zone 7 south—sow outdoors after the last spring frost date. Use annual euphorbias in mixed plantings. They also make attractive cut flowers: sear the stem ends over a candle flame or dip the ends in boiling water to seal in the sap and prolong their vase life. Plants self-sow.

E. cyanthophora P. 94

e. sigh-an-tho-FOR-ah. Annual Poinsettia, Fire-on-the-mountain, Painted Leaf. Sometimes listed as *E. heterophylla.* A shrubby, 1½- to 3-foot annual native to the United States and eastern Mexico. Grown for its showy leaves and bracts, which turn bright red at the stem tops like small poinsettias. Warm-weather annual.

E. lathyris P. 95

e. LATH-er-iss. Gopher Spurge, Mole Plant, Caper Spurge. A 1- to 4-foot biennial with leathery, lance-shaped, gray- to blue-green leaves. Bears 10- to 12-inch-wide umbels of yellow cyanthia in summer. Warm-weather annual.

E. marginata P. 95

e. mar-gin-AY-tah. Snow-on-the-mountain, Ghost Weed. A vigorous 1- to 3-foot-tall annual native to North America. Grown for its white-edged leaves and bracts, which are carried in loose clusters in summer and fall. Warm-weather annual.

Eustoma

you-STO-mah. Gentian family, Gentianaceae.

There are three species in this genus of annuals, biennials, and short-lived perennials native to the Americas. They are taprooted plants with rosettes of leaves topped by cup- or bell-shaped flowers in shades of lavender-blue, purple, pink, rose-purple, and white.

HOW TO GROW

Give these plants full sun and average, moist, well-drained soil. Neutral to alkaline pH is best. They do not grow well in areas with rainy, humid

Eustoma grandiflorum

summers and resent transplanting because of their taproots. Sow seeds indoors in individual pots 10 to 12 weeks before the last spring frost date. Press the tiny seeds into the soil surface, as light is necessary for germination. Seedlings germinate in 2 to 3 weeks at 65° to 70°F and are very slow-growing. Keep the soil on the dry side to prevent root rot. From Zone 7 south, try sowing outdoors a few weeks before the last frost date. From Zone 8 south, plants also can be grown as biennials: sow seeds in midsummer and move seedlings to the garden in midfall for bloom the following year. Pinch seedlings to encourage branching. Stake them with twiggy brush. Eustomas make excellent cut flowers and also can be added to beds and borders.

E. grandiflorum P. 96

e. gran-dih-FLOOR-um. Prairie Gentian, Texas Bluebell. Formerly *Lisianthus russellianus.* A 1- to 3-foot annual or biennial with fleshy, gray-green leaves. Bell-shaped, 2-inch-wide flowers with waxy or satiny-textured petals appear in spring and summer. Echo Series plants bear double flowers in a range of colors on 1½- to 2-foot plants; Heidi Series on 1½-foot ones. Mermaid Series plants are dwarf, to 8 inches, and do not require pinching. Cool-weather annual or biennial.

Evolvulus

ee-VOL-vue-lus. Morning glory family, Convolvulaceae.

There are about 100 species of *Evolvulus,* which are annuals, perennials, and subshrubs native to prairies and plains from North to South America. They bear entire, lance-shaped to ovate, silky-hairy leaves and small wheel- or bell-shaped flowers, either singly or in clusters. Unlike their relatives the morning glories (*Convolvulus* spp. and *Ipomoea* spp.), they do not climb: the botanical name is from the Latin *evolvere*, meaning "to untwist," in recognition of this fact.

HOW TO GROW

Evolvulus species thrive in full sun and poor to average, well-drained soil. Sow seeds indoors 8 to 10 weeks before the last spring frost date. Or take cuttings in spring or early summer to propagate plants for garden use or for overwintering indoors.

E. glomeratus P. 96

e. glom-er-AY-tus. A tender perennial or subshrub that's 1½ to 2 feet high and wide. Bears silky-hairy, silver-gray leaves and funnel- or bell-shaped, ½- to ¾-inch-wide lilac-pink or blue flowers. 'Blue Daze', also listed as a cultivar of *E. pilosus*, bears white, hairy leaves and pale blue flowers with white eyes. Tender perennial or warm-weather annual.

Exacum

EX-ah-come. Gentian family, Gentianaceae.

Some 25 species of tender annuals, biennials, and perennials belong to this genus of plants from the Middle East to India and Sri Lanka. They bear clusters of small wheel- to saucer-shaped flowers, which are fragrant and come in shades of blue and purple, as well as white and pink.

HOW TO GROW

Give exacum a spot in full sun to partial shade and rich, evenly moist, well-drained soil. These plants thrive in heat and humidity, but where summers are hot, they benefit from some shade during the hottest part of the day. Sow seeds indoors at least 10 to 12 weeks before the last spring frost date. Germinate at 65° to 70°F. Water regularly in summer and feed monthly. *Exacum* species are attractive as edging or container plants and when combined with other annuals in beds and borders.

E. affine P. 97

e. af-FIN-ee. Persian Violet. A compact, bushy, 5- to 12-inch-tall annual or short-lived perennial with shiny, rounded leaves. Clusters of lightly fragrant, ¾-inch flowers with a clump of golden yellow stamens and lavender-blue, pink, or white petals. Midget Series plants are especially compact, to 5 inches. Warm-weather annual.

Felicia

feh-LEE-cee-ah. Aster family, Asteraceae.

Commonly called blue marguerites or blue daisies, *Felicia* species are annuals, perennials, subshrubs, and shrubs native to South and tropical Africa. As their common names suggest, the 80 species in the genus bear daisylike flowers, which have yellow centers, or eyes, and petals in blue, lavender-blue, mauve-blue, or sometimes white.

HOW TO GROW

Blue marguerites thrive in full sun and light, poor to somewhat rich, very well drained soil that remains evenly moist. In frost-free climates—Zone 9 south—they can be grown outdoors as perennials; however, they do not grow well in hot, humid weather and also languish in cold, wet weather. Sow seeds indoors 6 to 8 weeks before the last spring frost date and germinate at 60° to 70°F, which generally takes 4 weeks. (Indoor sowing gives them a head start in areas where hot summer weather interferes with blooming.) Some gardeners prechill the seeds for 3 weeks to improve germination: sow them 3 weeks earlier and refrigerate the sown pots before moving them to a warmer spot for germinating. Or, in areas with cool summers, sow outdoors after the last frost date. Pinch seedlings once or twice to encourage branching. Take cuttings of perennials in spring to propagate for garden use or in late summer to overwinter the plants indoors. Use blue marguerites near the front of beds and borders as well as to add color to rock gardens. They also are handsome container plants.

F. amelloides P. 97

f. am-ell-OY-dees. Blue Daisy. This tender, bushy, 1- to 2-foot subshrub features a rounded habit and ovate leaves. It carries pale to deep blue, ¾- to 2-inch-wide, daisylike flowers with yellow centers from summer to fall. Tender perennial or warm-weather annual.

F. bergeriana P. 98

f. ber-ger-ee-AY-nah. Kingfisher Daisy. A low-growing annual reaching 8 to 10 inches and bearing gray-green, lance-shaped leaves. Bears rich, deep blue, 1½-inch, daisylike flowers with yellow or black centers in summer. Warm-weather annual.

F. heterophylla

f. het-er-oh-FILL-ah. A mounding, 15- to 20-inch-tall annual with lance-shaped, gray-green leaves. Bears ¾-inch-wide daisies in blue, or sometimes white or pink, in summer. Warm-weather annual.

Fuchsia

FEW-shah. Evening primrose family, Onagraceae.

Best known in North America as greenhouse pot plants, fuchsias are mostly tender shrubs and small trees, plus some climbers and trailers, native to mountainous areas in Central and South America as well as New Zealand and Tahiti. The genus contains some 100 species, and literally thousands of cultivars have been hybridized. They bear entire leaves and showy, often pendulous, flowers either singly or in clusters. Shades of pink, purple, and cream predominate, and many bear multicolored blooms.

HOW TO GROW

Give fuchsias partial shade, or morning sun and afternoon shade, as well as rich, well-drained, evenly moist soil. In areas with hot summers, shade is essential, as is regular, even daily, watering. This is especially true for plants grown in containers. Where hardy, grow them outdoors as shrubs or perennials. In the North, grow them as bedding plants replaced annually or as tender perennials overwintered indoors. They make outstanding plants for containers; trailing types are stunning in hanging baskets. Upright types can be trained into handsome standards. The flowers attract hummingbirds. Fuchsias are most often grown from cuttings. Take them in spring to propagate for garden use or in late summer to overwinter the plants. They also can be grown from seeds sown indoors in spring, but cultivars do not come true from seeds. Water deeply during dry weather, and feed pot-grown plants weekly during the summer with a balanced fertilizer. To overwinter, take cuttings, pot up entire plants, or move containers to a bright, cool (40° to 45°F) spot before the first fall frost. Keep them barely moist over winter. Prune overwintered plants to shape them in late winter or early spring: cut them back hard, if necessary, since they bloom best on new wood.

F. × hybrida P. 98

f. × HI-brih-dah. Common Fuchsia. Tender, much-hybridized shrubs, generally ranging from 1 to 2 feet in height and hardy only in frost-free areas, from Zone 10 south, although the plants can regrow from the roots in protected areas somewhat farther north. Pendent, tubular flowers that can be single, semidouble, or double, and often featuring two or more colors. Plants multicolored. Tender perennial or warm-weather annual.

F. magellanica P. 99

f. mag-el-LAN-ih-kah. Hardy Fuchsia. A tender shrub that can reach 10 feet in frost-free climates but is usually 2½ to 3 feet tall in the North, where it is killed to the ground each winter. Plants are root hardy to Zone 7 and with considerable winter protection will survive into Zone 6. Dainty, red and purple-red, ¾- to 1¼-inch-long flowers appear in summer. 'Aurea' is a semicascading plant with yellow leaves and red flowers. Tender perennial.

Gaillardia

gah-LAR-dee-ah. Aster family, Asteraceae.

Commonly called blanket flowers or simply gaillardias, the 30 species in this genus of aster-family plants are annuals, biennials, and perennials primarily native to North America. They bear rosettes of hairy leaves topped by single or double, daisylike flowers in shades of red, red-orange, maroon, and yellow over a long season in summer.

HOW TO GROW

Gaillardias thrive in full sun and average to rich, well-drained soil but also tolerate sandy soil and generally poor, dry conditions. They are drought- and salt-tolerant enough for seaside gardens. Too-rich soil yields floppy plants. Sow seeds of annual gaillardias indoors 6 to 8 weeks before the last spring frost date. Or sow them outdoors after the last frost.

Gaillardia pulchella

Either way, since light aids germination, just press the seeds into the soil surface. Plants bloom without deadheading, but removing the faded flowers promptly keeps the plants neat-looking and encourages new buds to form. Gaillardias add summer-long color to beds and borders, wildflower gardens, and containers. Also include them in plantings designed to attract butterflies. They make outstanding cut flowers.

G. pulchella

P. 99

g. pul-CHELL-ah. Blanket Flower, Indian Blanket. An erect, 1- to 1½-foot-tall annual with lance-shaped, grayish green leaves. Bears red, yellow, or red and yellow, 2-inch-wide, daisylike flowers with purple-black centers from summer to fall. 'Red Plume' bears rounded, fully double, red flowers on 1-foot plants. Warm-weather annual.

Gazania

gah-ZAY-nee-ah. Aster family, Asteraceae.

Gazanias, or treasure flowers as they are sometimes called, are native to tropical Africa, especially South Africa. They bear solitary, hot-colored, daisylike flowers atop leafless stems. The flowers close at night and in cloudy weather. There are 16 or so species of annuals and perennials in this genus, but most of the plants grown today are hybrids of species including *Gazania ringens* and *G. linearis.*

HOW TO GROW

Give gazanias full sun and poor to average, light, very well drained soil. They thrive in heat and dry soil and also tolerate salt spray. They do not bloom well in rich soil and tend to rot in areas with humid, wet summers or constantly wet soil. Grow gazanias as perennials from Zone 8 south. In

Gazania sp.

the North, start them each year from seeds, or overwinter the plants indoors. Sow seeds indoors 6 to 8 weeks before the last spring frost date. Barely cover the seeds with soil, as they need darkness for germination. Seedlings appear in 1 to 3 weeks at 60° to 65°F. Or sow outdoors after the last frost. Deadhead to prolong the bloom season. To overwinter, dig plants before the first hard fall frost and pot them up. Or take cuttings from shoots at the base of the plant in late summer or fall. Keep overwintered plants barely moist. Use gazanias in the front of beds and borders, as edging plants along paths, to add color to rock gardens, and in containers. They are ideal for seaside gardens and also attract butterflies.

G. Hybrids

P. 100

Tender perennials ranging from 8 to 12 inches with a rosette of spoon-shaped, often lobed leaves. Showy, 3- to 4-inch-wide, daisylike flowers bloom from summer to fall in shades of orange, bronze, gold, yellow, pink, red-orange, or white, sometimes in a solid color but often with bands, stripes, or spots of contrasting colors on the petals. 'Daybreak Mix' and 'Mini-Star Mix' plants are 8 inches tall, spreading to 10 inches, with flowers that usually have a zone of contrasting color. 'Sundance Mix' plants reach 10 to 12 inches. 'Silverlight' bears bright yellow flowers and woolly white leaves. 'Pink Beauty' bears silvery leaves and pink flowers. Tender perennial or warm-weather annual.

Gerbera

GERR-ber-ah. Aster family, Asteraceae.

While there are some 40 species of tender perennials in this genus, native from Africa to Asia and Indonesia, only one of them is commonly grown in gardens. *Gerbera* species bear solitary, daisylike flower heads above a rosette of pinnate, entire, or toothed leaves that are hairy underneath.

HOW TO GROW

Gerberas require full sun and average to rich, evenly moist, well-drained soil. They do not tolerate wet soil. In areas with very hot summers, partial shade in the afternoon is best. Sow seeds indoors in individual pots 12 weeks before the last spring frost date at 65° to 75°F. When sowing, just press the seeds into the soil surface, as they need light to germinate, which takes 2 to 3 weeks. When transplanting, set the crowns slightly above the soil surface to ensure good drainage. Deadhead regularly, and feed every month to 6 weeks. Grow gerberas outdoors as perennials from about

Zone 8 south; they may survive winters in Zone 7 if they are planted in a protected site and covered with a heavy layer of a dry mulch such as salt hay or weed-free straw. They are often grown as annuals, but older plants bloom best, so the plants are worth trying to overwinter. Plants are deep-rooted and resent transplanting, but container-grown ones can be brought indoors for overwintering: keep plants barely moist and cool (45° to 50°F), and provide sun and good air circulation. They can be propagated by division in spring, as well as from cuttings taken from the base of the plant in summer, which also can be used for overwintering. Use gerberas as edging plants, in mixed plantings, and in containers that are either set on a terrace or sunk to the rim in soil. They make outstanding, long-lasting cut flowers: cut them after they have fully opened, while the centers are still tight.

G. jamesonii **P. 100**

g. jame-SO-nee-eye. Transvaal Daisy, Barberton Daisy. A tender, 1 to 1½-foot perennial with deeply lobed leaves that are woolly underneath. Showy, waxy, 3- to 5-inch-wide, single or semidouble, daisylike flowers are carried on leafless stems from early to late summer in shades of orange-red, orange, red, yellow, pink, and cream. Tender perennial or warm-weather annual.

Gilia

GILL-ee-ah. Phlox family, Polemoniaceae.

There are some 25 to 30 species of *Gilia* primarily native to western North America. Most are annuals, although the genus contains some biennials and perennials. They have deeply divided, feathery leaves and tube-, funnel-, or bell-shaped flowers borne singly or in loose clusters.

HOW TO GROW

Full sun and average, well-drained soil are ideal. These plants are best for areas with cool summers or when started early enough so they bloom before hot weather arrives, since they do not tolerate heat and humidity. They will grow in very sandy soil. Sow seeds outdoors 2 to 3 weeks before the last spring frost date, or in fall in areas with mild winters—roughly Zone 8 south. Or sow indoors 6 to 8 weeks before the last frost and germinate at 50° to 65°F, but outdoor sowing is usually best. Stake plants with twiggy brush. Use gilias in drifts in mixed plantings. They also attract hummingbirds and butterflies and make attractive cut flowers. Plants self-sow.

G. capitata P. 101

g. cah-pih-TAH-tah. Queen Anne's Thimble. A feathery-leaved, 1½- to 2-foot-tall annual. Bears rounded, 1-inch-wide clusters of small lilac-blue flowers in summer. Cool-weather annual.

G. tricolor P. 101

g. TRI-cuh-lor. Bird's Eyes. A 1- to 1½-foot-tall annual with fernlike, deeply cut leaves. Lilac- to violet-blue, ½- to ¾-inch-wide flowers, each with an orange or yellow center and purple-blue spots, are borne from spring to late summer either singly or in small clusters. Cool-weather annual.

Glaucium

GLAU-see-um. Poppy family, Papaveraceae.

Glaucium species are named for their leaf color—the botanical name is from the Greek *glaukos*, "gray-green." There are about 25 species of annuals, biennials, and short-lived perennials in the genus, which are native to Europe, North Africa, the Middle East, and parts of Asia. The plants have yellow-orange sap and deeply cut leaves. Their showy, poppylike flowers have four papery petals. Each opens for only a day. They come in shades of yellow, orange, and red. Long, hornlike seedpods follow the flowers, thus the common name horned poppy.

HOW TO GROW

Horned poppies require full sun and poor to average, well-drained soil. They thrive in hot, dry sites as well as sandy soil and are good choices for seaside gardens. Sow seeds outdoors after the last spring frost. Indoors, sow in individual pots 6 to 8 weeks before the last spring frost date at 60° to 65°F. Germination takes 2 to 3 weeks. Like most poppies, they resent transplanting, but they can be moved if they are handled carefully and are still small. When sowing, barely cover the seeds with soil, as darkness is required for germination. From about Zone 6 south, to grow them as biennials, sow seeds outdoors in early summer or in fall. Plant horned poppies in drifts in wild gardens and mixed plantings. Plants self-sow.

G. corniculatum

g. cor-nick-you-LAY-tum. Red Horned Poppy. A silver-gray–leaved biennial reaching 1 to 1½ feet and spreading as far. Bears showy, 2-inch-wide, poppylike flowers in red, orange, or sometimes yellow from summer to fall;

most plants have a black blotch at the base of each petal. Biennial or cool-weather annual.

G. flavum P. 102

g. FLAY-vum. Yellow Horned Poppy. A short-lived, 1- to 3-foot perennial, normally grown as a biennial or annual, with blue-green leaves. Bears 2-inch-wide yellow to orange flowers in summer. Biennial or cool-weather annual.

Godetia *see Clarkia*

Gomphrena

gum-FREE-nah. Amaranth family, Amaranthaceae.

While gomphrenas bear flowers that resemble clovers, their blooms have a decidedly uncloverlike texture: they are composed of dense clusters of stiff, papery, brightly colored bracts borne beneath tiny, insignificant flowers. The plants flower from summer to frost and have softly hairy, lance-shaped to oval leaves. There are about 90 species in the genus—mostly annuals, but some perennials. They are native to Central and South America, as well as Australia.

HOW TO GROW

Full sun and average, well-drained soil are ideal. They thrive in hot weather and tolerate dry soil. Sow seeds indoors 6 to 8 weeks before the last spring frost date at 70° to 75°F. Germination takes 1 to 2 weeks. Water from below, and keep the soil barely moist, never wet. Or sow outdoors after the last spring frost. Either way, barely cover the seeds with soil, as darkness is required for germination. Pinch seedlings to encourage branching. While plants tolerate dry soil, water during dry weather for best performance. Use gomphrenas in plantings of annuals, as an edging for perennial gardens, and in containers. They make excellent cut or dried flowers and also attract butterflies. For drying, cut the blooms just as they open fully, and hang in bunches in a warm, dry, dark place.

G. globosa P. 102

g. glo-BOE-sah. Gomphrena, Globe Amaranth. A 1- to 2-foot annual with oval to oblong, 1½-inch-long flower heads in shades of pink, purple, or white. 'Buddy' bears purple flowers on 6-inch-tall plants. Gnome Series plants also are 6 inches tall and come in pink, white, and shades of purple. Warm-weather annual.

G. haageana **P. 103**

g. hog-ee-AY-nah. Gomphrena, Globe Amaranth. A 2-foot-tall annual with round, 1½-inch-wide flower heads in shades of pale red to reddish orange. 'Lavender Lady' bears pale purple flowers; 'Strawberry Fields', red ones on 30-inch plants. Warm-weather annual.

Gossypium

gos-SIP-ee-um. Mallow family, Malvaceae.

Gossypium species are best known as the agricultural crop cotton, but they also make interesting additions to ornamental plantings. Their showy, funnel- or bell-shaped flowers come in shades of yellow, cream, or rose-pink and are followed by capsules filled with seeds covered with the dense, hairy fibers we know as cotton. The leaves are large, palmately lobed, and/or veined. About 39 species of annuals, perennials, subshrubs, shrubs, and trees belong here.

HOW TO GROW

Cotton needs full sun, a light and rich soil, and a long, hot season to mature. Where summers are long and warm, from roughly Zone 8 south, sow seeds outdoors after the last frost, once the soil is warm and the weather settled. In the North, start seeds indoors at least 8 to 10 weeks before the last spring frost date to give plants enough of a head start so they can set seeds in the shorter season. Transplant after the last frost date, once the soil has warmed to 60°F and the weather has settled. Use cotton as an accent in mixed plantings. It also can be grown in containers.

G. hirsutum **P. 103.**

g. her-SUE-tum. Upland Cotton. A 2- to 5-foot-tall annual or perennial with large, gray-green, maplelike leaves. Cream or pale yellow, 4- to 6-inch-wide flowers, which fade to purple-pink, have five lobes, or petals. Warm-weather annual.

Gypsophila

jip-SOF-ih-lah. Pink family, Caryophyllaceae.

Best known as baby's breath, *Gypsophila* species are annuals and perennials native from the Mediterranean to central Asia. Most of the 100 species in the genus are found in dry, rocky, or sandy, alkaline soil. The name

Gypsophila is from the Greek *gypsos,* "chalk," and *philos,* "loving," and refers to the preference some species have for alkaline soils that are rich in chalk, a soft form of limestone high in calcium carbonate. They bear lance-shaped to linear, gray-green leaves and clouds of tiny, five-petaled, white or pink flowers that are star- or trumpet-shaped. One species is a popular annual.

HOW TO GROW

Give annual baby's breath *(G. elegans)* full sun or very light shade and rich, well-drained, evenly moist soil. Sow seeds outdoors a few weeks before the last spring frost date, or sow indoors 6 to 8 weeks before the last frost date; outdoor sowing is generally best. In areas with mild winters, sow seeds outdoors in fall. For continued bloom, sow new crops every 2 to 3 weeks until midsummer. Support tall cultivars with twiggy brush. Cut plants back hard after the first flush of bloom to encourage a second round of flowers. Use baby's breath as an airy filler in mixed plantings. Annual baby's breath is a good cut flower but unlike perennial baby's breath *(G. paniculata)* does not dry well.

G. elegans

P. 104

g. EL-eh-gans. Annual Baby's Breath. A well-branched, 1- to 2-foot annual with gray-green leaves. Produces masses of tiny, ½-inch, star-shaped flowers in white or pink in summer. 'Covent Garden' is an 18-inch-tall cultivar developed for use as a cut flower. 'Early Summer Lace' bears flowers in white and shades of pink. Cool-weather annual.

Hedychium

heh-DEE-chee-um. Ginger family, Zingiberaceae.

Commonly called ginger lilies or garland lilies, *Hedychium* species are tender perennials grown for their handsome foliage and erect trusses of fragrant flowers. The botanical name celebrates their fragrance: *Hedychium* is from the Greek *hedys,* "sweet," and *chion,* "snow." The plants grow from sturdy rhizomes and produce 1- to 2-foot-long, lance-shaped leaves in two parallel rows, or ranks, along reedlike stems. The tubular to trumpet-shaped flowers are borne in dense clusters from mid- to late summer and into fall; before they open, the flower buds resemble pine cones. Some 40 species belong to the genus; all are native to Asia, where they grow in moist, lightly wooded areas.

HOW TO GROW

Give ginger lilies full sun or partial shade and rich, constantly moist, well-drained soil. They thrive in areas with hot, rainy, humid summers. A site protected from wind is best. Where hardy—from Zone 8 or 9 south, depending on the species or cultivar—grow them outdoors as perennials. In areas where they are marginally hardy, try a site against a south-facing wall for extra winter protection, and protect them with a thick, dry mulch such as salt hay or weed-free straw over winter. In the North, grow them in containers, which can be brought indoors for overwintering, or in the ground, in which case dig the roots and overwinter them as you would cannas: store the rhizomes in barely damp vermiculite, peat, or sand in a cool (40° to 50°F), dry place. Feed ginger lilies monthly and water regularly throughout the summer. Feed container-grown plants every week or every 2 weeks. Standing the pots in shallow saucers kept filled with water helps keep the soil constantly moist. Gradually dry off plants in fall, and keep them on the dry side when dormant. Use these plants on the edges of woodland gardens, in mixed plantings in moist soil, or in large tubs or other containers on terraces.

H. coccineum P. 104

h. cock-SIN-ee-um. Red Ginger Lily. A 6- to 10-foot-tall tender perennial, hardy from Zone 8 south, with rounded trusses of 10-inch-long, red, pink, orange, or white flowers. Tender perennial.

H. coronarium

h. core-oh-NAIR-ee-um. White Ginger Lily, Garland Flower. A 6- to 10-foot tender perennial, hardy from about Zone 9 south, with extremely fragrant white flowers in 8-inch-long trusses. Tender perennial.

Helianthus

hee-lee-AN-thuss. Aster family, Asteraceae.

Known by gardeners and nongardeners alike as sunflowers, *Helianthus* species are annuals and perennials native to North, Central, and South America. The genus contains about 70 to 80 species of usually tall, often coarse plants with showy, daisylike flowers in shades of yellow and gold. The flowers, borne from summer to fall, consist of ray florets, or "petals," surrounding dense centers of disk florets, which produce the seeds. Sunflowers have large, coarse leaves that are oval or lance- or heart-shaped.

Both the common and botanical names celebrate the fact that these are plants for full sun: *Helianthus* is from the Greek *helios,* "sun," and *anthos,* "flower."

HOW TO GROW

Full sun and average soil that is moist but well drained are all these plants require. Sow annual sunflowers outdoors after danger of frost has passed. Or sow into individual pots indoors 4 to 6 weeks before the last spring frost date at 65° to 70°F. Germination takes about 2 weeks. Sunflowers are large plants best kept away from less vigorous neighbors; also, their roots give off a chemical that inhibits growth of some plants. Plant them in drifts at the back of borders and along fences, as accents, or in gardens designed to attract birds or butterflies. Use dwarf types in drifts alone or in mixed plantings as well as in containers. The flowers are lovely in fresh bouquets and can also be dried. Pick them just as the ray florets unfurl. Hang blooms destined for drying in a dark, warm place.

H. annuus P. 105

h. AN-yew-us. Annual Sunflower, Common Sunflower. A vigorous, fast-growing annual with roughly hairy, heart-shaped leaves that can range from 1 to 15 feet, depending on the cultivar. Flowers are single, semidouble, or double and range from 4 to 12 inches across or more. Many cultivars are available. Two developed for seed production are 6-foot-tall 'Mammoth Russian' and 11-foot 'Russian Giant'; both bear 10- to 12-inch-wide yellow flowers. 'Valentine' bears lemon yellow, 5- to 6-inch-wide, dark-centered flowers on 5-foot plants. 'Holiday' bears 3- to 5-inch, classic yellow sunflowers on well-branched, 5- to 7-foot plants. Dwarf cultivars include golden yellow, 10- to 15-inch-tall 'Big Smile' and 3-foot-tall 'Teddy Bear' with double, golden yellow flowers. 'Autumn Beauty' bears 8-inch-wide blooms in shades of yellow, bronze, maroon, and purple-red on well-branched, 5-foot plants. 'Velvet Queen' bears burgundy and maroon, 5-inch flowers on 5-foot plants. Warm-weather annual.

H. argophyllus

h. are-go-PHYLL-us. Silver-leaved Sunflower. A 3- to 6-foot annual native from Texas to Florida with heavily branched stems and white, silky-hairy, oval leaves. Bears 3-inch-wide flowers with yellow petals and dark purple centers. Warm-weather annual.

H. debilis ssp. *cucumerifolius*

h. deh-BILL-iss ssp. cue-cue-mer-ih-FOE-lee-us. Cucumber-leaved Sunflower. A 3-foot-tall annual native from Texas to Florida with hairy, toothed leaves and stems mottled in purple. Bears 5- to 6-inch-wide yellow flowers. 'Italian White' bears white to creamy yellow, 4- to 5-inch-wide flowers on well-branched, 4- to 5-foot-tall plants. Warm-weather annual.

Helichrysum

hell-ih-CRY-sum. Aster family, Asteraceae.

The genus *Helichrysum* contains some 500 species of annuals, perennials, and subshrubs with woolly or hairy leaves and yellow to golden flower heads. Unlike many aster-family plants, the blooms have only disk florets —they lack true "petals," or ray florets. Instead many have colorful, papery, petal-like bracts that surround the flower heads. While botanists have moved the best-known member of this genus—strawflowers, formerly *H. bracteatum,* are now listed as *Bracteantha bracteata*—the genus still contains tender perennials grown for their handsome foliage.

HOW TO GROW

Give these plants a site in full sun with poor to average, well-drained soil. Sow seeds indoors 6 to 8 weeks before the last spring frost date at 65° to 70°F. Just press the seeds into the soil surface, as they need light to germinate; germination takes 1 to 3 weeks. Perennial species can be replaced annually, but they also are easy to grow from cuttings taken in summer, which can be used to overwinter the plants. They also can be propagated by division in spring. Water during very dry weather. Trim species grown for foliage as needed to keep them shapely. On species grown for foliage, many gardeners remove the flowers as they appear. Use *Helichrysum* species as fillers in low mixed plantings, as edging plants, as well as in containers.

H. bracteatum see Bracteantha bracteata

H. italicum ssp. *serotinum* P. 105

h. ih-TAL-ih-cum ssp. ser-oh-TYE-num. Curry Plant. Formerly *H. angustifolium.* A tender, densely branched, 1½-foot subshrub with narrow, grayish white, woolly leaves that have an intense, currylike fragrance but no culinary value. Clusters of tiny, ⅛-inch, bottlebrush-like, golden yellow flowers appear from summer to fall. Tender perennial or warm-weather annual.

H. petiolare

P. 106

h. pee-tee-oh-LAIR-ee. Licorice Plant. A tender, shrubby, 1½- to 2-foot-tall species with trailing stems that spread 5 feet or more and small, woolly, heart-shaped leaves. Bears small, rounded, cream-colored flowers from summer to fall. 'Limelight' bears silvery lime-green leaves. 'Variegatum' bears gray-green leaves marked with cream. Tender perennial or warm-weather annual.

Heliotropium

he-lee-oh-TROWP-ee-um. Borage family, Boraginaceae.

Heliotropium contains some 250 species of annuals, perennials, subshrubs, and shrubs with entire, roughly hairy leaves and flattened to rounded clusters of small, funnel-shaped flowers in shades of lavender, purple, white, or sometimes yellow. They are native to tropical and subtropical regions in the Americas as well as the Canary Islands and islands of the Pacific. One species is a popular tender perennial or annual grown for its richly fragrant flowers.

HOW TO GROW

Select a site in full sun or partial shade andwith rich, well-drained soil. In areas with hot summers, a site with afternoon shade is best. Sow seeds indoors 10 to 12 weeks before the last spring frost date at 70° to 75°F. Germination takes 4 to 6 weeks. Pinch seedlings and young plants to encourage branching and bushy growth. Move them outdoors a few weeks after the last frost date, once the soil has warmed to about 60°F and the weather has settled. Water regularly and feed plants monthly, especially container-grown ones. Deadheading prolongs bloom. Grow heliotropes *(H. arborescens)* as bedding plants replaced annually, or overwinter them indoors in a bright, cool (50° to 55°F) spot. Even in Zone 10, they need protection from the coldest temperatures. Seed-grown plants are slow and will vary in fragrance and color; for uniform plants and quick results, propagate by cuttings. Take them in late summer for overwintering indoors, or bring in whole, container-grown plants to use as stock plants for cuttings in spring. Prune to shape plants in late winter or early spring: cut them back hard, if necessary. Pinch to encourage bushy growth. Use heliotropes in containers and mixed plantings; dwarf types are good edging plants. They can also be grown as standards or shrubs overwintered indoors. Their flowers attract butterflies.

H. arborescens P. 106

h. are-bore-ESS-cens. Heliotrope, Cherry Pie. A tender shrub that can reach 4 feet but is considerably shorter in containers, with oval to lance-shaped, dark green leaves. Showy, 3- to 4-inch-wide clusters of tiny flowers in lavender, violet, or white in summer. Many, but not all, cultivars have a rich vanilla-like fragrance. 'Marine' is a dwarf, 1½-foot-tall cultivar. Tender perennial or warm-weather annual.

Helipterum

H. manglesii see Rhodanthe manglesii
H. roseum see Rhodanthe chlorocephala ssp. *rosea*

Hesperis

HESS-per-iss. Cabbage family, Brassicaceae.

Loose clusters of fragrant, four-petaled flowers characterize the 30 species of biennials and perennials in this genus of plants native from Europe to China and Siberia. The botanical name commemorates the fact that the flowers are most fragrant near nightfall—*Hesperis* is from the Greek *hespera,* meaning "evening." One species has naturalized in eastern North America and is a popular addition to wildflower gardens.

HOW TO GROW

A site with partial shade and rich, evenly moist, well-drained soil is best for dame's rocket *(H. matronalis).* Plants grow in full sun with even moisture and also tolerate full shade. Sow seeds outdoors in spring or from midsummer to fall where the plants are to grow. Or sow seeds indoors 8 to 10 weeks before the last spring frost date. When sowing, just press the seeds into the soil surface, as they need light to germinate. Germination takes about 3 weeks at 70° to 75°F. Plants self-sow; cut back plants after they have set seed. Or propagate by cuttings taken in spring from shoots at the base of the plant. Use dame's rocket in wildflower gardens and other semiwild plantings, as well as to attract moths.

H. matronalis P. 107

h. may-tro-NAL-iss. Dame's Rocket, Sweet Rocket. A 2- to 3-foot biennial or short-lived perennial with toothed, ovate to oblong leaves. Carries loose clusters of 1¼- to 1½-inch-wide, four-petaled flowers in white or pinkish purple from late spring to midsummer. Biennial.

Hibiscus

hi-BISS-kus. Mallow family, Malvaceae.

Both hardy and tender plants belong to the genus *Hibiscus*—over 200 species of annuals, perennials, shrubs, and trees belong here. They bear showy, funnel-shaped flowers, each with a prominent central column consisting of the stamens and pistil. The flowers have five petals and are borne either singly or in clusters. The leaves are entire to palmately lobed.

HOW TO GROW

Hibiscus thrive in full sun, warm temperatures, and rich, well-drained soil. For annual hibiscus, sow seeds outdoors after danger of frost has passed and the soil has warmed. Since plants take about 3 months to bloom from seeds, they need a head start in northern gardens, roughly Zone 6 north. Where seasons are short, sow indoors in individual peat pots 8 to 10 weeks before the last spring frost date at 50° to 55°F. Transplant after the weather has settled in spring (especially north of Zone 6 and in any area where spring is cool and rainy). Seedlings resent transplanting, so handle them carefully. Feed with a balanced fertilizer in midsummer. Annuals self-sow in mild climates. Grow Chinese hibiscus *(H. rosa-sinensis)* outdoors as a shrub in Zones 10 and 11; in areas where plants are marginally hardy, try a site against a south-facing wall for extra winter protection. In the North, grow Chinese hibiscus in containers and overwinter indoors in a bright, cool (40° to 45°F) spot; prune in spring as needed to shape. Feed container-grown plants monthly. Water all hibiscus regularly and deeply in dry weather. Use hibiscus grown as annuals in mixed beds and borders, combining them with bold annuals and perennials, as well as shrubs. Use Chinese hibiscus in containers on terraces or decks; they can be trained as standards. Hummingbirds will visit hibiscus flowers.

H. acetosella

h. ah-see-toe-SELL-ah. Formerly *H. eetveldeanus.* An annual or short-lived tender perennial with lobed, maplelike leaves that ranges from 2 to 5 feet tall. Carries yellow or purple-red, 2½- to 4-inch-wide flowers in late summer and fall, but only in areas with very long growing seasons. A maroon-purple–leaved cultivar sold under the names 'Red Shield' and 'Red Sentinel' is grown for its handsome foliage. Tender perennial or warm-weather annual.

H. manihot see Abelmoschus manihot

H. rosa-sinensis P. 107

H. ROE-sah sye-NEN-sis. Chinese Hibiscus, Hawaiian Hibiscus. A tender shrub or small tree that can range from 5 to 10 feet in height but stays smaller when grown in containers in the North. It bears toothed, dark green leaves and showy flowers that range from 4 to 7 inches or more across, depending on the cultivar. Flowers may be single, semidouble, or double, and colors include scarlet, pink, orange-red, apricot-orange, yellow, gold, and cream. Tender perennial.

H. trionum P. 108

H. tri-ON-um. Flower-of-an-hour. A 1- to 2-foot-tall annual or tender, short-lived perennial that has become a weed in some parts of North America. It bears palmate, three- to five-lobed leaves and from summer to fall carries an abundance of 2- to 3-inch-wide, brown-centered, yellow flowers that last a day or less. Tender perennial or warm-weather annual.

Hordeum

HOAR-day-um. Grass family, Poaceae.

Some 20 species of annuals and perennials belong to this genus, including the agricultural crop barley. *Hordeum* species have narrow leaves and rounded, plumy flower heads. One species is commonly grown as an ornamental grass and is used in dried flower arrangements.

HOW TO GROW

Full sun and average, well-drained soil suffice for these easy-to-grow plants. Sow seeds outdoors a few weeks before the last spring frost date or in late fall for germination the following spring. (Plants resent transplanting and are best started outdoors where they are to grow.) To use the flower heads of squirrel-tail grass *(H. jubatum)* for drying, cut them just before the flower buds open and hang them in small bunches in a warm, dry, dark place. This species also adds attractive texture to mixed beds and borders. Plants self-sow and can become weedy.

H. jubatum

P. 108

h. jue-BAY-tum. Squirrel-tail Grass, Fox-tail Barley. A 2-foot-tall annual or perennial grass, hardy from Zone 4 south, with arching leaves. Bears feathery, 5-inch-long flower spikes that are green flushed with pale pink or purple and ripen to beige. Hardy perennial or cool-weather annual.

Humulus

HEW-mew-lus. Hemp family, Cannabidaceae.

The two species that belong to this genus are the vines commonly called hops. They feature attractive, deeply lobed, palmate leaves and bear male and female flowers on separate plants. One species, Japanese hop *(Humulus japonicus)*, is commonly grown as an annual.

HOW TO GROW

Give Japanese hop plants full sun or partial shade and average to rich, evenly moist but well-drained soil. They also need a sturdy trellis upon which to climb. Sow seeds indoors 8 to 10 weeks before the last spring frost, and place the sown pots in the refrigerator for 2 to 3 weeks before moving them to a warmer (70° to 75°F) spot for germinating. Germination takes 3 to 4 weeks. Or sow seeds outdoors in spring a few weeks before the last frost date, or in fall for germination the following spring. Or propagate by cuttings taken in spring or summer. Plants self-sow and can become weedy; pull up unwanted seedlings as they appear. Use this vigorous vine to create temporary privacy screens, or train it over an arbor to add shade to a sitting area.

H. japonicus

P. 109

h. jah-PON-ih-kus. Japanese Hops. A vigorous, tender perennial climber that can reach 10 feet or more in a single season. Lobed, maplelike leaves and small, oval spikes of greenish flowers appear from mid- to late summer. Plants self-sow abundantly from about Zone 4 south. 'Variegatus' features leaves streaked and mottled with white and comes true from seeds. Cool-weather annual.

Hunnemannia

hun-eh-MAN-ee-ah. Poppy family, Papaveraceae.

Only one species belongs to the genus *Hunnemannia*, a tender perennial native to Mexico commonly called Mexican tulip poppy. It closely resembles California poppy (*Eschscholzia* spp.) and has deeply divided, blue-green leaves and glossy, cup-shaped, four-petaled flowers, borne from summer to fall. Botanists distinguish plants in the two genera because *H. fumariifolia* has separate sepals, while in *Eschscholzia* species they are united to form a cap.

HOW TO GROW

Plant Mexican tulip poppies in full sun and average, well-drained soil. They thrive in heat and do not tolerate shade or wet soil. Sow seeds outdoors in spring several weeks before the last spring frost date. Or sow indoors in individual pots 6 to 8 weeks before the last spring frost date at 55° to 60°F. Germination takes 2 to 3 weeks. Handle the plants carefully at transplanting, as they resent root disturbance; for this reason, they aren't generally overwintered. Use tulip poppies in mixed plantings in beds and borders as well as in containers. They also make excellent cut flowers.

H. fumariifolia P. 109

h. few-mare-ee-ih-FO-lee-ah. Mexican Tulip Poppy, Mexican Golden-cup. A tender, 2- to 3-foot perennial with ferny, blue-green leaves. Bears 2- to 3-inch-wide, golden yellow flowers with glossy petals from midsummer to frost. Tender perennial grown as a cool-weather annual.

Hymenostemma paludosum *see Leucanthemum paludosum*

Hypoestes

hy-poe-ES-tees. Acanthus family, Acanthaceae.

There are about 40 species of *Hypoestes*, which are tender perennials, subshrubs, and shrubs from South Africa, Madagascar, and Southeast Asia. They bear ovate, sometimes toothed, leaves and small spikes of two-lipped flowers from late summer to frost. One species is grown as a foliage plant, both indoors as a houseplant and outdoors as a foliage accent in bedding displays.

HOW TO GROW

Give these plants a site in partial shade and rich, evenly moist, well-drained soil. Sow seeds indoors 10 to 12 weeks before the last spring frost date. Plants are fast and easy to grow from cuttings taken in spring or summer. Pinch plants to encourage branching and bushy growth. Grow them as bedding plants replaced annually or as tender perennials — keep plants in containers so they are easy to bring in, take cuttings in late summer, or dig the plants and pot them up for overwintering. Feed container-grown plants monthly during the growing season. Use these plants to add foliage color to shady plantings and mixed containers.

H. phyllostachya P 110.

h. fill-oh-STAY-kee-ah. Polka-dot Plant, Freckle Face. A 1-foot-tall subshrub with ovate leaves spotted with pink. Bears tiny spikes of pink to lilac flowers in summer and fall. 'Splash' has leaves heavily dotted with large spots of bright pink. 'Confetti Mix' produces plants spotted with pink and white. Tender perennial or warm-weather annual.

Iberis

EYE-ber-iss. Cabbage family, Brassicaceae.

Better known as candytufts, *Iberis* species are annuals, perennials, and subshrubs grown for their rounded clusters of flowers, which are sometimes fragrant. The genus contains about 40 species that thrive in alkaline, fast-draining soils and are found from Spain and Southern Europe, through North Africa, to Turkey and Iran. They bear linear to ovate leaves, and their showy flower clusters are made up of tiny four-petaled flowers, which usually have two larger and two smaller flowers.

HOW TO GROW

Give annual candytufts full sun or partial shade in areas with hot summers and poor to average, well-drained soil that remains evenly moist. A neutral to alkaline pH is best. Sow seeds outdoors after danger of frost has passed. From Zone 8 south, annual candytufts can be sown in late summer or early fall for bloom the following year. Or sow seeds indoors in individual pots 6 to 8 weeks before the last spring frost date at 65° to 70°F. Germination takes 2 to 3 weeks. Transplant with care. Sow new crops every 2 weeks until midsummer for continued bloom. Deadhead to prolong bloom, and pull up plants once they begin to die. Plants self-sow in mild climates. Use annual candytufts in beds of annuals, as fillers among perennials, or in containers. They also make excellent cut flowers.

I. amara P. 110

i. am-AH-rah. Rocket Candytuft. A 6- to 18-inch-tall, branching annual with spoon-shaped leaves. Bears rounded, 4- to 6-inch-tall clusters of mildly fragrant white to lilac-white flowers in summer. 'Giant White Hyacinth Flowered' features good fragrance and is an especially good cut flower. Cool-weather annual.

I. umbellata P. 111

i. um-bell-AY-tah. Globe Candytuft. A mounding, well-branched 6- to 12-inch annual with linear to lance-shaped leaves. Flattened, 2-inch-wide clusters of fragrant flowers appear in shades of white, pink, lilac, purple, and red in summer. 'Flash Mix' plants come in an especially wide range of colors. Cool-weather annual.

Impatiens

im-PAY-shens. Balsam family, Balsaminaceae.

The genus *Impatiens* contains about 850 species of annuals, perennials, and subshrubs with brittle, succulent stems; fleshy leaves; and spurred, asymmetrical flowers. The flowers have five petals, although the lower petals on each flower are fused together to form two lobed pairs. Cultivated forms of impatiens bear single or double flowers; in some species they are hooded. In addition to beloved annuals, jewelweed *(I. capensis)* belongs here. It is also called touch-me-not, a name that celebrates another characteristic of all impatiens: the seeds are contained in an explosive capsule that flings seeds in all directions when touched. Hummingbirds visit many species of impatiens.

HOW TO GROW

Give impatiens partial to full shade and rich, evenly moist, well-drained soil. New Guinea impatiens grow best in full sun to very light shade. Sow seeds indoors 8 to 10 weeks before the last spring frost date. Germination

Impatiens wallerana

takes 2 to 3 weeks at 70° to 75°F (germinate garden balsam, *I. balsamina,* slightly cooler—60° to 65°F). Use a sterile seed-starting mix, and just press the seeds into the soil surface, since light aids germination. To combat damping off, which can be a problem, water only from below, but provide high humidity by covering the pots with plastic until seedlings appear. Do not set plastic-covered pots or flats in sun, since they can quickly overheat. Grow seedlings at around 60°F. Transplant to the garden several weeks after the last spring frost date, once night temperatures remain above 50°F. Perennials, including New Guinea impatiens and garden impatiens *(I. walleriana),* are easy to propagate by cuttings taken in spring or summer. They can be grown as bedding plants replaced annually or as tender perennials: to overwinter them, take cuttings, dig and pot up plants, or keep them in containers. Use impatiens to add summer-long color to shade gardens, either planted in large drifts or interspersed among perennials, as well as in containers. Dwarf types make excellent edgings for paths and beds. Some species, especially garden balsam *(I. balsamina),* self-sow.

I. balsamina

P. 111

i. bal-sah-MEE-nah. Garden Balsam. A 1- to 2½-foot-tall annual with lance-shaped leaves and single or double flowers borne along the main stem in the leaf axils from summer to early fall. Flowers come in shades of pink, white, red, and purple. 'Tom Thumb Mix' plants are 8 to 12 inches tall. 'Camellia Flowered Mix' yields 2-foot, double-flowered plants. Warm-weather annual.

I. glandulifera

i. gland-you-LIF-er-ah. Himalayan Jewelweed. Formerly *I. roylei.* A somewhat coarse, 1- to 3-foot annual with ovate to lance-shaped leaves. Bears clusters of fragrant, 1½-inch-long, lavender to rose-purple flowers. This species is native to the Himalayas but has naturalized in North America. Warm-weather annual.

I. New Guinea Hybrids

P. 112

Hybrid, tender, subshrubby perennials developed by crossing various species from New Guinea, including *I. schlecteri.* They bear lance-shaped leaves on 12- to 14-inch-tall plants that can be green, bronze, or variegated with yellow or cream. Flat-faced, 2- to 2½-inch-wide flowers appear from summer to frost in shades of rose, red, salmon, lilac-pink, and white. Many cultivars are cutting-propagated, but 'Spectra Mix' is a strain that comes true from seeds. Tender perennial or warm-weather annual.

I. walleriana

P. 112

i. wall-er-ee-AH-nah. Garden Impatiens, Busy Lizzie, Patience Plant. Tender, subshrubby, ½- to 2-foot-tall perennials with rounded to lance-shaped, green leaves that may be flushed with bronze. Showy, flat-faced, single or double, 1- to 2½-inch-wide flowers borne in abundance from summer to frost. Many cultivars are available, most mixes with a wide range of colors, including pale and dark pink, lavender, rose, white, salmon, red, and orange-red; bicolors also are available. 'Super Elfin Mix' plants are 6 inches tall. 'Confection Mix' produces a large percentage of double-flowered plants. Mini-Hawaiian Series plants are miniature, with well-branched plants and leaves and flowers under 1 inch. Tender perennial or warm-weather annual.

Ipomoea

eye-poe-MEE-ah. Morning glory family, Convolvulaceae.

Ipomoea is a large and diverse genus consisting of about 500 species. The best-known garden plants are climbing annuals and tender perennials—the genus name is from the Greek *ips,* "worm," and *homoios,* "resembling"—but the genus also contains nonclimbing annuals and perennials along with a few shrubs and trees. Botanists have classified and reclassified the plants contained here, so several species are still listed under other names. Closely related to *Convolvulus* species, *Ipomoea* species bear funnel- or bell-shaped flowers, either singly or in clusters in the leaf axils. Hummingbirds are attracted to the blooms, especially of red-flowered species and cultivars.

HOW TO GROW

A site in full sun and average, well-drained, evenly moist soil is ideal. Most require strings, a trellis, or other support upon which to climb. Sow seeds indoors in individual pots 6 to 8 weeks before the last spring frost date. Germination takes from 1 to 3 weeks at 65° to 70°F. Seedlings need a stake to climb on even when they are still fairly small; otherwise the vines will become entangled. Transplant a few weeks after the last frost, once temperatures remain above 45°F. Or sow outdoors 2 weeks after the last frost date. Install the required trellis *before* outdoor sowing. Either way, to speed germination, carefully nick the seed coats with a knife or file and/or soak the seeds for 24 hours in warm water before sowing. In addition to seeds, perennials can be propagated by cuttings taken in spring or summer, which can be used to overwinter the plants, if desired. Use these plants to climb and cover all manner of structures from deck railings and fences to trellises. They also can be trained over shrubs. Some, including foliage cultivars of *I. batatas,* are effective clambering among perennials and annuals in mixed plantings or in containers.

I. alba

P. 113

i. AL-bah. Moonflower. Formerly *Calonyction aculeatum* and *I. bona-nox.* A tender perennial climber that can reach 15 feet in a single season. Large, rounded leaves with heart-shaped bases. Bears fragrant, white, 5- to 5½-inch-wide flowers that open at dusk from early or midsummer to frost. The flowers attract night-flying moths. Warm-weather annual or tender perennial.

I. batatas

P. 113

i. bah-TAH-tas. Sweet Potato. A tender perennial grown in food gardens for its fleshy, sweet, edible roots. Plants can climb or spread 10 feet or more in a single season, and to 20 feet or more in frost-free climates. They bear rounded to heart-shaped leaves that can be entire or lobed and 1-inch-wide, pale purple flowers in summer. While even cultivars developed for vegetable gardens have attractive foliage, often flushed with purple, several are grown for their leaves alone: 'Blackie' bears dark, purple-black, maplelike leaves; 'Margarita' has chartreuse, heart-shaped leaves; 'Pink Frost' has arrow-shaped leaves marked with green, white, and pink, which require protection from direct sun. All are hardy from Zone 9 south and produce tubers, which can be dug before frost and used to overwinter the plants farther north. Warm-weather annual or tender perennial.

I. coccinea

i. cock-SIN-ee-ah. Red Morning Glory, Star Morning Glory. Formerly *Quamoclit coccinea.* A vigorous 6- to 12-foot annual climber with ovate or deeply toothed leaves. Bears small clusters of scarlet, ¾-inch-wide trumpets in summer. Warm-weather annual.

I. hederacea

i. hed-er-AY-cee-ah. Formerly *Pharbitis hederacea.* A 6- to 10-foot annual climber with rounded, three-lobed leaves. Bears small clusters of ¾- to 1½-inch-wide, blue, purple, or purple-red flowers in summer. 'Fugi Mix' and 'Roman Candy' feature variegated leaves. Warm-weather annual.

I. lobata

P. 114

i. low-BAH-tah. Spanish Flag, Exotic Love. Formerly *Mina lobata, Ipomoea versicolor,* and *Quamoclit lobata.* A tender perennial climber most often grown as an annual that ranges from 6 to 15 feet in height. Bears lobed leaves and dense, one-sided racemes of slightly curved, narrow, tubular flowers that are ½ to ¾ inch long. Buds and flowers initially are red but turn orange, yellow, then cream as they age. 'Citronella' bears lemon yellow flowers that age to white. Tender perennial or warm-weather annual.

I. × *multifida* **P. 114**

i. × mul-TIFF-ih-dah. Cardinal Climber. A 3- to 6-foot annual climber, the result of a cross between *I. coccinea* and *I. quamoclit.* Bears deeply lobed leaves and crimson, 1-inch-wide, salverform flowers, which have a slender tube with a flared and flattened face. Warm-weather annual.

I. nil **P. 115**

i. NIL. Morning Glory. Formerly *I. imperialis.* A vigorous annual or tender, short-lived perennial that can reach 15 feet in a single season. Bears ovate, sometimes lobed, leaves and 2- to 4-inch-wide, white-tubed flowers in shades of pale to deep blue, red, purple, or white from midsummer to fall. 'Early Call Mix' is fast from seeds and a good choice for areas with short growing seasons. Platycodon Series bears purple, red, or white, single or semidouble flowers. 'Chocolate' bears pale red-brown flowers. 'Scarlett O'Hara' bears red flowers. Warm-weather annual.

I. purpurea

i. pur-PUR-ee-ah. Common Morning Glory. Formerly *Convolvulus purpureus* and *Pharbitis purpurea.* A 6- to 10-foot annual climber with broad, rounded to lobed leaves and trumpet-shaped, 2½-inch-wide, white-throated flowers in shades of blue, purple-blue, pink, red, and white in summer; white flowers with stripes of color also are available. Warm-weather annual.

I. quamoclit **P. 115**

i. QUAM-oh-clit. Cypress Vine, Star Glory. Formerly *Quamoclit pennata.* A 6- to 20-foot annual climber with deeply cut leaves. Bears scarlet, ¾-inch-wide flowers in summer. Warm-weather annual.

I. tricolor **P. 116**

i. TRI-cuh-lor. Morning Glory. Formerly *I. rubrocaerulea.* A vigorous annual or short-lived tender perennial reaching 10 to 12 feet in a season. Bears 3-inch-wide flowers with white throats in shades from pale blue to purple in summer. 'Heavenly Blue' bears sky blue flowers with white throats. 'Crimson Rambler' bears red flowers with white throats. 'Pearly Gates' has white flowers. Warm-weather annual.

Ipomopsis

ip-oh-MOP-sis. Phlox family, Polemoniaceae.

This genus contains 24 species of annuals, biennials, and perennials, plus one shrub, that were once included in the genus *Gilia.* Most are native to western North America, although standing cypress *(Ipomopsis rubra)* is native from South Carolina and Florida to Texas. They bear entire to deeply cut, featherlike leaves and showy clusters of tubular flowers in shades of red, pink, violet, yellow, and white.

HOW TO GROW

Plant in full sun and average, very well drained soil. The species discussed here thrive in sandy soil. They can be grown as annuals or biennials, but growing them as biennials yields the showiest flower display and is the best option where plants are hardy. To grow them as annuals, sow seeds outdoors 2 to 3 weeks before the last spring frost date; sow in fall in areas with mild winters (from Zone 6 south). Or sow indoors 6 to 8 weeks before the last frost, and germinate at 50° to 65°F, but outdoor sowing is usually best. To grow them as biennials, sow seeds outdoors in mid- to late summer. Keep the soil on the dry side, since wet conditions lead to root rot, especially in winter. Use them in drifts in mixed plantings as well as wild gardens. The flowers attract hummingbirds as well as moths and also make attractive additions to bouquets. Plants self-sow.

I. aggregata P. 116

i. ag-greh-GAH-tah. Skyrocket, Scarlet Gilia. A 2-foot-tall biennial bearing large panicles of tubular to funnelform, ¼- to 1½-inch-long flowers in red, pink, yellow, or nearly white. Biennial or cool-weather annual.

Ipomopsis aggregata

I. rubra

P. 117

i. RUE-brah. Standing Cypress. A 3- to 6-foot biennial with feathery leaves and narrow panicles of scarlet flowers dotted with red and yellow inside. Biennial or cool-weather annual.

Iresine

EYE-reh-sign. Amaranth family, Amaranthaceae.

Colorful foliage is the hallmark of *Iresine* species, which are commonly referred to as blood leaf. About 80 species of plants native to South America and Australia belong to this genus, including annuals, tender perennials, both erect and climbing, and subshrubs. They bear simple, unlobed leaves that often are brilliantly marked with red or yellow. The insignificant flowers are white or greenish.

HOW TO GROW

Full sun and rich, evenly moist, well-drained soil are best. Plants grow in partial shade but show best leaf color in sun. Since asexual propagation yields uniform-looking plants identical to their parents, cuttings are the best choice for propagation. Grow them as bedding plants replaced annually or as tender perennials. If you start from seeds, sow indoors 8 to 10 weeks before the last spring frost date and germinate at 55° to 60°F. Take cuttings anytime. Move plants to the garden several weeks after the last frost date, once temperatures consistently stay in the 50s. Water regularly and feed monthly during the growing season. Pinch regularly to encourage branching and bushy growth. To overwinter plants indoors, take cuttings in late summer, and keep them on the dry side. Use blood leaves as edging plants or to add season-long foliage color to beds and borders. They tolerate shearing, so make a good edging for knot gardens and also are used in carpet bedding displays.

I. herbstii

P. 117

i. HERB-stee-eye. Painted Blood Leaf, Beefsteak Plant, Chicken Gizzard. A well-branched, bushy annual or short-lived tender perennial that can reach 5 to 6 feet in the tropics but is usually a foot tall when grown in the North. Rounded, waxy, 2½- to 3-inch-long leaves are variegated or have contrasting veins: colors include green, yellow, red, purple-red, and orange-red. The leaf surface may be puckered. 'Aureoreticulata' features green leaves with yellow veins. 'Brilliantissima' has shocking red-pink leaves blotched with purple-brown. Tender perennial or warm-weather annual.

I. lindenii **P. 118**

i. lin-DEN-ee-eye. Blood Leaf. A tender perennial that can reach 3 feet in the tropics but is considerably shorter in northern gardens. Grown for its glossy, ovate to lance-shaped, dark red leaves, leafstalks, and stems. Tender perennial or warm-weather annual.

Kochia scoparia forma *trichophylla* *see Bassia scoparia* forma *trichophylla*

Lablab

LAB-lab. Pea family, Fabaceae.

The one species that belongs to this genus—*Lablab purpureus*—is a tender, climbing perennial known under such common names as hyacinth bean, bonavist, lablab, and Indian or Egyptian bean. It is widely grown from North Africa to India for its edible beans and pods, but in North America it is primarily appreciated as an ornamental because of its rose-purple flowers and glossy purple-maroon fruit.

HOW TO GROW

Full sun and average to rich, well-drained soil are ideal. Plants need strings, netting, or a trellis upon which to climb. Sow seeds indoors in individual pots 6 to 8 weeks before the last spring frost date at 65° to 75°F. Germination takes 2 weeks. Or, in areas with long growing seasons—roughly Zone 7 south—sow outdoors after the last frost, once the soil has warmed to 60°F. Soak seeds in warm water for 24 hours before sowing, and barely cover them with soil. Plants tolerate poor, dry soil, but for best growth water regularly and feed once or twice when plants are still small to give them a good start. Use hyacinth beans to decorate trellises, walls, pergolas, and railings. They are effective when combined with other annual vines.

L. purpureus **P. 118**

l. pur-PUR-ee-us. Hyacinth Bean, Lablab. Formerly *Dolichos lablab* and *D. purpureus.* A vigorous, fast-growing, tender vine, ranging from 6 to 20 feet in height and hardy only in Zones 10 and 11. Bears palmate leaves and clusters of fragrant, rose-purple, ½- to 1-inch-long, pealike flowers. The flowers are followed by flat, glossy, maroon-purple pods that are quite showy. The pods and beans are edible, but strong-tasting, and dry beans can cause an allergic reaction in some people: soak the beans in hot water and discard the water to eliminate this danger. Tender perennial or warm-weather annual.

Lagenaria

lah-jen-AIR-ee-ah. Squash family, Cucurbitaceae.

Lagenaria species, commonly known as bottle gourds, often are overlooked by gardeners interested in growing ornamentals. These climbing or sprawling plants feature large leaves that are rounded to heart-shaped, or sometimes lobed. They climb via tendrils and bear separate male and female five-petaled flowers. Flowers are followed by fruit that can exceed 3 feet in length. The botanical name is from the Greek *lagenos,* "flask." Of the six species of annuals and perennials in the genus, one is grown for its variously shaped fruits, which can be dried and used to make items such as birdhouses, dried-flower vases, toys, musical instruments, and serving containers and utensils.

HOW TO GROW

Full sun; rich, well-drained soil; and plenty of space will satisfy gourds. In areas with long growing seasons, the vines can climb or spread to 30 feet in a single season. Sow seeds indoors in individual pots no more than 4 weeks before the last spring frost date. Germination takes about 1 week if the soil is kept warm, about 75°F. Transplant with care after the last frost date, once the weather has settled and the soil has warmed up to at least 50°F. In areas with long growing seasons, sow seeds outdoors after the soil has reached 60°F. Larger gourds require a longer season to set and ripen fruit: birdhouse gourds can be direct-sown from about Zone 7 south, while kettle should be given a head start indoors from about Zone 8 south. Use gourds as fast, temporary, inexpensive ground covers in new gardens and under shrubs. They will climb trees and trellises if permitted; just don't let them engulf shrubs you value. They also will cover eyesores. The best way to dry the gourds is to wait until they turn brown on the plants and then cut them with several inches of stem attached. If frost threatens, however, harvest immediately. Spread them out in a dry, warm

(70°F or warmer), airy spot until they turn light brown or straw-colored and are light in weight. This can take several months for larger types. Handle undried gourds carefully, as they break easily and bruised spots tend to rot during the drying process. Some experts wipe down the outside of the gourds every few weeks with a 10 percent bleach solution (1 part bleach, 9 parts water). Inspect the drying gourds regularly, and discard any that show signs of rot.

L. siceraria P. 119

l. sis-er-AIR-ee-ah. Bottle Gourd, White-flowered Gourd, Calabash. A vigorous climbing annual, to 30 feet, with heart-shaped leaves, white flowers, and fruit in various shapes and sizes. Cultivars are named by the shapes of the fruit, or gourds: 'Hercules Club', 'Long-Handled Dipper', 'Kettle', and 'Birdhouse' are a few of the cultivars/shapes available. Warm-weather annual.

Lagurus

LAG-ur-us. Grass family, Poaceae.

One species belongs to this genus: hare's tail grass *(Lagurus ovatus)*, a native of sandy soils in the Mediterranean. It is grown for its fluffy, rounded flower heads, which both the common and botanical names commemorate. *Lagurus* is from the Greek *lagos*, "hare," and *oura*, "tail."

HOW TO GROW

Select a site with full sun and poor to average soil that is light, even sandy, and very well drained. Plants tolerate dry soil. Sow seeds indoors 6 to 8 weeks before the last spring frost date at 55°F. Germination takes 2 to 3 weeks. Or sow outdoors 2 to 3 weeks before the last frost date where the plants are to grow. In mild climates—roughly Zone 7 south—sow seeds outdoors in late summer or fall for bloom the following year. Use hare's tail as an edging plant, in mixed plantings, and in containers. It makes an attractive cut or dried flower. Harvest the flower heads just before they mature (either cut them or pull up the plants), and hang in a warm, dry place. Plants self-sow.

L. ovatus P. 119

l. oh-VAY-tus. Hare's Tail Grass. A clumping annual, to 20 inches in height, with narrow leaves. In summer, plants bear greenish white, 2½-inch-long plumes that may be tinted with purple; they ripen to creamy tan. 'Nanus' is 5 inches tall. Warm-weather annual.

Lantana

lan-TAN-ah. Vervain or Verbena family, Verbenaceae.

Showy, domed clusters of flowers characterize the cultivated lantanas, or shrub verbenas as they are sometimes called. Some 150 species of tender shrubs and perennials, native to the Americas and South Africa, belong to this genus, but gardeners primarily grow cultivars of two species. *Lantana* species bear simple, toothed, wrinkled leaves and dense clusters of salverform flowers, which have a slender tube with a flared, flattened face. The flowers, which attract both hummingbirds and butterflies, have five lobes and are arranged in rounded or flattened heads.

HOW TO GROW

Full sun and poor to average, well-drained soil are ideal. Lantanas are hardy in Zones 10 and 11, where they can be grown outdoors as shrubs (they survive a light frost but not a hard freeze). In areas where they are marginally hardy, try a site against a south-facing wall for extra winter protection, and cover them when frost threatens. North of Zone 10, grow them as bedding plants replaced annually or as tender perennials kept in containers and overwintered indoors in a bright, cool (40° to 45°F) spot. Sow seeds indoors 12 to 15 weeks before the last spring frost date. Germination takes 6 to 8 weeks at 70° to 75°F. Soak seeds in warm water for 24 hours before sowing. Pinch seedlings to encourage branching. Transplant to the garden after the last frost date once the soil has warmed to 50°F. Lantanas are also easy to grow from cuttings taken in spring or summer,

Lantana montevidensis

and cuttings are best if you want a particular color, since cultivars do not come true from seeds. (Seeds yield plants in a mix of colors.) Consider buying or overwintering a stock plant from which to take cuttings. Water deeply during dry weather, and feed pot-grown plants monthly in summer. Prune to shape plants in late winter or early spring; cut them back hard, if necessary. Use lantanas as bedding plants or in containers either set on terraces or sunk to the rim in the soil.

L. camara

P. 120

l. cam-AH-rah. Lantana. A tender, 3- to 6-foot shrub with ill-smelling, slightly toothed leaves. Bears 1- to 2-inch-wide flower heads of ⅓-inch-wide blooms in shades of yellow, pink, cream, red, lilac, and purple, often with multiple colors in each head. Tender perennial or warm-weather annual.

L. montevidensis

P. 120

l. mon-teh-vih-DEN-sis. Weeping Lantana. A tender, spreading ½- to 3-foot-tall shrub that can be used to form a dense ground cover. Bears ovate to lance-shaped, coarsely toothed leaves and ¾- to 1¼-inch-wide clusters of ½-inch-wide, rose-lilac flowers. Tender perennial or warm-weather annual.

Lathyrus

LATH-ur-rus. Pea family, Fabaceae.

Lathyrus species are annuals and perennials with showy, butterfly-like flowers that botanists call papilionaceous: they have a large, upright petal, called a banner or standard, and two side, or wing, petals. The two lower petals are joined at the base to form a sheath, called a keel. Many of the 150 species in the genus climb by means of tendrils on the leaves, which are pinnate, meaning divided into leaflets arranged in a featherlike fashion.

HOW TO GROW

Give sweet peas *(L. odoratus)* full sun to partial shade and rich, well-drained soil. They are best in areas with cool summers, although in the South they can be grown for winter or spring bloom; pull them up and replace them once hot weather arrives and they begin to languish. Sow seeds outdoors in early spring as soon as the soil can be worked, about 5 weeks before the last spring frost date. Or sow indoors 6 to 8 weeks before the last frost. Germination takes 2 to 3 weeks at 55° to 60°F. Either way, to speed germination, nick the hard seed coats with a file or knife and/or soak them in warm water for 24 hours before sowing. Climbing types require twiggy brush, strings, or a trellis upon which to climb. Water regularly and mulch the plants to keep the soil cool and moist. Feed monthly. Deadheading prolongs blooming.

L. odoratus P. 121

l. oh-dor-AH-tus. Sweet Pea. A bushy or climbing annual with winged stems that can reach as much as 6 to 8 feet tall. Bears small clusters of fragrant, 1½- to 2-inch-wide flowers in shades of lavender, rose-pink, purple-pink, white, and purple. Standards and keels may be the same or different colors. Old-fashioned cultivars are more likely to be fragrant; modern ones have been selected for range of color, size of flowers, and habit, rather than fragrance. 'Old Spice Mix' and 'Painted Lady' are two old cultivars that bear fragrant, 1-inch blooms and climb to 5 to 6 feet. 'Knee-Hi Mix' plants are dwarf, ranging from 1½ to 2 feet tall; tendril-less 'Explorer Mix' plants grow to 14 inches. Cool-weather annual.

Laurentia axillaris *see Solenopsis axillaris*

Lavatera

lah-vah-TARE-ah. Mallow family, Malvaceae.

Some 25 species of annuals, biennials, perennials, subshrubs, and shrubs belong to this genus, which is widely distributed from the Mediterranean to central Asia and Russia, Australia, and California. Most are plants of dry, rocky soils. They bear leaves that usually are palmately lobed and are grown for their showy, five-petaled flowers in shades of pink and white. The blooms are saucer- or funnel-shaped and resemble small hibiscus.

HOW TO GROW

Full sun and average, well-drained soil are ideal. Too-rich soil yields abundant foliage but few flowers. Sow seeds outdoors where the plants are to grow in early spring, a few weeks before the last spring frost date when the soil is still cool. Or sow indoors in individual pots 6 to 8 weeks before last frost at 70°F. Transplant with care. Taller types may require pea stakes or other support. Use lavateras in mixed plantings. Dwarf cultivars can be grown in containers. All make excellent cut flowers.

L. trimestris

P. 121

l. tri-MES-tris. Lavatera, Tree Mallow. A 2- to 4-foot, well-branched annual. Bears funnel-shaped, 3- to 4-inch-wide flowers singly in leaf axils. Flowers come in white and pale to reddish pink. 'Mont Blanc' and 'Mont Rose' are compact 2-foot-tall cultivars. 'Silver Cup' bears rose-pink flowers on 3-foot plants. Cool-weather annual.

Layia

LAY-ee-ah. Aster family, Asteraceae.

The genus *Layia* contains 15 species of annuals native to the western United States, primarily California. Commonly called tidy tips, they bear narrow, toothed to pinnately lobed leaves. The daisylike flower heads have yellow centers, and the petals, more properly called ray florets, are toothed at the tip and come in yellow or white, as well as yellow with white tips.

HOW TO GROW

Give tidy tips a site with full sun or light shade and poor to average, moist but well-drained soil. Plants thrive in sandy soil, and very rich conditions yield floppy growth. They also grow best in areas with cool summers; where hot summers prevail, start seeds indoors to give plants a chance to bloom before hot weather sets in. Sow seeds outdoors where the plants are to grow after the last spring frost date. Or sow indoors 6 to 8 weeks before the last frost at 70° to 75°F. Germination takes 1 to 3 weeks. In mild climates — roughly Zone 7 south — sow seeds in fall for bloom the following spring. Water during very dry weather. Use tidy tips in mixed plantings, on banks, as well as in rock gardens. They make excellent cut flowers.

L. platyglossa

P. 122

l. plah-tee-GLOSS-ah. Tidy Tips. Formerly *L. elegans*. A 1- to 1½-foot-tall annual with featherlike, slightly hairy, gray-green leaves. Bears 2-inch-wide daisies with golden yellow centers and yellow petals tipped with white from summer to fall. Cool-weather annual.

Leonotis

lee-oh-NO-tis. Mint family, Lamiaceae.

Native mostly to South Africa, the 30 species of *Leonotis* are square-stemmed annuals, perennials, subshrubs, and shrubs with aromatic, lance-shaped to ovate leaves. They bear clusters of showy, two-lipped flowers in tiers at the leaf nodes along upright stems, with each tier consisting of densely clustered flowers arranged around the stem. The blooms come in red-orange, scarlet, and orange, as well as white. Both the common name lion's ear and the botanical name, which is from the Greek *leon,* "lion," and *ous,* "ear," refer to the notion that the flowers' corollas (petals) resemble lion's ears.

HOW TO GROW

Give lion's ears a site in full sun or partial shade and average, well-drained soil. Good choices for seaside gardens, they can be grown outdoors in Zones 10 and 11. In the North, grow them as bedding plants replaced annually or as tender perennials overwintered indoors in a bright, cool (50° to 65°F) spot. Sow seeds indoors 8 to 10 weeks before the last spring frost date at 55° to 65°F. Or start them from cuttings taken in spring or summer, which can be used to propagate the plants for the garden or for overwintering. Pinch seed-grown or young cutting-grown plants to encourage branching. Transplant to the garden after the last frost date, once the soil has warmed to 50°F. Water regularly in dry weather. Stake as necessary. Prune to shape plants in late winter or early spring: cut them back hard, if necessary. Use lion's ears in mixed beds and borders or in containers, either set on terraces or sunk to the rim in the soil.

L. leonurus P. 122

l. lee-oh-NUR-us. Lion's Ear. A tender shrub that can reach 6 feet but is considerably smaller in the North. Bears aromatic, lance-shaped leaves and 2½-inch-long, orange-red to scarlet flowers in fall and will continue to bloom into winter if you bring it indoors. Tender perennial.

L. ocymifolia

l. ah-sim-ih-FOE-lee-ah. Lion's Ear. A tender perennial that can reach 10 feet but is smaller in the North. Bears ovate, aromatic leaves with toothed margins and whorls of 1½-inch-long orange flowers in late summer and fall. Tender perennial.

Leucanthemum

leu-CAN-theh-mum. Aster family, Asteraceae.

Leucanthemum contains some 25 species of annuals and perennials, many of which were once included in the genus *Chrysanthemum.* They bear daisylike flower heads, which usually have white "petals," or ray florets, and yellow centers consisting of densely packed disk florets. The botanical name is from the Greek *leukos,* "white," and *anthemon,* "flower." One species is a popular annual.

HOW TO GROW

Full sun and average, well-drained, evenly moist soil are ideal. Sow seeds indoors 6 to 8 weeks before the last spring frost date at 65° to 70°F. Or sow outdoors where the plants are to grow on the last frost date. When sowing, just press the seeds into the soil surface, as light aids germination. Pinch young plants to promote bushy growth. Deadheading prolongs bloom. Plants may self-sow. Use annual leucanthemums at the front of beds and borders as well as in rock gardens.

L. paludosum P. 123

l. pal-you-DOE-sum. Formerly *Chrysanthemum paludosum, Melampodium paludosum* and *Hymenostemma paludosum.* A bushy, spreading, 2- to 6-inch-tall annual with spoon-shaped leaves. Bears masses of solitary, ¾- to 1¼-inch-wide, daisylike flowers with white petals and yellow centers in summer. Cool-weather annual.

Limnanthes

lim-NAN-theez. Meadow foam family, Limnanthaceae.

Native wildflowers from the western United States, *Limnanthes* species bear cup-shaped, five-petaled flowers and deeply cut, featherlike leaves. Of the 17 species in the genus, all low-growing annuals, one is cultivated.

HOW TO GROW

Choose a planting site with full sun or partial shade and rich, moist, well-drained soil. Sow seeds outdoors where the plants are to grow several weeks before the last spring frost date, while the soil is still cool and light frost is possible. Seeds germinate in about 3 weeks. In areas with mild winters—roughly Zone 7 south—sow seeds in fall for spring bloom; protect them with a light mulch of weed-free straw over winter. Plants grow best in areas with cool summers and die or languish when hot weather arrives. Use these plants for early color in mixed beds and borders. Plants self-sow.

L. douglasii P. 123

l. dug-LASS-ee-eye. Fried Eggs, Meadow Foam, Poached-egg Plant. A spreading annual with fleshy, feathery leaves that can reach 6 inches in height and width. Bears masses of fragrant, 1-inch-wide, golden yellow flowers with white-edged petals from summer to fall. Cool-weather annual.

Limonium

lih-MOAN-ee-um. Plumbago family, Plumbaginaceae.

Many gardeners know *Limonium* species as statice, a former botanical name for this genus of 150 species of perennials, subshrubs, and some annuals and biennials. Leaves range from simple and entire to deeply lobed and featherlike; generally they are clustered in a rosette at the base of the plant. They produce small spikes of papery flowers in summer and fall that are arranged in larger panicles.

HOW TO GROW

Provide full sun and average, well-drained soil. Statices are good plants for sandy soils and seaside gardens. Sow seeds indoors 6 to 8 weeks before the last spring frost date at 65° to 75°F. Germination takes 2 to 3 weeks. Or sow outdoors after the last frost date. Add statice to mixed plantings. They are ideal candidates for cutting gardens and are top-notch dried flowers. Harvest when most of the flowers in the spray have opened fully, and hang in small bunches in a warm, dark place to dry.

L. sinuatum P. 124

l. sih-nu-AH-tum. Statice. A 1½-foot-tall tender perennial, hardy from Zone 8 south, with showy clusters of brightly colored, ½-inch-long, funnel-shaped flowers in shades of violet, lavender, yellow, pink, orange, salmon, and white. Pacific or California Series plants feature cultivars in separate colors, including 'American Beauty' (deep rose) and 'Gold Coast' (deep yellow). Warm-weather annual.

L. suworowii see Psylliostachys suworowii

Linanthus

lih-NAN-thus. Phlox family, Polemoniaceae.

Some 35 species of annuals and perennials belong to the genus *Linanthus,* once included in *Gilia,* a closely related genus. Native from the western United States, Mexico, and Chile, they bear deeply cut leaves and bell- to funnel-shaped, five-petaled flowers. The flowers come in shades of blue, lavender, white, pink, or yellow and somewhat resemble flowers of *Linum* species, commonly known as flax. The botanical name commemorates this resemblance: it is from the Greek *linon,* "flax," and *anthos,* "flower."

HOW TO GROW

Full sun and average, well-drained soil are ideal. These plants grow well in sandy soil and are best for areas with cool summers; or start them early enough to bloom before hot weather arrives, since they do not tolerate heat and humidity. Sow seeds outdoors where the plants are to grow 2 to 3 weeks before the last spring frost date or in fall in areas with mild winters—roughly from Zone 7 south. Or sow indoors in individual pots 6 to 8 weeks before the last frost, at 50° to 65°F, but outdoor sowing is usually best. Stake plants with twiggy brush. Use *Linanthus* species in drifts in mixed plantings or wild gardens. They also make attractive cut flowers. Plants self-sow.

L. grandiflorus P. 124

l. gran-dih-FLOOR-us. Mountain Phlox. A 1- to 2-foot annual with dense heads of 1¼-inch-wide flowers in shades of purplish pink, lavender, or white in spring and summer. Cool-weather annual.

L. nuttallii

nut-TAL-lee-eye. A 4- to 8-inch-tall tender perennial, hardy from Zone 8 south. Bears clusters of funnel-shaped, white, ½-inch-wide flowers in summer. Cool-weather annual.

Linaria

lin-AIR-ee-ah. Figwort family, Scrophulariaceae.

Sometimes called spurred snapdragons, *Linaria* species have two-lipped flowers with jaws that open like snapdragons (*Antirrhinum* spp.) but with a spur at the base. The genus contains about 100 species of annuals, biennials, and perennials with ovate, linear, or lance-shaped leaves and erect or trailing stems. Their flowers are carried in erect racemes from spring to fall and come in shades of yellow, orange, white, pink, purple, and red.

HOW TO GROW

Linarias thrive in full sun and average to rich soil that is light and well drained. Most linarias are plants of dry, sandy or rocky soil; they don't tolerate wet soil. Sow seeds outdoors where the plants are to grow a few weeks before the last spring frost date. Or sow indoors 6 to 8 weeks before the frost date at 55° to 60°F. Germination takes 2 weeks. Some gardeners start 3 weeks earlier and chill the sown pots in the refrigerator before moving them to a warmer spot for germinating. Water plants during dry weather. Cut them back after the first flush of bloom to encourage new flowers to form. Use linarias in mixed plantings and wild gardens. They attract hummingbirds and make excellent cut flowers. Plants self-sow.

L. maroccana P. 125

l. mah-rock-AN-ah. A ½- to 2-foot-tall annual from Morocco with linear leaves and loose clusters of ½-inch-long flowers in violet-purple, lavender, pink, white, yellow, and orange. The lower lip, called the palate, is usually marked with yellow or orange. 'Fairy Bouquet' bears ¾-inch flowers on 9-inch plants in a range of colors. Cool-weather annual.

Linum

LIE-num. Flax family, Linaceae.

This genus contains some 200 species of annuals, biennials, perennials, subshrubs, and shrubs commonly called flax. They bear simple, generally narrow, leaves and clusters of five-petaled, funnel- to saucer-shaped flowers. Flowers come in blue, lavender, white, yellow, red, and pink. Common flax *(Linum usitatissium),* source of the fiber from which linen is made, belongs here; the botanical name is the Latin word for that plant.

HOW TO GROW

Full sun and average to rich, light, well-drained soil are ideal. Sow seeds outdoors where the plants are to grow a few weeks before the last spring frost date. They also can be started in individual pots 6 to 8 weeks before the last frost date, but outdoor sowing is generally best. Or, where winters are mild — roughly Zone 7 south — sow outdoors in late summer or fall for bloom the following year. Use flaxes in mixed plantings with annuals or perennials. They do not make good cut flowers, as they wilt quickly after picking. Plants self-sow.

L. grandiflorum P. 125

l. gran-dih-FLOOR-um. Flax. A 1½- to 3-foot annual with gray-green leaves. Bears saucer-shaped, 1½- to 2-inch-wide flowers in shades of lilac-blue, red, white, and pink. Cool-weather annual.

Lobelia

loe-BEE-lee-ah. Bellflower family, Campanulaceae.

While most of the 365 to 370 species in this diverse genus are annuals and perennials, *Lobelia* also contains shrubs, treelike plants, and even an aquatic species that grows partially submerged. Most are native to the Americas; the treelike species, which can reach 10 to 30 feet, are from East Africa. All produce simple leaves and tubular flowers that are slit almost to the base to form two lips; the top lip has two lobes, the bottom one, three. Flowers are borne singly or in erect racemes or panicles and come in shades of blue, lilac, violet, red, pink, white, and yellow.

HOW TO GROW

Choose a planting site with full sun to partial shade and rich, evenly moist soil. In the South, a site that receives shade during the hottest part of the day is essential. Sow seeds indoors at 65° to 75°F from 8 to 10 weeks before the last spring frost date. Use a sterile seed-starting mix, and just press the seeds into the surface of the soil, as they need light to germinate. Water only from below to prevent damping off. Germination takes 2 to 3 weeks. Transplant a few weeks after the last frost date, once the weather has settled and temperatures remain above 40°F. Water regularly during dry weather. Feed every 2 weeks for best bloom. Use lobelias in mixed plantings, as edgings, and in containers. Their flowers attract butterflies.

L. erinus P. 126

l. er-EYE-nus. Edging Lobelia. A popular, much-hybridized, trailing or bushy tender perennial from South Africa. Plants range from 4 to 9 inches tall and bear linear leaves sometimes flushed with maroon-bronze. Bears small clusters of ½-inch flowers from early summer to frost. Cascade Series features trailing 8-inch-tall plants suitable for baskets. Rainbow Series plants are 5 inches tall and excellent for edging. They include 'Crystal Palace' with blue flowers and bronze leaves, 'Rosamond' with cherry red, white-eyed flowers and green leaves, and 'White Lady' with white flowers and green leaves. Warm-weather annual.

Lobularia

lob-you-LAIR-ee-ah. Cabbage family, Brassicaceae.

Dense, rounded clusters of fragrant flowers characterize the five species that belong to this genus of plants native to the Mediterranean and Canary Islands. They bear narrow, simple leaves and grow in sunny, dry spots with rocky or sandy soil. One species, *Lobularia maritima,* better known as sweet alyssum, is a popular annual.

HOW TO GROW

Give sweet alyssum full sun or partial shade and average, well-drained soil. Grows well in evenly moist soil but also tolerates dry conditions. Sow seeds indoors 6 to 8 weeks before the last spring frost date at 65° to 70°F. Germination takes 1 to 2 weeks. Or sow outdoors where the plants are to grow several weeks before the last frost date, when the soil is cool and light frost is still possible. Or sow in fall for spring bloom the following year. When sowing, just press the seeds into the soil surface, as light is required for germination. Water regularly for best performance. Shear plants back by one-half after the first flush of bloom to encourage new flowers to form. Plants self-sow. Use sweet alyssum as a ground cover, in mixed plantings, in containers, as an edging, and in paving cracks. It is a good choice for seaside gardens.

Lobularia maritima

L. maritima P. 127

l. mah-RIT-ih-mah. Sweet Alyssum. Formerly *Alyssum maritimum*. A spreading, well-branched, 2- to 12-inch-tall annual with linear, gray-green leaves. Bears masses of rounded, 1- to 3-inch-wide clusters of tiny, four-petaled flowers in white as well as shades of pink, rose-red, violet, and lilac from spring to fall. Many cultivars are available, including white-flowered, 3- to 4-inch-tall 'Snow Cloth' and 'Carpet of Snow'; Basket Series, which are 4-inch plants available in separate colors or a mix; purple-flowered, 4-inch 'Royal Carpet'; and 4-inch 'Rosie O'Day', with rose-pink blooms. Cool-weather annual.

Lonas

LOW-nas. Aster family, Asteraceae.

Despite its common name, African daisy, the one species that belongs in this genus is an annual from the Mediterranean. Another common name, yellow ageratum, is perhaps more apt: it bears dense clusters of buttonlike flower heads consisting of all disk florets—they lack the "petals" or ray florets of many aster-family plants. The foliage is deeply divided and featherlike.

HOW TO GROW

Choose a site with full sun and average, well-drained soil. Plants tolerate dry soil but flower better in evenly moist conditions. Sow seeds indoors 8 to 10 weeks before the last spring frost date at 60° to 65°F. Or sow outdoors after the last frost date, once the soil has warmed up a bit. Either way, barely cover the seeds with soil, as darkness is required for germination. Yellow ageratum makes an unusual addition to mixed plantings and also is an outstanding cut or dried flower. Harvest the blooms as soon as they are fully open, and hang them in bunches in a dark, warm, airy spot to dry.

L. annua P. 128

l. AN-yew-ah. Yellow Ageratum, African Daisy. Formerly *L. inodora*. A 1-foot-tall annual with dense, rounded, 3- to 5-inch-wide clusters of small, round, buttonlike flower heads. Warm-weather annual.

Lotus

LOW-tus. Pea family, Fabaceae.

Lotus species are annuals, perennials, and subshrubs, primarily native to the Mediterranean, and are no relation to the water-garden plants commonly called lotuses (*Nelumbo* spp.). Some 150 species belong here, all bearing leaves divided into three or more leaflets and pea-shaped flowers. Flowers are most often carried in clusters but also singly or in pairs.

HOW TO GROW

Select a site with full sun and average, well-drained soil. These plants tolerate a wide range of soils, including dry and sandy as well as alkaline to acid. Somewhat dry soil is better than moist conditions. Plants are most often grown from cuttings rather than seeds. Sow seeds indoors 8 to 10 weeks before the last spring frost date at 65° to 75°F. Grow *Lotus* species as bedding plants replaced annually or tender perennials. Take cuttings in summer for garden use or to overwinter the plants indoors. Over winter, keep plants in a bright, cool (50°F), well-ventilated spot. Prune in spring as necessary, and replace plants that become too woody. Use these plants in containers, baskets, and mixed plantings.

L. berthelotii P. 128

l. ber-theh-LOW-tee-eye. Lotus Vine, Parrot's Beak, Coral Gem. A trailing, tender subshrub, hardy from about Zone 9 south, that reaches 6 to 8 inches but can spread several feet. Bears bunches of silver-green, needle-like leaves and orange-red to scarlet, 1¼- to 1½-inch-long flowers with black centers. Flowers are carried singly or in pairs from spring to summer. *L. maculatus* is a similar species that produces yellow, 1-inch-long flowers tipped with red-orange or red. Tender perennial or warm-weather annual.

Lunaria

loo-NAIR-ee-ah. Cabbage family, Brassicaceae.

Commonly called honesty, money plant, silver dollar, and just simply lunaria, the three species that belong to this genus are annuals, biennials, or perennials native from Europe to western Asia. They bear toothed, heart-shaped to somewhat triangular leaves and showy racemes of four-petaled, cross-shaped flowers from late spring to summer. The flowers

Lunaria annua

are followed by sprays of round, flat seedpods, called siliques, that split along their edges. When the walls, or valves, fall off, they reveal the silvery, papery partitions that make these plants valued additions to dried arrangements.

HOW TO GROW

Plant lunarias in full sun or partial shade and rich, evenly moist, well-drained soil. Sow seeds outdoors anytime from a few weeks before the last spring frost date to early fall. Or sow indoors 6 to 8 weeks before the last frost, although outdoor sowing is generally best. Money plant *(L. annua)* produces foliage the first year and blooms the second. To use the seedpods for dried arrangements, harvest them just as they begin to turn from green to brown, and gently loosen the valves covering the silvery partitions by rubbing them between your fingers. Leave some seeds to ripen on the plants, as plants self-sow. Use lunarias in shade gardens, along shrub borders, and in semiwild areas.

L. annua

P. 129

l. ANN-yew-ah. Money Plant, Honesty. A ½- to 1-foot-tall biennial — to 3 feet in bloom — with ½-inch-wide, rose-purple or sometimes white flowers. Plants are hardy in Zones 5 to 9. 'Variegata' bears handsome, white-edged leaves, which are evergreen, with red-purple flowers and comes true from seeds. Biennial.

Lupinus

lu-PIE-nus. Lupine. Cabbage family, Brassicaceae.

There are about 200 species of lupines, which are annuals, perennials, subshrubs, and shrubs with palmate leaves and showy clusters of pealike flowers. The flowers, which are borne in spikelike panicles or sometimes whorls, have an upright petal, called a standard; two side or wing petals; and two lower petals joined at the base to form a sheath, called a keel. Lupines primarily are native to the Americas, the Mediterranean, and North Africa.

HOW TO GROW

Select a site with full sun and average, well-drained soil. Most lupines need cool, moist conditions and usually fail in hot, humid climates. Where hot summers prevail, sow seeds early so they have time to bloom before torrid weather arrives. Sow seeds outdoors several weeks before the last spring frost date. Or sow indoors in individual pots 6 to 8 weeks before the last frost date at 55° to 65°F. Germination takes 2 to 3 weeks. Transplant with care. Either way, chip the hard seed coats with a knife or file, or soak them in warm water for 24 hours before sowing. Use lupines in beds and borders, as well as meadows and wild gardens. The flowers attract hummingbirds and make attractive cut flowers. Plants self-sow.

L. hartwegii

l. hart-WEDGE-ee-eye. A 2- to 3-foot-tall annual with dense, 8-inch-long spikes of flowers from summer to fall. Blooms are ½ inch long and pale lavender-blue with a rose-pink blush on the upright standards. Cool-weather annual.

L. luteus

l. LOO-tee-us. Yellow Lupine. A 2-foot-tall annual with 10-inch-long spikes of golden yellow, ½- to ¾-inch-long flowers in summer. Cool-weather annual.

L. nanus

l. NAY-nus. Sky Lupine. A bushy, 1½- to 2-foot annual with 8-inch-long spikes of lavender-blue, white, or bicolor, ½-inch-wide flowers in summer. Cool-weather annual.

L. texensis

P. 129

l. tex-EN-sis. Texas Bluebonnet. A 10- to 12-inch annual with dense, 3-inch-long racemes of blue to violet-blue ½-inch-wide flowers in summer. Cool-weather annual.

Lychnis

LICK-niss. Pink family, Caryophyllaceae.

Lychnis contains some 15 to 20 species of biennials and perennials. They bear five-petaled flowers with tube-shaped bases and flattened faces with petals that are rounded, notched, or sometimes fringed at the tips. Flowers are carried singly on branched stems or in small, rounded clusters. The plants have rounded, often hairy, leaves. *Lychnis* species are quite similar to *Silene* species and share the common names campion and catchfly. There's no wonder they look so similar, since the two genera differ only in the number of styles (the narrow stalk that joins the stigma and ovary of a pistil, the female part of a flower) in the flowers. *Lychnis* species have five, or sometimes four, styles, while *Silene* species have three, or sometimes four.

HOW TO GROW

Full sun or partial shade and average, well-drained soil are ideal. Plants tolerate dry soil as well. Sow seeds outdoors in spring several weeks before the last spring frost date or in fall. Or sow indoors in pots 10 to 12 weeks before the last spring frost, and chill the sown pots in the refrigerator for 2 weeks before moving them to a warmer (70°F) spot for germination. However you sow, just press the seeds into the surface of the growing medium. Use these plants in beds and borders. They make fine cut flowers. Plants self-sow.

L. coronaria P. 130

l. cor-oh-NAIR-ee-ah. Rose Campion, Mullein Pink, Dusty Miller. A biennial or short-lived perennial, hardy in Zones 4 to 8, with rosettes of woolly, silver-gray leaves. Carries branched clusters of 1- to 1¼-inch-wide flowers on 2½- to 3-foot-tall stems. Blooms have rounded, notched petals and appear in magenta-pink or white in mid- to late summer. Biennial.

L. coeli-rosa see Silene coeli-rosa.

Machaeranthera

mat-cheer-AN-ther-ah. Aster family, Asteraceae.

These natives of western North America bear daisylike flower heads, either singly or in clusters, and leaves with spiny tips and margins that often are toothed or pinnately lobed or cleft. There are about 26 species in the genus, most native to plains and prairies with dry, well-drained soil.

HOW TO GROW

Give tahoka daisy *(Machaeranthera tanacetifolia)* full sun or light shade and average to rich, well-drained soil. Plants are best in areas with cool summers; a spot with light shade during the hottest part of the day may help them cope with hot weather, but they tend to be short-lived in hot, humid climates. Sow seeds indoors 8 to 10 weeks before the last spring frost, and chill the sown pots in the refrigerator for 2 weeks before moving them to a warmer (50° to 60°F) spot for germination, which takes 3 to 4 weeks. Or sow outdoors in spring a few weeks before the last frost date or in early fall for bloom the following year. Either way, just press the seeds into the soil surface. Use tahoka daisies in wild gardens and mixed plantings. They make excellent cut flowers.

M. tanacetifolia P. 130

m. tan-ah-cee-tih-FOE-lee-ah. Tahoka Daisy. Formerly *Aster tanacetifolius.* A bushy, 1- to 2-foot annual or biennial with abundant, 2-inch-wide, daisy-like flowers with yellow centers and pale purple "petals," or ray florets. Biennial or cool-weather annual.

Malcomia

mal-COE-mee-ah. Cabbage family, Brassicaceae.

Commonly called stocks, *Malcomia* species bear racemes of four-petaled, cross-shaped flowers in shades of pink, purple, white, and red from summer to fall. The genus contains about 35 species of annuals and perennials native from the Mediterranean to central Asia — not Virginia, as the common name of *M. maritima* might suggest.

HOW TO GROW

Full sun to light shade and average to rich, well-drained soil are ideal. Neutral to slightly alkaline pH is best. Stocks are best in areas with cool summers and are especially intolerant of warm nighttime temperatures. A spot with light shade during the hottest part of the day is best. Sow seeds outdoors a few weeks before the last spring frost date, simply raking them into the soil surface. For continued bloom in cool climates, sow new crops every 4 weeks through late summer. Or sow outdoors in fall for bloom the following year. In areas with hot, humid summers, start them early enough to bloom before hot weather arrives. Use stocks in mixed beds and borders, along pathways, and in cracks between paving. They are good choices for seaside gardens. Plants self-sow.

M. maritima

P. 131

m. mah-RIT-ih-ma. Virginia Stock. A ½- to 1½-foot-tall annual with oval, softly hairy, gray-green leaves. Bears loose spikes of fragrant, purplish pink, pink, lavender, red, or white flowers. Cool-weather annual.

Malope

MAL-oh-pay. Mallow family, Malvaceae.

Native from the Mediterranean to western Asia, *Malope* species are tall, bushy annuals or perennials with ovate, lobed or entire leaves and showy, five-petaled, saucer-shaped flowers in shades of pink, white, rose-purple, or violet-blue, often with veins in a darker shade. The flowers are borne singly on long stalks in the leaf axils. There are four species, one of which is commonly grown.

HOW TO GROW

Give annual mallow *(M. trifida)* full sun and average, well-drained, evenly moist soil. It is best in areas with cool summers, and a spot with light shade during the hottest part of the day is best. Sow seeds indoors in individual pots 8 to 10 weeks before the last spring frost date. Chill the sown pots in the refrigerator for 3 weeks before moving them to a warmer (65° to 75°F) spot for germination, which takes 2 to 4 weeks. Transplant with care. Or sow seeds outdoors 2 to 3 weeks before the last frost date. In areas with hot, humid summers, start seeds as early as possible so the plants can bloom before hot weather arrives. For continued bloom in cool climates, sow new crops every 4 weeks through late summer. Use annual mallow in mixed beds and borders. It is a good choice for seaside gardens, where cool conditions prevail, and also makes an attractive cut flower. Stake plants with brushy twigs as needed. Plants self-sow.

M. trifida

P. 131

m. try-FID-ah. Annual Mallow, Malope. An erect 2- to 3-foot annual with hairy, ovate leaves and 2- to 3-inch-wide, trumpet-shaped flowers in shades from rose- and purple-red to magenta-pink and white from summer to fall. Cool-weather annual.

Mandevilla

man-deh-VILL-ah. Dogbane family, Apocynaceae.

For the most part, Mandevilla species are woody-stemmed or perennial climbers, often with tuberous roots. About 120 species native to Central and South America belong here. They have simple leaves, have milky sap in their stems, and bear funnel-shaped flowers with five broad "petals," or lobes, either singly or in small racemes.

HOW TO GROW

Give mandevillas full sun to light shade and average to rich soil that is moist but well drained. A site with dappled shade during the hottest part of the day is beneficial. They require a trellis or other support upon which to climb. Where hardy—in Zones 10 and 11—grow these plants outdoors. In the North, grow them in large containers and treat them as tender perennials or as annuals. Start plants from cuttings taken in late spring or summer. Or sow seeds at 65° to 70°F in spring. When plants are growing actively, water regularly and feed monthly. Bring container-grown plants indoors before the first fall frost and overwinter indoors in a sunny, warm (60° to 65°F) spot. Prune overwintered plants in late winter or early spring; cut them nearly to the ground, if necessary, and they will produce new shoots from the base of the plant that will still bloom the same year. Water moderately during winter.

M. × *amoena* 'Alice DuPont' P. 132

m. × ah-MEE-nah. A woody-stemmed climber that can reach 20 feet or more in frost-free regions but is considerably shorter when grown in the North. Bears racemes of up to 20 funnel-shaped, 3- to 4-inch-wide, rich pink flowers. Tender perennial or warm-weather annual.

Martynia fragrans *see Proboscidea louisianica*

Matthiola

mat-thee-OH-lah. Cabbage family, Brassicaceae.

Commonly called stock, *Matthiola* species are closely related to wallflowers (*Erysimum* spp.) and bear dense racemes of sweetly scented, four-petaled flowers and lance-shaped or lobed leaves. Two of the 55 species of annuals, biennials, perennials, and subshrubs that belong to the genus are commonly grown in gardens.

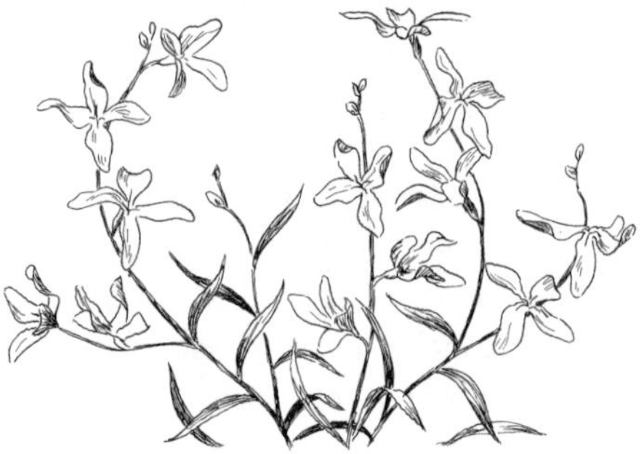

Matthiola longipetala

HOW TO GROW

Full sun to light shade and average to rich, well-drained soil are ideal. Neutral to slightly alkaline pH is best. Stocks are best in areas with cool summers and are especially intolerant of warm nighttime temperatures. Sow seeds indoors 6 to 8 weeks before the last spring frost date at 50° to 65°F. Germination takes 1 to 3 weeks. To prevent damping off, sow in a sterile seed-starting mix, water only from below, and let the medium dry out slightly between waterings. Or sow outdoors after the last frost date. When sowing, simply press the seeds into the soil surface, as light is required for germination. From Zone 9 south, also sow seeds from late summer to early fall for bloom the following spring. Use stocks in mixed beds and borders as well as in containers, especially in spots where their fragrance can be enjoyed. They make excellent cut flowers and are good choices for seaside gardens.

M. incana P. 132

m. in-CAH-nah. Common Stock, Gillyflower. A ½- to 3-foot-tall tender perennial or subshrub, hardy only in Zones 7 and 8, with felty, gray-green leaves. Bears dense, erect clusters of spicy-scented, single or double, 1-inch-wide flowers in shades of pink, white, red, mauve, and purplish pink. 'Ten-Week Mix' plants are quicker to bloom than many cultivars and are a good choice for most North American gardens, where plants decline when hot weather arrives. Tender perennial or cool-weather annual.

M. longipetala ssp. *bicornis* P. 133

m. lon-gih-PET-ah-la ssp. bi-CORN-iss. Night-scented Stock. A 1 to 1½-foot-tall annual with loose racemes of ¾-inch, pink, mauve, or purple flowers that release their strong, sweet fragrance at night. Cool-weather annual.

Maurandella and *Maurandya*

mawr-ran-DELL-ah, mau-RAN-dee-ah. Figwort family, Scrophulariaceae.

The tender perennials in these two closely related genera formerly belonged to *Asarina. Maurandella* contains one species native to the southwestern United States and Mexico, and *Maurandya* contains two species found from Mexico through Central America. Plants in both genera bear two-lipped tubular to trumpet-shaped blooms in summer and fall.

HOW TO GROW

Select a site with full sun and average soil that is moist but well drained. Dappled shade during the hottest part of the day is beneficial, as is neutral to slightly alkaline pH. Where hardy—from Zone 9 south—grow these plants outdoors year-round. In the North, grow them as bedding plants replaced annually or as tender perennials overwintered in a sunny, cool (55° to 60°F) spot. Sow seeds indoors about 12 weeks before the last spring frost date at 55° to 60°F. Or start plants from cuttings in spring or in midsummer to overwinter them. Water regularly and feed monthly during the growing season. Keep plants slightly dry over winter. Use these plants to cover trellises or other supports.

Maurandella antirrhiniflora

m. an-tih-rye-nih-FLOR-ah. Violet Twining Snapdragon. Formerly *Asarina antirrhiniflora.* A 3- to 6-foot, wiry-stemmed climber with shallowly lobed, ovate to triangular leaves. Bears tubular to trumpet-shaped, 1¾-inch-long flowers with flaring purple or violet lobes. Tender perennial or warm-weather annual.

Maurandya scandens P. 133

m. SCAN-dens. Chickabiddy, Creeping Gloxinia. Formerly *Asarina scandens.* A 6- to 15-foot, woody-based perennial with angular, heart-shaped to roughly arrowhead-shaped leaves. Bears 1½- to 2-inch-long, trumpet-shaped flowers with flaring violet, lavender, or pink lobes. *M. barclayana* is a similar species. Tender perennial or warm-weather annual.

Melampodium paludosum *see Leucanthemum*

Melianthus

mel-ee-AN-thus. Melianth family, Melianthaceae.

Handsome foliage and nectar-rich flowers are the hallmark of the six species of tender evergreen shrubs in the genus *Melianthus.* All are native to South Africa and bear aromatic leaves that are divided in a featherlike fashion (pinnate) into toothed leaflets. The common name honey bush refers to the fact that their small flowers, which are borne in erect racemes, bear copious amounts of nectar. The botanical name refers to this characteristic as well—it is from the Greek *meli,* "honey," and *anthos,* "flower."

HOW TO GROW

Melianthus species are best in full sun and average to rich, well-drained soil that remains evenly moist but is never wet. Where hardy, grow them outdoors as perennials or shrubs. Plants killed to the base in winter will resprout from the roots, performing as perennials rather than shrubs, provided temperatures don't fall much below 23° to 25°F and they are protected with a thick, dry mulch such as salt hay or weed-free straw over winter. Wet soil in winter may kill the plants, though. Where hardy, they will spread vigorously by suckers. In the North, grow them as tender perennials and overwinter them indoors, or treat them as annuals. Sow seeds indoors 8 to 10 weeks before the last spring frost date at 55° to 65°F. Or take cuttings from shoots at the base of the plant in spring or summer. The plants also can be propagated by division or by digging up suckers that appear near the plants in spring. Bring plants in before hard frost in fall, and keep them barely moist over winter in a bright, cool (55° to 65°F) spot. *Melianthus* species are handsome container plants and also are effective as foliage accents in beds and borders.

M. major P. 134

m. MAY-jor. Honey Bush. A 6- to 10-foot tender shrub with arching, featherlike, gray-green leaves that are 1 to 1½ feet long and have up to 17 sharply toothed leaflets. Bears 1- to 2-foot-long racemes of small, red-brown, ill-scented flowers from spring to midsummer, which are followed by attractive, green, bladderlike seedpods. Tender perennial or warm-weather annual.

Mentzelia

ment-ZEE-lee-ah. Loasa family, Loasaceae.

Native from the southwestern United States to Mexico and the West Indies, *Mentzelia* species bear poppylike, orange, yellow, or white flowers with 5 to 10 petals. Commonly called blazing stars, there are 60 species of annuals, biennials, and subshrubs in the genus. One species is commonly grown for its handsome foliage and fragrant flowers.

HOW TO GROW

Full sun and average, well-drained soil are ideal. A warm, protected site is best. *Mentzelia* species are taprooted and resent transplanting, so sow seeds outdoors after the last spring frost date. From Zone 9 south, sow outdoors in fall or very early spring. Or try starting seeds indoors in individual pots 6 to 8 weeks before the last frost date, and transplant with care. Cut plants back to about 2 inches after the first main flush of bloom; regular watering also encourages repeat bloom. Use these plants in mixed beds and borders as well as wild gardens.

M. lindleyi P. 134

m. LIND-lee-eye. Blazing Star. Formerly *Bartonia aurea.* A well-branched, ½- to 2-foot-tall annual with deeply cut, featherlike leaves. Bears golden yellow, 2- to 3½-inch-wide flowers that are fragrant at night. Cool-weather annual.

Mesembryanthemum criniflorum *see Dorotheanthus bellidiformis*

Michauxia

mih-SHOW-ee-ah. Bellflower family, Campanulaceae.

Stunning but little known to American gardeners, the seven species of *Michauxia* are native to well-drained, rocky soils from the eastern Mediterranean to southwestern Asia. They are biennials or short-lived perennials with a rosette of irregularly toothed or lobed leaves and tall spikes or racemes of blue or white flowers. While their relatives the bellflowers (*Campanula* spp.) bear flowers with 5 lobes, or "petals," *Michauxia* species have flowers with 7 to 10 lobes.

HOW TO GROW

Give these plants full sun and average, well-drained soil with a neutral to alkaline pH. They grow well in sandy or stony soil and need a spot protected from wind. Sow seeds indoors 8 to 10 weeks before the last spring frost date at 70°F. Or sow outdoors on the last spring frost date either where the plants are to grow or in a nursery bed. (Move seedlings sown in a nursery bed to where they are to flower in fall or the following spring.) Water regularly in dry weather. Plants are hardy from Zone 7 south; protect them in the garden over winter with a dry mulch such as evergreen boughs or salt hay. In the North, keep plants in pots the first year and overwinter them indoors in a cool, sunny spot or in a cold frame. Use *Michauxia* species in beds and borders and along the front of shrub plantings. Plants die after flowering, either the second or third year from seeds, but they may self-sow.

M. tchihatchewii P. 135

m. chat-CHEFF-ee-eye. A tender, 5- to 7-foot perennial, hardy from Zone 7 south, with lance-shaped, toothed leaves. Each rosette of leaves produces a stiff, branched raceme of 1¼-inch-wide white flowers with slightly reflexed petals in midsummer. Biennial.

Mimulus

MIM-you-lus. Figwort family, Scrophulariaceae.

Commonly called monkey flowers, *Mimulus* species are annuals, perennials, and shrubs with tubular, two-lipped flowers. There are about 150 species in the genus, mostly native to damp areas in the Americas as well as Africa, Asia, and Australia. They bear linear to nearly round leaves that can be toothed or lobed and carry snapdragon-like flowers with five lobes, or "petals." Plants bloom from spring to fall in shades of red, pink, yellow, and orange, and the flowers are often spotted with contrasting colors. Both the common and botanical names refer to the cheerful, funny-faced flowers: *Mimulus* is from the Latin *mimus*, variously translated as "little buffoon" or "mimic actor."

HOW TO GROW

Grow the species covered here in full sun to partial shade and rich, moist to wet soil. These plants grow best in areas with cool, wet summers. In areas with hot summers, give them a site that receives dappled shade in the afternoon. Sow seeds indoors 14 to 15 weeks before the last frost date, merely pressing seeds into the soil surface, and chill the sown pots in the refrigerator for 3 weeks before moving them to a warmer (70°F) spot for germinating, which takes 1 to 3 weeks. Pinch plants to encourage branching and bushy growth. Water regularly especially in hot weather; the soil should never dry out. Deadhead to encourage new flowers to form. They can be propagated by division in spring and by cuttings in spring or summer, which can be used to overwinter the plants. Or keep plants in pots year-round and simply sink them to their rims in the soil in summer. In winter, keep them in a sunny, well-ventilated, cool (50°F) spot. Use *Mimulus* in moist beds and borders, bog gardens, and containers. The flowers attract hummingbirds. Plants self-sow.

M. × *hybridus* P. 135

m. × HI-brih-dus. Hybrid Monkey Flower. Well-branched, 6- to 12-inch tender perennial, hardy from Zone 7 south. Bears tubular flowers with flared, 2-inch-wide faces, usually in shades of orange-red, red, and yellow, often spotted with a contrasting color. Tender perennial or cool-weather annual.

M. luteus

m. LOO-tee-us. Yellow Monkey Flower, Monkey Musk. A vigorous, 1-foot-tall tender perennial, hardy from Zone 7 south. Bears broadly ovate, toothed leaves and pairs of ¾- to 2-inch-long yellow flowers with red- or purple-red–spotted throats and petals from late spring to midsummer. Tender perennial or cool-weather annual.

Mina lobata *see Ipomoea lobata*

Mirabilis

meer-AB-il-iss. Four-o'clock family, Nyctaginaceae.

Mirabilis contains some 50 species of annuals and tender, tuberous-rooted perennials native to the Americas. They bear ovate leaves and trumpet-shaped flowers with flared, flattened faces that have five lobes, or "petals," as they are sometimes called. One species is a popular, old-fashioned annual. The botanical name is from the Latin word *mirabilis,* meaning "wonderful."

HOW TO GROW

Full sun to partial shade and average, well-drained soil are ideal. Sow seeds outdoors on the last spring frost date. Or sow indoors 6 to 8 weeks before the last frost date at 55° to 65°F. Germination takes 1 to 3 weeks. From Zone 7 south, sow seeds outdoors in fall for bloom the following year. Either way, just press the seeds into the soil surface, as light is required for germination. For best bloom, water regularly and feed monthly. North of Zone 10, grow these plants as bedding plants replaced annually or as tender perennials: either start new plants from seeds each year or dig the tuberous roots after a light fall frost and store them in barely damp vermiculite, peat, or sand in a cool (40° to 50°F), dry place, as you would dahlias. In Zones 10 and 11, grow them outdoors year-round as perennials. Where marginally hardy, mulch heavily in fall. Use these plants in beds and borders. Their flowers attract hummingbirds and moths.

M. jalapa P. 136

m. jah-LAH-pah. Four-o'clock, Marvel of Peru. A bushy, tender, 2-foot-tall perennial, hardy from Zone 10 south but often forming self-sowing colonies north of that zone. Bears ovate leaves and fragrant, 2-inch-long flowers in pink, red, magenta, yellow, and white, sometimes with stripes or other markings of more than one color on each flower. Flowers on the same plant can be different colors. Each flower opens in the afternoon and dies by morning. Warm-weather annual or tender perennial.

Moluccella

mol-yew-CHELL-ah. Mint family, Lamiaceae.

Square stems and two-lipped, tubular flowers identify the four species of *Moluccella* as relatives of mints (*Mentha* spp.) and salvias (*Salvia* spp.). All are annuals or short-lived perennials native from the Mediterranean to northwestern India. From summer to fall, they bear erect stalks of fragrant but insignificant flowers, each surrounded by a large, showy, saucer- or cup-shaped calyx.

HOW TO GROW

Select a site in full sun to light shade and poor to average, well-drained soil. Plants grow well in sandy soil. Sow seeds indoors in individual pots 8 to 10 weeks before the last spring frost date, and chill the sown pots in the refrigerator for 2 weeks before moving them to a warmer (60°F) spot for germinating, which takes 1 to 4 weeks. Or, from about Zone 5 south, sow outdoors a few weeks before the last frost date. In areas with mild winters — Zone 6 or 7 south — sow outdoors in fall for bloom the following year. When sowing, just press the seeds into the soil surface, as light is necessary for germination. Water regularly during dry weather. Use them near the middle or back of beds and borders and in cottage-style gardens. Stake plants when they are still small; otherwise they tend to sprawl. They make excellent cut and dried flowers. For fresh use, cut them when they have reached the desired length. For drying, cut when still green or once they begin to turn beige. Plants may self-sow.

M. laevis

P. 136

m. LAY-vis. Bells-of-Ireland, Shell Flower, Molucca Balm. A 2- to 3-foot-tall annual with ovate, scalloped leaves. Bears erect, 1-foot-long stalks of tiny, fragrant, white flowers surrounded by cup-shaped, pale green calyces, which turn papery once seeds form. Cool-weather annual.

Myosotis

my-oh-SO-tis. Bugloss family, Boraginaceae.

Known to gardeners and nongardeners alike as forget-me-nots, *Myosotis* species are erect or sprawling annuals, biennials, and perennials with hairy leaves and clusters of tiny, trumpet- to funnel-shaped flowers in shades of blue, violet, pink, and white. The blooms have five "petals," or lobes, flat faces, and a contrasting yellow or white eye. Some 50 species belong to this widespread genus: plants are native in woods, meadows, and boggy spots mostly in Europe and New Zealand but also Asia and North and South America.

HOW TO GROW

Give *M. sylvatica* full sun or light shade and any well-drained, moist soil. Shade during the hottest part of the day is best in hot climates. Sow seeds indoors 8 to 10 weeks before the last spring frost date at 65° to 70°F. Germination takes 1 to 4 weeks. To prevent damping off, sow in a sterile seed-starting mix, water only from below, and let the medium dry out slightly between waterings. Or sow outdoors several weeks before the last frost date. In areas with mild winters — roughly from Zone 6 south — sow seeds in fall for bloom the following spring, or sow in midsummer to grow plants as biennials. When sowing, barely cover the seeds with soil, as they require darkness for germination. Use forget-me-nots in wild gardens, interplant them with bulbs, and use them at the front of beds and borders. Pull plants up after flowering to prevent excessive self-sowing.

M. sylvatica P. 137

m. syl-VAT-ih-cah. Forget-me-not. A 5- to 12-inch-tall, tufting biennial or short-lived perennial with ovate or lance-shaped, gray-green leaves. Bears clusters of ⅜-inch-wide, saucer-shaped flowers in spring and early summer. Many cultivars are available. Ball Series plants are compact and 6 inches tall; Victoria Series plants reach 4 inches. Cool-weather annual or biennial.

Nemesia

neh-ME-see-ah. Figwort family, Scrophulariaceae.

Nemesia contains some 50 species of annuals, perennials, and subshrubs native to South Africa, where they are found in scrubby, disturbed sites inland as well as sandy soils near the coast. They bear showy, spurred or pouched, two-lipped flowers either singly or in small racemes. The flowers have four upper lobes, or "petals," and one or two large, flared lower ones.

HOW TO GROW

These plants require full sun and average to rich, well-drained soil that remains evenly moist. They are best in areas with mild summers and need cool nighttime temperatures to bloom well. To prolong bloom in hot climates, give them dappled shade in the afternoon. Sow seeds indoors 8 to 10 weeks before the last spring frost date at 55° to 65°F. Germination takes 1 to 3 weeks. To prevent damping off, sow in a sterile seed-starting mix, water only from below, and let the medium dry out slightly between waterings. Pinch to encourage bushy growth. Transplant with care, as the plants are brittle. In areas with mild summers, such as the Pacific Northwest, sow outdoors after the last frost date, and sow new crops every 6 weeks through late summer. Water regularly. Use nemesias in mixed beds and borders and in containers. They are good choices for seaside gardens in areas with cool summers.

N. strumosa P. 137

n. stru-MOE-sah. A 6- to 12-inch-tall annual with toothed or entire, lance-shaped, hairy leaves. Bears racemes of 1-inch-wide flowers in shades of red, pink, yellow, lavender-blue, purple, or white in mid- and late summer. Flowers may be a solid color or bicolor, with upper and lower lips in contrasting colors. Cool-weather annual.

Nemophila

nem-oh-FILL-ah. Water leaf family, Hydrophyllaceae.

Native to western North America, the 11 species of *Nemophila* are spreading or prostrate annuals with saucer- or bell-shaped, five-petaled flowers in shades of blue or white.

HOW TO GROW

Full sun or partial shade and rich, moist, well-drained soil are ideal. Although plants tolerate full sun in areas with cool summer weather, a site that receives dappled shade is best in areas where summers bring heat and humidity. They stop blooming once warm, humid weather arrives. Where hot summers prevail, start seeds indoors 6 to 8 weeks before the last spring frost date to give plants a chance to bloom before torrid weather sets in. Germination takes 1 to 3 weeks at 55°F. Or sow seeds outdoors several weeks before the last frost date. In mild climates — roughly Zone 7 south — sow seeds in fall for bloom the following spring. Water regularly and mulch to keep the soil cool. Use nemophilas in mixed plantings and in wildflower gardens. Plants self-sow.

N. maculata P. 138

n. mac-you-LAH-tah. Five-spot. A fleshy-stemmed, 6- to 12-inch-tall annual with pinnate, or featherlike, leaves. In summer it carries 1¾-inch-wide flowers that are white with a purple spot at the tip of each petal. Cool-weather annual.

N. menziesii P. 138

n. men-ZEE-see-eye. Baby Blue Eyes. A spreading, 8-inch-tall annual with pinnate, or featherlike, leaves. Usually bears 1½-inch-wide blue flowers with lighter blue centers, but forms with white or pale blue flowers are available, as well as ones spotted, blotched, or striped with dark blue or violet. Cool-weather annual.

Nicandra

nye-CAN-drah. Nightshade family, Solanaceae.

Only one species belongs to this genus, *Nicandra physaloides*, an old-fashioned garden favorite grown for its bell-shaped flowers, which are followed by berries encased in inflated, papery, green calyxes. Apple of Peru, one common name for the plant, celebrates its origin in that country and also calls attention to the ornamental fruit. It is also sometimes called shoo fly plant, because old-time gardeners believed it repelled flies.

HOW TO GROW

Select a planting site with full sun or partial shade and rich, moist, well-drained soil. Plants thrive in heat and humidity. Sow seeds indoors 6 to 8 weeks before the last spring frost date at 60° to 65°F. Germination takes 2 to 3 weeks. Or sow seeds outdoors, either a few weeks before the last frost date or in fall for germination the following spring. Use apple of Peru in mixed plantings and informal, cottage-style or wild gardens. The decorative fruit is attractive in dried arrangements. Plants self-sow and can become weedy in warm climates.

N. physaloides P. 139

n. fy-sal-OY-deez. Apple of Peru, Shoo Fly Plant. A well-branched, 2- to 3-foot-tall annual with rounded, wavy-margined leaves. Bears short-lived, 1½-inch-wide, shallowly bell-shaped flowers from summer to fall. The flowers, borne in abundance, are light purple-blue and are followed by inedible berries in lantern-shaped calyxes. Warm-weather annual.

Nicotiana

nih-koe-shee-AH-nah. Nightshade family, Solanaceae.

The ornamental members of this genus are commonly known as flowering tobaccos or simply nicotianas. Some 67 species of annuals, biennials, perennials, and shrubs belong here, including the commercial crop tobacco *(Nicotiana tabacum)*. Native to tropical regions in the Americas as well as Australia, they bear undivided leaves, often covered with sticky hairs, and clusters of flowers with narrow, tubular bases and flaring, flat- to cup-shaped faces from summer to frost. Many nicotianas have flowers that open only in late afternoon or early evening and are fragrant at night.

Nicotiana alata

HOW TO GROW

Select a site with full sun or partial shade and rich, evenly moist, well-drained soil. A site with dappled afternoon shade is beneficial in areas with hot summers. Sow seeds indoors 6 to 8 weeks before the last spring frost date at 70° to 75°F. Germination takes 2 to 3 weeks. Or sow outdoors after the last frost date. Either way, just press the tiny seeds into the soil surface, as light is required for germination. Water during dry weather. Deadhead to keep plants neat-looking and encourage new flowers to form. Add nicotianas to mixed plantings, and site fragrant types close to sitting areas where you can enjoy them after dark. The flowers attract moths and hummingbirds. Plants self-sow.

N. alata P. 139

n. ah-LAH-tah. Flowering Tobacco. This short-lived, 1½- to 5-foot tender perennial, hardy in Zones 10 and 11, bears ovate to spoon-shaped leaves and 4-inch-long flowers. The species bears very fragrant, greenish white or yellowish flowers that open at night on 4- to 5-foot plants. Cultivars are usually 1½ to 2 feet tall and bear flowers in shades of pink, red, white, and chartreuse. They remain open in the daytime but usually are not fragrant. Nicki Series plants bear fragrant flowers in a range of colors on 1½-foot plants. Warm-weather annual.

N. langsdorfii P. 140

n. langs-DOR-fee-eye. Flowering Tobacco. A 5-foot-tall annual with large ovate leaves and airy clusters of small, 2-inch-long, green flowers with tubular bases and bell-like faces. Warm-weather annual.

N. × *sanderae*

n. × SAND-er-eye. Flowering Tobacco. A tender, 2-foot-tall perennial with rounded, wavy-edged leaves and loose panicles of trumpet-shaped, 2-

inch-wide flowers in shades of red, pink, purple-pink, and white. Heat-resistant Domino Series plants are 1 to 1½ feet tall. Warm-weather annual.

N. sylvestris P. 140

n. syl-VES-tris. Flowering Tobacco. A 3- to 5-foot annual or short-lived perennial, hardy in Zones 10 and 11, with a rosette of large, rounded leaves up to 3 feet long. Bears clusters of fragrant, white, 3½-inch-long trumpets. Warm-weather annual.

Nierembergia

near-em-BER-gee-ah. Nightshade family, Solanaceae.

Commonly called cup flowers, *Nierembergia* species are slender-stemmed annuals, perennials, and subshrubs with upturned, cup- or bell-shaped flowers and entire, often spoon-shaped or linear leaves. Some 20 species native to South America belong here.

HOW TO GROW

Full sun and rich, evenly moist, well-drained soil are ideal for all but *N. repens,* which prefers dry, even sandy, conditions. Partial shade in the afternoon is best in areas with hot summers. Sow seeds indoors 8 to 10 weeks before the last spring frost date at 55° to 65°F. Germination takes 2 to 4 weeks. Or sow outdoors in spring a few weeks before the last frost date or in fall. Water regularly, especially in hot weather. Perennials can be propagated by cuttings in summer or early fall. Species covered here are hardy from Zone 7 south. Use cup flowers in containers and mixed plantings. *N. repens* also looks great in cracks between paving stones, as an edging, ground cover, and in rock gardens, but where hardy it can become invasive.

N. caerulea P. 141

n. see-RUE-lee-ah. Formerly *N. hippomanica* var. *violacea.* A well-branched, 8-inch-tall tender perennial with cup-shaped, lavender-blue, ¾-inch flowers in summer. Tender perennial or cool-weather annual.

N. repens P. 141

n. RAY-pens. White Cup. A creeping, mat-forming tender perennial that reaches 2 inches in height and spreads to 2 feet or more. Bears white, 1- to 2-inch-wide, bell-shaped flowers with yellow centers in summer. Tender perennial or cool-weather annual.

N. scoparia

n. sko-PAR-ee-ah. Formerly *N. frutescens.* A shrublike, 1½- to 3-foot-tall tender perennial with pale lilac-blue, 1-inch-wide, tubular flowers with yellow centers. Tender perennial or cool-weather annual.

Nigella

nye-JEL-ah. Buttercup family, Ranunculaceae.

Nigella contains 20 species of bushy annuals native to the Mediterranean and western Asia. They bear deeply cut, feathery leaves and flowers in shades of lavender-blue, purple, pink, and white. The flowers have 5 petal-like sepals and from 5 to 10 true petals, which are somewhat smaller. In some species, the flowers are surrounded by a ruff (technically called an involucre) of branched, threadlike, green bracts, a characteristic that leads to the common name love-in-a-mist. The flowers, borne in summer, are followed by inflated seed capsules that are often used in dried arrangements.

HOW TO GROW

A site with full sun and average, well-drained soil is all these easy-to-grow plants require. They are happiest in cool weather. Sow seeds outdoors several weeks before the last spring frost date, barely covering the seeds with soil. Or sow indoors in individual pots 6 to 8 weeks before the last frost date at 65° to 70°F. Outdoor sowing is generally best. For continued bloom in cool climates, sow new crops every 4 weeks through late summer. Or sow outdoors in fall for bloom the following year. Water during dry weather. Deadheading prolongs bloom but prevents the formation of the ornamental seedpods. Use nigellas in mixed beds, as fillers among perennials, or as cut flowers, or dry the seedpods. Plants self-sow.

N. damascena P. 142

N. dam-ah-SEEN-ah. Love-in-a-mist, Devil-in-a-bush. A 1½- to 2-foot annual with 1¾-inch-wide flowers in shades of lavender-blue, purple, violet, pink, rose-red, and white. The flowers are surrounded by a showy involucre of branched, threadlike bracts. Plants in the Persian Jewels Series are 16 inches tall and come in an array of rich colors. Cool-weather annual.

N. hispanica P. 142

n. hiss-PAN-ih-kah. Fennel Flower. A 1½-foot annual with deeply cut but not threadlike leaves and 2½-inch-wide, blue, faintly fragrant flowers with maroon-red stamens that lack an involucre of bracts. Cool-weather annual.

Nolana

no-LAH-nah. Nightshade family, Solanaceae.

Commonly called Chilean bellflowers, the 18 *Nolana* species are all native to Chile and Peru. They are well-branched, prostrate or sprawling annuals, perennials, and subshrubs with simple, sometimes fleshy, leaves; many are covered with sticky hairs. Their flowers, which open only in sunny weather, are bell-shaped, with five "petals," or lobes, and come in shades of lavender-blue, purple, pink, or white. Some experts classify *Nolana* in the Nolana family, Nolanaceae.

HOW TO GROW

Full sun and average, well-drained soil are ideal. They grow well in poor, somewhat dry soil and are best in areas with cool summers, where they are suitable for seaside gardens. Sow seeds outdoors several weeks before the last frost date. Or sow indoors 6 to 8 weeks before the last frost date at 60°F. Established plants need watering only during very dry weather. Use Chilean bellflowers as edging plants, in mixed plantings, as well as in containers.

N. humifusa

n. hew-mih-FEW-sah. A spreading, 6-inch-tall tender perennial or subshrub, hardy from Zone 9 south, that can spread to 1½ feet. Carries 1-inch-wide, lilac-blue flowers with white throats and darker purple streaks in summer. Cool-weather annual.

N. paradoxa P. 143

n. pair-ah-DOX-ah. An 8- to 10-inch-tall annual or perennial bearing 2-inch-wide, purple-blue flowers with yellow throats and white eyes. Cool-weather annual.

Ocimum

AH-see-mum. Mint family, Lamiaceae.

Ocimum contains 35 species of annuals, perennials, and shrubs native to tropical Africa and Asia. They bear aromatic leaves that are opposite and

Ocimum basilicum

linear to rounded in shape and carry spikes of small, tubular, two-lipped flowers in summer. Of these, one species is well-known to gardeners and cooks alike: common or sweet basil, the culinary herb renowned for its aromatic, spicy-tasting leaves.

HOW TO GROW

Give basil a site in full sun and fairly rich, well-drained, evenly moist soil. Too-rich soil yields plants with lots of foliage, but the leaves have a reduced oil content and therefore less flavor and fragrance. Sow seeds indoors 4 to 6 weeks before the last spring frost date at 60° to 70°F. Germination takes 1 to 2 weeks. Transplant after the last frost date once the soil has warmed to 60°F and the weather has settled. In areas with long growing seasons — roughly Zone 8 and south — seeds can be sown outdoors in spring after the soil has warmed up to about 60°F. Pinch seedlings to encourage branching and bushy growth. Water regularly. To encourage the production of more leaves, pinch off the flower stalks as they appear. To renew plants in midsummer, cut them back by half, then water and feed. Plants can be dug in late summer and overwintered in a sunny, cool (60°F) spot. Harvest leaves just before flowers appear and dry or freeze them. Use basil in mixed plantings, herb gardens, and containers. Purple-leaved cultivars and Thai basils are especially ornamental. Compact, small-leaved types such as 'Spicy Globe' make effective edging plants.

O. basilicum PP. 143, 144

o. bah-SIL-ih-cum. Common or Sweet Basil. A variable, ½- to 2-foot-tall annual or short-lived perennial with narrowly oval to rounded leaves. Bears whorls of ½-inch-long white flowers sometimes flushed with pink or purple. Many cultivars are available. 'Genovese' is a classic, spicy-flavored Italian cultivar to 30 inches tall; 'Genovese Compact' is similar but stays under 18 inches. 'Spicy Globe' bears ¼- to ½-inch-long leaves on compact 6- to 8-inch plants. Lemon basil, or 'Citriodora', has a lemon fragrance and flavor. Thai basils, including 'Siam Queen', have a spicy, basil-clove fragrance and flavor plus handsome purple flower spikes in summer and fall. 'Dark Opal', 'Red Rubin', and 'Purple Ruffles' bear handsome foliage in shades of purple and are also useful for cooking and vinegars. Tender perennial or warm-weather annual.

Oenothera

ee-no-THAIR-ah. Evening primrose family, Onagraceae.

The 125 species in this genus are commonly called sundrops, evening primroses, golden eggs, or just oenotheras. They are annuals, biennials, and perennials mostly native to North America (a few species are from South America), enjoyed for their showy, sometimes fragrant, flowers in brilliant yellow, white, or pink. The four-petaled flowers are usually saucer- to cup-shaped and borne singly or in clusters. They open in either the morning or the evening, depending on the species, and although individual flowers fade quickly, they are borne in abundance over a long season in summer.

HOW TO GROW

Full sun and poor to average, well-drained soil are ideal conditions for these plants. Sundrops tolerate dry, rocky soil. Too-rich soil yields lots of foliage but few flowers. To grow plants as annuals, sow seeds indoors in individual pots 8 to 10 weeks before the last spring frost date at 65° to 70°F. Germination takes 1 to 4 weeks. Or sow seeds outdoors in spring several weeks before the last frost date or in fall for bloom the following year. For plants to be treated as biennials, sow seeds up to midsummer in a nursery bed or indoors, and move them to where they will bloom in fall or the following spring. However you sow, barely cover the seeds with soil, as darkness aids germination. Always transplant with care: many oenotheras have taproots and resent being disturbed. Water during very dry weather. Plants may stop blooming in hot, dry weather. Some species self-sow.

O. biennis P. 144

o. bi-EN-nis. Evening Primrose. A 3- to 5-foot annual or biennial, hardy in Zones 4 to 8, with a rosette of lance-shaped, somewhat sticky, toothed leaves. Carries fragrant, bowl-shaped, 2-inch-wide flowers that open pale yellow and age to gold from summer to fall. Biennial or cool-weather annual.

Omphalodes

om-fah-LO-deez. Bugloss family, Boraginaceae.

Grown for their forget-me-not–like flowers, the 28 species of *Omphalodes* are annuals, biennials, and perennials native to Europe, North Africa, Asia, and Mexico. They bear simple, oblong to ovate leaves and blue or white flowers, which are usually carried in small terminal clusters. The flowers have five "petals," or lobes, flat faces, and a paler-colored eye in the center. Both the botanical name and the common names navelwort and navelseed refer to the seeds, which are actually nutlets that have a depressed spot on them: *Omphalodes* is from the Greek *omphalos,* "navel," and *oides,* "resembling."

HOW TO GROW

Give Venus's navelwort *(O. linifolia)* full sun and light, rich, well-drained soil. Most other species prefer partial shade. Sow seeds outdoors in spring a few weeks before the last spring frost date. Or sow indoors at 65° to 70°F in individual pots 10 to 12 weeks before the last frost, and move hardened-off plants to the garden after danger of hard frost has passed. Outdoor sowing is generally best, because the plants resent transplanting. Germination takes 2 to 4 weeks. Use Venus's navelwort in mixed plantings and as a cut flower. Plants self-sow.

O. linifolia P. 145

o. lin-ih-FOE-lee-ah. Venus's Navelwort. A 1- to 1½-foot-tall annual with spatula-shaped leaves and airy, terminal racemes of faintly scented, white or pale blue, ½-inch-wide flowers from spring to summer. Cool-weather annual.

Onopordum

on-oh-POR-dum. Aster family, Asteraceae.

Sometimes called cotton thistles because their leaves and stems are covered with woolly, cobweblike hairs, the 40 species of *Onopordum* are biennials native to Europe, the Mediterranean, and western Asia. They bear deeply lobed, spiny leaves as well as winged, branched stems that also are spiny. The flowers are round and thistlelike, with spiny bases, and come in shades of purple, purplish pink, pink, violet, or sometimes white. The genus name sometimes is spelled *Onopordon.*

HOW TO GROW

Select a site in full sun to light shade with rich, evenly moist, well-drained soil. They grow well in heavy soils; neutral to slightly alkaline pH is best. Sow seeds outdoors after the last spring frost date. Sow either where the plants are to bloom or into a nursery bed, and move the plants to their final location in fall or the following spring. Or sow indoors 8 to 10 weeks before the last frost date at 55° to 60°F. Use drifts of these thistles at the back of informal perennial gardens and in semiwild plantings. Deadhead regularly in order to curtail self-sowing, and cut plants down after they finish flowering.

O. acanthium P. 145

o. ah-CAN-thee-um. Scotch Thistle, Cotton Thistle. A taprooted biennial with a rosette of spiny, deeply cut, gray-green, foot-long leaves. Bears erect, branching stems ranging from 3 to 9 feet in height with 1½- to 2-inch-wide, pale rose-purple or white flower heads in summer. Biennial.

Origanum

or-ih-GAN-um. Mint family, Lamiaceae.

Commonly known as marjorams or oreganos, *Origanum* species are tender or hardy perennials and subshrubs native from the Mediterranean to western Asia. About 20 species belong to the genus, all bearing opposite, aromatic leaves on square stems and spikelike clusters of tiny, two-lipped flowers. The flowers are tubular to funnel-shaped and have prominent, often colorful, bracts beneath them that remain showy for several weeks.

HOW TO GROW

Plant marjoram in full sun and poor to average, well-drained soil. Plants grow well in dry, rocky soil, and neutral to alkaline pH is best. Where hardy, tender perennials can be grown outdoors year-round, but this is generally practical only in dry climates, as they resent excessive soil moisture, especially in winter. Sow seeds indoors 6 to 8 weeks before the last spring frost date at 55° to 65°F. Germination takes 2 weeks. Or sow seeds outdoors several weeks before the last spring frost date. Pinch seedlings to encourage branching. Perennials can be propagated in spring by cuttings taken from shoots at the base of the plant or by division. Perennials can be overwintered in a sunny, well-ventilated, cool (40° to 50°F) spot. Keep them barely moist in winter. Use marjorams in mixed plantings, raised beds, herb gardens, and containers.

O. calcaratum

o. cal-car-AH-tum. Formerly *O. tournefortii.* A 1-foot-tall tender subshrub, probably hardy only from Zone 8 south, with rounded, hairy, gray leaves on arching stems and small clusters of pink flowers. Tender perennial or warm-weather annual.

O. majorana P. 146

o. mah-jo-RAY-nah. Sweet Marjoram, Knotted Marjoram. A 2- to 3-foot subshrub with aromatic, rounded, gray-green leaves on arching stems. Clusters of white to pink, ⅜-inch flowers from early to late summer. Warm-weather annual, biennial, or tender perennial.

Osteospermum

oss-tee-oh-SPER-mum. Aster family, Asteraceae.

Grown for their showy, daisylike flowers in shades of yellow, white, or pink, *Osteospermum* species are native from South Africa to the Arabian Peninsula. About 70 species of annuals, perennials, and subshrubs belong to the genus. They are closely related to *Dimorphotheca* species, and plants in both genera share the common names Cape marigold, African daisy, and star of the veldt. Like many other aster-family plants, *Osteospermum* species bear flowers consisting of sterile, petal-like ray florets (the "petals") around a dense cluster of fertile disk florets (the "eye"), which produce the seeds. (*Dimorphotheca* species bear fertile ray florets.) The flowers are borne from midsummer to fall. The leaves are narrow to oval with lobed, toothed, or entire margins.

HOW TO GROW

Select a site in full sun and average to poor soil that is light and well drained. Plants thrive in heat, tolerate dry soil, and perform best in areas with a long growing season; they do not do as well in areas with hot, humid, rainy summers. Sow seeds indoors 6 to 8 weeks before the last spring frost date at 60° to 65°F. Germination takes about 2 weeks. Or, from Zone 9 south, sow seeds outdoors. (Plants are considered hardy from Zone 10 south, but in a protected site with perfect drainage, some plants may survive Zone 9 winters.) Either way, barely cover the seeds with soil, and try to avoid wetting the foliage when watering to prevent fungal diseases. Deadheading prolongs bloom. Perennials can be propagated by cuttings taken in spring or summer. Try overwintering plants in a sunny, well-ventilated, cool (50°F) spot: they require very well drained soil that is evenly moist but never wet. Prune in spring. Use osteospermums in containers, or add them to mixed plantings in beds and borders.

O. ecklonis P. 147

o. eck-LON-iss. A sprawling subshrub with gray-green leaves, this species can range from 2 to 5 feet tall and spread to 4 feet. Bears 2- to 3-inch-wide, daisylike flowers with violet-blue centers and white petals that are violet-blue on the undersides. 'Silver Sparkler' bears 3-inch-wide flowers and white-edged leaves. Tender perennial or warm-weather annual.

O. jucundum P. 147

o. ju-KUN-dum. Formerly *Dimorphotheca barberae.* A mounding, ½- to 2-foot perennial with gray-green leaves and 2-inch-wide, magenta-purple daisies with petals that are darker on the undersides. Warm-weather annual or tender perennial.

Oxypetalum caeruleum *see Tweedia caerulea*

Papaver

PAH-pah-ver. Poppy family, Papaveraceae.

Although many plants are commonly called poppies, *Papaver* is the genus of the true poppies, which are grown for their showy, bowl- or cup-shaped flowers with silky, crepe-paper-textured petals. Some 70 species of annuals, biennials, and perennials belong here. They bear simple to deeply cut, fernlike leaves, and their stems contain milky latex. Blooms come in hot colors—orange, orange-red, scarlet, hot pink, and yellow—as well as soft pink, pale yellow, and white. The flowers are followed by distinctive, rounded seed capsules.

HOW TO GROW

Give poppies full sun and average to rich, evenly moist, well-drained soil. A site protected from wind is best, and in areas with hot summers, a spot with morning sun and afternoon shade provides beneficial heat protection. Sow seeds outdoors several weeks before the last spring frost date, when the soil is cool and frost is still possible. Or sow outdoors in late summer or fall for flowers the following spring; from Zone 8 south, fall sowing is best. Or sow indoors in individual pots 6 to 8 weeks before the last spring frost date at around 60°F; transplant with care. Outdoor sowing is generally best. However you sow, barely cover the seeds with soil, as darkness aids germination. In areas with cool summers, sow new crops every 6 weeks to prolong bloom. Iceland poppy *(P. croceum)* grows best in areas with cool nights and warm days, and plants die out in midsummer in areas with hot, humid summers. Although hardy, it is commonly grown as a biennial because younger plants are more vigorous; pull up plants that overwinter after blooming the first time to make room for younger, more vigorous ones. Use poppies in beds and borders. They make fine cut flowers, but the stems need to be seared to prolong vase life: Cut them when the buds begin to open. Recut the stems once they are in the house, and immediately dip the tips into an inch or two of boiling water for a few seconds. Or sear the ends with a match. Stand the flowers in cold water for several hours before arranging. Sear the ends of the stems again if you cut them while arranging. Plants self-sow freely; deadhead to curtail this tendency.

P. commutatum P. 148

p. com-mew-TAH-tum. A 1½-foot-tall annual bearing 3-inch-wide, brilliant red flowers with black spots at the base of each petal in summer. Cool-weather annual.

P. croceum P. 148

p. CRO-cee-um. Iceland Poppy, Arctic Poppy. Formerly *P. nudicaule.* A 1- to 2-foot perennial, hardy in Zones 2 to 8, usually grown as a biennial or annual. Bears showy, 3- to 5-inch-wide flowers in spring and early summer in the full range of poppy colors. Hardy perennial, biennial, or cool-weather annual.

P. rhoeas P. 149

p. ROW-ee-as. Flanders Poppy, Corn Poppy, Field Poppy. A 2- to 3-foot annual with 3-inch-wide, bowl-shaped, single or double flowers. The species bears brilliant red blooms, but cultivars in pastel shades also are available. The popular Shirley Series poppies bear single, semidouble, or double blooms in the full range of poppy colors, with petals that lack black spots at the base. Cool-weather annual.

P. somniferum P. 149

p. som-NIF-er-um. Opium Poppy, Bread Poppy. A 3- to 4-foot annual with blue-green leaves and bowl-shaped, 3- to 4-inch-wide flowers in shades of pink, mauve, white, and red. Double-flowered forms are available. The seeds of this species are the source of poppy seeds, which are used in breads and other confections. Cool-weather annual.

Pelargonium

pel-ar-GO-nee-um. Geranium family, Geraniaceae.

Pelargonium contains about 230 species of tender perennials, subshrubs, shrubs, and succulents, including the popular garden plants widely known as geraniums. Most species are native to South Africa, but gardeners mostly grow cultivated varieties that belong to one of several horticultural groups, including zonal geraniums, ivy-leaved geraniums, regal or Martha Washington geraniums, and scented-leaved geraniums. In general, *Pelargonium* species bear rounded to deeply cut or fernlike leaves that often are hairy and/or aromatic. The five-petaled, star- or saucer-shaped flowers are borne in rounded clusters that resemble umbels. Most geraniums bloom from spring to frost; in frost-free regions, many bloom year-round.

HOW TO GROW

Give most geraniums full sun to light shade and rich, well-drained soil. A neutral to slightly alkaline pH is best. In areas with very hot summers, give them partial shade during the hottest part of the day. Regal geraniums grow best in areas with cool summers and prefer partial shade. Where hardy, grow geraniums outdoors as perennials. Most are hardy only from Zone 10 south, but some species survive winters in colder climates, especially in a protected site with dry winter mulch. In the North, grow geraniums as bedding plants replaced annually or as tender perennials. Sow seeds indoors about 14 to 16 weeks before the last spring frost date at 70° to 75°F. Germination takes 1 to 3 weeks. Or propagate by 4-inch cuttings taken in late summer for overwintering or from overwin-

Pelargonium × hortorum

tered plants in winter or early spring to grow plants for the garden. Transplant seed- or cutting-grown plants after all danger of frost has passed. Pinch plants to encourage branching. Water container-grown plants regularly, and feed at least monthly. Deadhead plants regularly. To overwinter, bring container-grown plants indoors in fall, and keep them nearly dry in a bright, cool (40°F), frost-free place. Or keep them slightly warmer (50° to 55°F), and keep the soil barely moist. To root cuttings, remove all but three leaves, and let the cuttings dry for about 6 hours to seal the stem ends. Then dust the ends with rooting powder and stick them in pots filled with sterilized sharp sand. (To sterilize, pour boiling water over the sand.) Water thoroughly, then keep the cuttings on the dry side, but do not allow them to wilt. Pot in individual 3-inch pots once they have rooted, and treat them as you would overwintered plants. Repot and cut back overwintered plants in late winter, then feed twice a month beginning in early spring once plants are growing actively. Grow geraniums in beds and borders and in containers. Scented types are appropriate additions to herb gardens. Hummingbirds will visit geranium flowers.

Ivy Geraniums P. 150

Cultivars of *P. peltatum* with fleshy, lobed, ivylike leaves and trailing stems that can reach 3 to 4 feet. They bear 1½- to 2-inch-wide clusters of single or double flowers in shades of pink, mauve, lilac, and white and are ideal for hanging baskets. Summer Showers Series plants can be grown from seeds and come in a range of colors. Tender perennials.

Regal Geraniums

A group of cultivars commonly listed as *P. × domesticum* and also called Martha Washington geraniums. Plants bear rounded, sometimes lobed or toothed, leaves on 1- to 4-foot plants. Single or sometimes double flowers are carried in 2- to 4-inch-wide clusters and come in solid colors or combinations of red, purple, pink, white, maroon, and orange. Angel geraniums, the result of a cross between regal geraniums and *P. crispum*, bear showy, regal-like flowers and sometimes scented leaves. Tender perennials.

Scented geraniums

P. 151

A mix of species and cultivars fall into the scented group, most of which bear small clusters of single, 1-inch-wide flowers. 'Mabel Grey' bears lemon-scented, deeply cut leaves and 2-inch-wide clusters of pale purple flowers. Nutmeg geranium, sold as *P.* × *fragrans* and *P.* 'Fragrans' bears gray-green, nutmeg-scented leaves and 1- to 1¼-inch-wide clusters of white flowers. Coconut-scented geranium *(P. grossularioides)* bears lobed, coconut-scented leaves; red stems; and small, star-shaped, magenta-pink flowers. Other scented geraniums featuring the fragrances that their names imply include apple geranium *(P. odoratissimum)*, peppermint geranium *(P. tomentosum)*, rose geranium (*P. graveolens* or *P.* 'Graveolens'), 'Lime', 'Prince of Orange', 'Peppermint Lace', and 'Lemon Rose'. Tender perennials.

Zonal geraniums

P. 150

Commonly listed as *P.* × *hortorum*, these are better known as bedding or common geraniums. They are succulent-stemmed tender perennials with rounded leaves that may or may not exhibit the dark maroon band, or "zone," that gave these plants their name. Showy, 3- to 5-inch-wide clusters of 1-inch-wide flowers appear from early summer to frost. Single-flowered types bear five petals per flower and are most common. They include such seed-grown cultivars as 'Big Red', 'Freckles' (pink dotted with white), and 'Neon Rose'. "Rosebud" geraniums bear double flowers with centers that do not open, like rosebuds. "Stellar" geraniums have single, star-shaped flowers; 'Bird Dancer' bears dark-zoned, maplelike leaves and pink, star-shaped flowers in 3-inch-wide clusters. Fancy-leaved geraniums fall here, too, and are grown primarily for their showy leaves. 'Mr. Henry Cox' has leaves marked with cream, yellow, green, purple-maroon, and red. 'Vancouver Centennial' has lobed gold leaves with maroon-brown center splotches and red-orange, star-shaped flowers. Tender perennials.

Pennisetum

pen-ih-SEE-tum. Grass family, Poaceae.

Pennisetums, also called fountain grasses, are grown for their feathery, bottlebrush or bushy, foxtail-like seed heads, which are produced over handsome clumps of arching, linear leaves. The botanical name refers to the feathery flowers: it is from the Greek *penna*, "feather," and *seta*, "bristle." The genus contains about 120 species of annuals as well as hardy and tender perennials.

HOW TO GROW

Give pennisetums full sun and average to rich, well-drained soil. Sow seeds indoors 6 to 8 weeks before the last spring frost date at 65° to 70°F. Or sow outdoors on the last frost date. Water regularly, especially during dry weather. Where hardy, they can be grown outdoors year-round. In the North, grow them as bedding plants replaced annually or as tender perennials: dig the plants indoors to bring them in for overwintering in a sunny, cool (55° to 60°F) spot. In areas where they are marginally hardy, mulch them heavily with salt hay, weed-free straw, or another dry mulch over winter. Plants self-sow and may become invasive.

P. setaceum P. 151

p. seh-TAY-cee-um. Fountain Grass. A tender, 3-foot-tall perennial, hardy from Zone 9 south, with plumelike, 1-foot-long, pinkish or purplish flower heads in late summer and fall. 'Purpureum', also listed as 'Atropurpureum', bears purple leaves and red-pink flowers. 'Burgundy Giant' reaches 5 feet and has purple-maroon leaves. Tender perennial or warm-weather annual.

P. villosum P. 152

p. vil-LOW-sum. Feathertop. A tender, 2-foot-tall perennial, hardy from Zone 9 south, with plumy, cylindrical, 4- to 5-inch-long, green or white flowers that mature to purplish seed heads. Tender perennial or warm-weather annual.

Penstemon

PEN-steh-mon. Figwort family, Scrophulariaceae.

Primarily native to North and Central America, *Penstemon* species are perennials and subshrubs with linear to lance-shaped leaves and panicles of tubular or bell-shaped, two-lipped flowers in shades of lavender, purple, purple-blue, lilac-blue, pink, red, yellow, and white. The 250 species in the genus are found in a wide range of habitats—cool, moist, western mountains; dry plains and deserts; and both dry and moist woodlands and prairies in the eastern half of the country. Since many penstemons will not grow well outside their native habitats, for best results with these plants, match the requirements of the species to the site and soil conditions in your garden.

HOW TO GROW

Unless otherwise noted, give the penstemons listed here full sun to partial shade and rich, well-drained, evenly moist soil. They grow best in areas with cool summers; in areas with hot summers, give plants a site with shade in the afternoon to help them cope. In general, even most hardy perennial species will be short-lived out of their native range and are best treated as annuals, biennials, or short-lived perennials. Fortunately, plants self-sow and also can be propagated by cuttings in spring or summer or division in spring. Sow seeds indoors 8 to 10 weeks before the last spring frost date at 55° to 65°F. When sowing, just press the seeds onto the soil surface, as light can help germination. Water during dry weather, and deadhead regularly. Where plants are marginally hardy, cover them with a dry winter mulch such as evergreen boughs or weed-free straw in late fall. Penstemons, sometimes called beard-tongues, are attractive in beds and borders and make excellent cut flowers. Their flowers attract hummingbirds.

P. campanulatus P.

p. cam-pan-you-LAH-tus. A tender, 1- to 2-foot perennial, hardy from Zone 7 south. Bears loose racemes of bell-shaped, violet or rose-purple, 1½-inch-long flowers in early summer. Tender perennial.

P. Hybrids PP. 152, 153

Sometimes sold as gloxinia penstemon (*P. × gloxinioides,* although this is a listed name of no botanical standing for hybrids between *P. hartwegii* and *P. cobaea*). Both hardiness and adaptability of the hybrids are variable: most are hardy from Zone 7 south and do best in gardens on the West Coast, because of their preference for cool summers. Treat them as biennials or short-lived perennials in the East. Hybrids sold as gloxinia penstemons bear tubular, bell-shaped flowers that are 1½ to 2 inches long and as wide. Plants range from 1½ to 2 feet. 'Midnight' bears violet-purple, bell-shaped flowers on 1½-foot plants and tolerates the heat and humidity of the Southeast.

Pentas

PEN-tas. Madder family, Rubiaceae.

Of the 40 or so species of perennials, biennials, subshrubs, and shrubs that belong to this genus, one is a tender perennial grown for its showy flowers in shades of pale pink, mauve, magenta, purple-red, lilac, or white flowers. Commonly called star clusters, *Pentas* species bear hairy, ovate or lanceolate leaves and rounded or flat clusters of tubular to bell-shaped flowers, each with five lobes, or "petals." They are native in tropical Africa, the Arabian Peninsula, and Madagascar.

HOW TO GROW

Star clusters thrive in full sun and rich, well-drained soil. They are hardy in Zones 10 and 11, where they can be grown outdoors year-round. In the North, grow them as bedding plants replaced annually or as tender perennials overwintered indoors. Sow seeds indoors 8 to 10 weeks before the last spring frost date at 60° to 65°F. Pinch seedlings to encourage branching. Transplant to the garden after the last frost date, once the soil has warmed to 50°F. *Pentas* species also are easy to grow from cuttings taken any time of year. Water during dry weather, and feed pot-grown plants monthly in summer. To overwinter, either take cuttings or keep plants in containers. Gradually withhold water in fall; set them in a bright, cool (55° to 60°F) spot; and keep plants on the dry side over winter. Prune to shape plants in late winter or early spring: cut them back hard, if necessary. Or use overwintered plants as stock plants and take cuttings. Star clusters make showy additions to beds and borders and fine container plants. Their flowers attract hummingbirds.

P. lanceolata P. 153

p. lan-cee-oh-LAH-tah. Star Cluster, Star Flower, Egyptian Star Cluster. A woody-based perennial or subshrub that can reach 6 feet in frost-free climates but generally is from 1 to 2 feet tall in northern gardens. Bears rounded, 3- to 4-inch-wide clusters of ½-inch-wide flowers. Tender perennial.

Perilla

peh-RIL-lah. Mint family, Lamiaceae.

Six species of annuals native from India to Japan belong to the genus *Perilla.* Closely related to coleus *(Solenostemon scutellarioides),* these plants also are grown for their showy, often richly colored, foliage. Like coleus, they bear erect spikes of insignificant, two-lipped flowers. One species is a vigorous annual grown as a foliage plant for the lush, tropical air it adds to gardens.

HOW TO GROW

Give perillas full sun to partial shade and very rich, moist, well-drained soil. Sow seeds indoors in individual pots 10 to 12 weeks before the last spring frost date at 65° to 70°F. Or sow outdoors after the last frost date. When sowing, just press the seeds onto the soil surface, as light is required for germination. Pinch plants to encourage branching and bushy growth. Transplant with care a week or so after the last frost date, once the weather has settled. Perillas also can be propagated by cuttings, which can be used to overwinter the plants indoors. Or cut back plants, and pot them up for overwintering. Plants self-sow with abandon and can become invasive.

P. frutescens P. 154

p. fru-TES-cens. Beefsteak Plant, Chinese Basil, False Coleus. A 1- to 3-foot annual with broadly ovate, deeply toothed leaves and 6-inch-tall spikes of tiny white flowers. The species has green leaves, but 'Atropurpurea' bears deep red-purple leaves and *P. frutescens* var. *crispa* (also listed as *P. nankinensis*) bears purple to bronze leaves with frilled, deeply toothed margins. Warm-weather annual.

Persicaria

per-sih-CARE-ee-ah. Buckwheat family, Polygonaceae.

Commonly called knotweeds because of their characteristic knobby, jointed-looking stems, *Persicaria* species are annuals, perennials, and subshrubs that bear erect spikes or panicles of small, densely packed flowers that are funnel-, bell-, or cup-shaped. The genus, which contains from 50 to 80 species distributed worldwide, includes both ornamental and weedy species. Plants in this genus were formerly listed as *Polygonum* species.

HOW TO GROW

Knotweeds grow in full sun and any moist soil. They also tolerate partial shade. Too-rich soil tends to encourage rank growth. Sow seeds indoors 6 to 8 weeks before the last spring frost date at 70° to 75°F. Germination takes about 3 weeks. Or sow outdoors after the last frost date. Diminutive *P. capitata* makes a fine ground cover, while prince's feather *(P. orientale)* is useful at the back of mixed plantings. Both species self-sow.

P. capitata P. 154

p. cap-ih-TAH-tah. Formerly *Polygonum capitatum.* A tender, 3-inch-tall perennial, hardy in Zones 8 and 9, with rounded leaves and ½-inch-wide, pink flower heads of tiny, bell-shaped blooms in summer. Warm-weather annual or tender perennial.

P. orientale P. 155

p. or-ee-en-TAL-ee. Prince's Feather, Princess Feather, Kiss-me-over-the-garden-gate. Formerly *Polygonum orientale.* A 3- to 5-foot-tall annual with large, 4- to 8-inch-long, heart-shaped leaves. Bears arching, branched, 2- to 3-inch-long spikes of tiny, bell-shaped, pink, rose-red, or white flowers from late summer to fall. Warm-weather annual.

Petroselinum

peh-tro-seh-LIN-um. Carrot family, Apiaceae.

Better known as a resident of vegetable and herb gardens, parsley *(Petroselinum crispum)* is one of the three species, all biennials, in this genus of plants native to the Mediterranean. They grow from thick, carrotlike rootstocks and bear flat-topped compound umbels of tiny, white, star-shaped flowers.

HOW TO GROW

Plant parsley in full sun and rich, evenly moist, well-drained soil. It grows best in cool weather: in areas with hot summers, give plants partial shade, especially during the hottest part of the day. Sow seeds indoors in individual pots 8 to 10 weeks before the last frost date at 65° to 70°F. Germination takes 3 weeks. Transplant with care; plants are taprooted and resent being disturbed. Or sow outdoors several weeks before the last frost date, as soon as the soil can be worked. Mark the site, as germination is slow. When sowing, soak the seeds overnight in warm water before sowing, and cover them with soil, as darkness aids germination. Water regularly in dry weather and mulch, especially in areas with hot summers, to keep the soil cool. Parsley plants are hardy from Zone 5 south and will overwinter and flower the following year. Some gardeners pull up plants after the first year; others let them flower, since the blooms attract beneficial insects. Caterpillars of swallowtail butterflies feed on the foliage. Use curled parsley in containers, as edgings, and in low mixed plantings. Flat-leaved parsley is less ornamental but adds attractive, dark green foliage color to mixed plantings. Harvest the leaves as soon as they are large enough to use, and dry or freeze them. When harvesting, cut rather than pull the leaves off the plants to avoid disturbing the roots.

P. crispum P. 155

p. KRIS-pum. Parsley. Two types of this ½- to 2½-foot biennial are grown. Curled parsley bears dark green, finely cut, curled leaves; flat-leaved or Italian parsley has glossy, flat, deeply cut leaves. Cool-weather annual or biennial.

Petunia

peh-TUNE-yah. Nightshade family, Solanaceae.

The trumpet-shaped blooms of petunias are a familiar sight in summer. While the genus contains some 40 species of annuals and tender perennials, all native to South America, hybridizers have produced countless cultivars, which are much more commonly grown than the species. Petunias are sprawling to erect plants with sticky-hairy, ovate to lance-shaped leaves and trumpet- to saucer-shaped flowers. Flowers are borne from summer to frost and come in shades of pink, salmon, red, rose-pink, burgundy, violet, lilac, and yellow. Hybrids with stripes, edges, or veins in contrasting colors also are available. Some botanists believe that several of the species (not commonly grown until recently) should belong to the genus *Calibrachoa;* others include them all in *Petunia.* Since all are cultivated in the same manner, gardeners can continue enjoying these plants while the debate rages.

HOW TO GROW

Petunias thrive in full sun or light shade and average to rich soil that is moist but well drained. They tolerate poor soil and are good choices for seaside gardens. A site protected from wind is best. Sow seeds indoors 10 to 12 weeks before the last frost date at 65° to 70°F. Just press the dustlike seeds onto the soil surface, as light is required for germination, which takes 1 to 3 weeks. Water from below to avoid washing the seeds out of the pots. Pinch plants to encourage branching and bushy growth. Water regularly, and deadhead to encourage new flowers to form. Feed container-grown plants every two weeks. Cut back plants that become scraggly. Cutting them back by half in late summer will encourage new growth and flowers until fall; some plants, including *P. integrifolia,* benefit from shearing two or three times during the season. Plants self-sow, but hybrids do not come true from seeds. Petunias are usually grown as annuals, but they are tender perennials and can be overwintered indoors in a bright, cool (55° to 65°F) spot. They also can be propagated by cuttings taken in spring or summer, and cuttings are the best bet for propagating double-flowered forms, which produce a large percentage of singles when grown from seeds. Use petunias as edging plants, in mixed plantings, and in all manner of containers, from hanging baskets and window boxes to large tubs, where they are effective combined with other annuals. Their flowers attract both hummingbirds and moths.

P. × hybrida P. 156

p. × HI-brih-dah. Hybrid or Common Petunias. Gardeners should pay attention to groups within this species, which includes all the commonly grown hybrids, since new cultivars are introduced annually, replacing ones already on the market. Most series of cultivars come in the full range of petunia colors. Grandiflora petunias bear large, 4-inch-wide flowers, which are easily damaged by rain and wind and are best for sheltered spots only. Ultra and Storm Series grandifloras show improved resistance to weather. Multiflora petunias are bushier plants that bear smaller but more abundant flowers, to 2 inches across. Wave Series multifloras are vigorous, densely branched plants that can be used as ground covers. Both Grandiflora and Multiflora plants are 12 to 14 inches tall and can spread to about 3 feet. Fantasy Series plants, which are sold as Mulliflora petunias, bear an abundance of 1- to 1½-inch-wide flowers on densely branching plants that spread to about 8 inches. Tender perennial or warm-weather annual.

P. 'Million Bells'

Sold as a cultivated form of *Calibrachoa* (kal-ih-brah-KOE-ah), this group of hybrids comes in violet-blue, pink, magenta, and white and bears an abundance of small, 1-inch-wide flowers on densely branching 8-inch-tall plants with trailing, spreading stems. Tender perennial or warm-weather annual.

P. Supertunia and Surfinia Group **P. 157**

A group of compact, heavy-blooming hybrids developed by crossing various cultivars with *P. integrifolia.* Plants are propagated by cuttings only. They bear 2- to 3-inch-wide flowers in purple-blue, pink, white, fuchsia, lavender-blue, and purple-red. Feed every two weeks for best performance. Tender perennial.

P. integrifolia **P. 157**

p. in-teg-rih-FOE-lee-ah. A spreading, shrubby tender perennial, hardy from Zone 8 south, that can reach 2 feet in height. Bears 1½-inch-wide, magenta-pink flowers with dark centers from spring to frost. 'Alba' bears white flowers. Tender perennial or warm-weather annual.

Phacelia

fah-CEE-lee-ah. Waterleaf family, Hydrophyllaceae.

Native to North and South America, *Phacelia* contains about 150 species of annuals, biennials, and perennials that bear clusters of nectar-rich flowers in shades of blue, violet, or white. The flowers have five lobes, or "petals," and are either tubular or bell- or bowl-shaped. Leaves are usually deeply cut in a pinnate, or featherlike, fashion.

HOW TO GROW

Give annual species full sun and well-drained soil. They are best for areas with cool summers and do not tolerate heat and humidity. In areas where summer heat and humidity prevail, start them early enough so they bloom before hot weather arrives, then replace them with summer-blooming, heat-tolerant annuals. Sow seeds outdoors several weeks before the last spring frost date; sow in fall in areas with mild winters— roughly Zone 8 south. Or sow indoors in individual pots 6 to 8 weeks before the last frost at 50° to 55°F; transplant with care. Outdoor sowing is generally best. When sowing, cover the seeds with soil, as darkness aids germination. Stake plants with twiggy brush. Use *Phacelia* species in mixed plantings or wildlife gardens, where their nectar-rich flowers attract insects.

P. campanularia **P. 158**

p. cam-pan-you-LAIR-ee-ah. California Bluebell. A compact, well-branched, ½- to 1-foot-tall annual with sticky-hairy leaves. Bears loose clusters of upturned, 1-inch-wide, bell-shaped blooms in dark blue from late spring to summer. Cool-weather annual.

P. tanacetifolia

p. tan-ah-cee-tih-FOE-lee-ah. Fiddleneck. A 1- to 3-foot-tall annual with dense, curved clusters of ½-inch-wide, blue or lavender-blue flowers in summer. Cool-weather annual.

Phaseolus

pha-see-OH-lus. Pea family, Fabaceae.

The best-known plants in this genus of 20 species of annuals and perennials are commonly grown in vegetable gardens—green beans and lima beans. *Phaseolus* species are primarily climbing plants with twining stems, three-part leaves, and clusters of pea-shaped flowers. One species is grown both as an ornamental for its showy flowers and as a food plant for its edible pods and seeds.

HOW TO GROW

Give scarlet runner bean *(P. coccineus)* full sun and average to rich, moist but well-drained soil. Plants require a trellis or strings to climb or can be trained over shrubs. They thrive in heat and humidity but stop setting seeds when temperatures are over 90°F. Sow seeds indoors in individual pots 4 to 6 weeks before the last spring frost date at 60° to 70°F. Germination takes 1 to 2 weeks. Or sow outdoors 2 weeks after the last spring frost once the soil has warmed up and the weather has settled. Water plants regularly in dry weather. Keep beans picked to encourage new flowers to form. They are most tender when harvested at 4 inches or less. Plants produce tuberous roots, and in areas where the ground doesn't freeze, they can be killed back by frost but will resprout from the roots. In addition to being handsome climbers, scarlet runner beans attract hummingbirds, butterflies, and bees to the garden.

P. coccineus P. 158

p. cock-SIN-ee-us. Scarlet Runner Bean. A twining climber that can reach 8 to 12 feet in a single season. Loose racemes of 1¼-inch-wide scarlet flowers appear from early summer to frost. 'Albus' bears white flowers. 'Hammond's Dwarf' is a 1½-foot-tall, nonclimbing cultivar suitable for pots. Warm-weather annual or tender perennial.

Phlox

FLOX. Phlox family, Polemoniaceae.

While the best-known phlox are hardy perennials, this genus of 70 species also contains annuals and a few shrubs. Nearly all are native North American wildflowers — one species is from Siberia. They bear showy clusters of salverform flowers, meaning the flowers have a slender tube at the base and an abruptly flared and flattened face. The flowers have five lobes, or "petals," and bear simple, linear to ovate leaves. One species is a popular annual.

HOW TO GROW

Grow annual phlox *(Phlox drummondii)* in full sun and average to rich, moist, well-drained soil. They thrive in cool weather and tend to die out in areas where hot, humid conditions prevail in summer. Sow seeds outdoors several weeks before the last spring frost date. Or sow indoors in individual pots 6 to 8 weeks before the last frost date at 55° to 65°F. Germination takes 2 to 3 weeks. When sowing, cover seeds with soil, as they require darkness to germinate. Transplant with care, as plants resent being moved. Sow seeds in fall for early spring bloom in areas with mild winters; where summers are cool, sow new crops of seeds every 4 to 6 weeks to lengthen the bloom season. Pinch seedlings when they are 3 inches tall to encourage branching. Feed plants monthly and water regularly. Deadhead to prolong bloom, and cut plants back to within 2 inches of the soil if they become leggy. Use annual phlox in containers and mixed plantings. They make excellent cut flowers, and their flowers attract hummingbirds.

P. drummondii P. 159

p. drum-MON-dee-eye. Annual Phlox, Drummond Phlox. A much-hybridized, 4- to 18-inch-tall annual with clusters of purple, lavender, salmon, pink, or red, single or double blooms that are 1 inch wide. Dwarf Beauty Series plants are 8 inches tall; 'Dolly Mix', 4 inches tall. For cut flowers, look for taller cultivars, such as 1½- to 2-foot-tall 'Tapestry'. Cool-weather annual.

Phormium

FOR-mee-um. Agave family, Agavaceae.

This genus of tender perennials contains two species, both native to New Zealand, grown for their dramatic grassy or irislike clumps of sword-shaped leaves, each folded lengthwise in a V. They bear erect panicles of small flowers in summer. Maoris traditionally used fiber from the leaves in basket making, and the botanical name is from the Greek *phormos*, "basket." The common name New Zealand flax also refers to this use.

HOW TO GROW

Give these plants full sun and rich, moist, well-drained soil. Where hardy, generally from Zone 9 south, grow them outdoors as perennials. In areas where they are marginally hardy, select a sheltered, south-facing site and protect plants with a thick layer of dry mulch such as salt hay or weed-free straw over winter. Or grow plants in tubs or large containers and overwinter them indoors in a bright, cool (45° to 50°F) spot. Most gardeners start plants from divisions, which is the only way to acquire the choice cultivars. Or sow seeds indoors 10 to 12 weeks before the last spring frost date at 60° to 65°F. Germination can take from 1 to 6 months. Water plants regularly in summer, especially container-grown specimens, which can be left in saucers filled with water to keep them moist. Feed plants monthly. Use phormiums as specimen plants and for vertical accents in containers. Set pot-grown plants on terraces, or sink them to the rim in garden soil.

P. tenax **P. 159**

p. TEN-ax. New Zealand Flax. A tender, clump-forming perennial with leaves that range from 3 to 9 feet long and clusters of dark red, 2-inch-long flowers in summer. The species bears green leaves with red or orange edges. 'Bronze Baby' is a 2- to 3-foot plant with arching bronze leaves. 'Sundowner' reaches 6 feet and has leaves striped in bronze, green, and rose-pink. 'Dazzler' reaches 3 feet and bears arching, bronze-maroon leaves with red and pink stripes. Tender perennial.

Phygelius

fy-GEE-lee-us. Figwort family, Scrophulariaceae.

Commonly called Cape fuchsias, *Phygelius* species are tender shrubs or subshrubs native to South Africa that spread by suckers. They bear bluntly toothed, ovate-lanceolate leaves and racemes of showy flowers, which appear from summer to fall. The flowers are tubular and have five lobes, or "petals," that curve backward. Two species belong to the genus. They are not closely related to fuchsias (*Fuchsia* spp.), although the flowers bear a superficial resemblance. Botanically, they are more similar to other figwort-family members such as penstemons (*Penstemon* spp.).

HOW TO GROW

Cape fuchsias thrive in full sun and rich, moist, well-drained soil. They tolerate hot, dry conditions, too. In very hot climates, a site with shade during the hottest part of the day is best. Where hardy, grow them outdoors as shrubs; in areas where they are marginally hardy, try growing them as perennials, since they can be killed to the ground and will resprout from the roots. For extra winter protection, try a site against a south-facing wall and cover them with a dry mulch such as salt hay or weed-free straw. In the North, grow them in containers and overwinter them indoors in a bright, cool (40° to 45°F) spot. Sow seeds indoors 6 to 8 weeks before the last spring frost date at 70° to 75°F. Germination takes about 2 weeks. Plants also can be propagated in spring either by cuttings or by digging up suckers that appear around the plants. Use cape fuchsias in containers, shrub borders, and mixed plantings. Their flowers attract hummingbirds.

P. aequalis P. 160

p. ee-QUAL-iss. A tender, 3-foot-tall-shrub, hardy from Zone 7 south, with 10- to 12-inch-long panicles of 2½-inch-long trumpets, which are pink with red petals and yellow throats. 'Yellow Trumpet' bears creamy yellow flowers. Tender perennial.

P. × *rectus* P. 160

p. × RECK-tus. A 3- to 5-foot tender shrub, hardy from Zone 8 south, with 6- to 12-inch-long panicles of 2½-inch-long red flowers. Cultivars include 'Moonraker' with greenish yellow flowers, 'African Queen' in salmon-orange, and 'Winchester Fanfare' in shell pink. Tender perennial.

Platystemon

plat-ee-STEM-on. Poppy family, Papaveraceae.

Platystemon contains one species native to grasslands, deserts, and chaparral in the western United States. Commonly called cream cups, it is an erect or sprawling annual with hairy, gray-green, linear to narrow, lance-shaped leaves and an abundance of small poppylike flowers.

HOW TO GROW

Plant cream cups in full sun and average, loose, well-drained soil. They tolerate dry soil, but extremely hot, humid weather may cause plants to die back (or die off); fortunately, they generally recover once cooler conditions return. Sow seeds outdoors in fall or several weeks before the last spring frost date, when the soil is still cool. Barely cover the seeds with soil. Or sow indoors in individual pots 6 to 8 weeks before the last spring frost date and transplant with care. Outdoor sowing is generally best. Water during dry weather. Use cream cups as edgings, at the front of shrub borders, in rock gardens, and in mixed plantings. Plants self-sow.

P. californicus P. 161

p. cal-ih-FOR-nih-kus. Cream Cups. A well-branched, 4- to 12-inch-tall annual that can spread to 9 or 10 inches. Bears 1-inch-wide, six-petaled, creamy yellow flowers. Cool-weather annual.

Plectranthus

pleck-TRAN-thus. Mint family, Lamiaceae.

Some 350 species of annuals, perennials, and shrubs belong to this genus from tropical Africa, Asia, Australia, and the Pacific islands. They have square, sometimes succulent, stems that can be erect or trailing. Gardeners most often value them for their showy leaves, which can be heart-shaped to rounded with scalloped, toothed, or wavy margins. The foliage is often aromatic and somewhat hairy. The plants produce erect clusters of small, tubular, two-lipped flowers in shades of pale pink, mauve, white, or lilac in summer.

HOW TO GROW

Give these plants a site in dappled shade and average to rich, well-drained soil. Grow them as bedding plants replaced annually or as tender perennials overwintered in a bright, cool to warm (60° to 70°F) spot. (They also make fine houseplants.) Sow seeds indoors 8 to 10 weeks before the last spring frost date at 65° to 75°F. Transplant after the last frost date once temperatures remain above 45°F. They root easily from cuttings taken any time of year, and cuttings — or simply digging up rooted stems — are the best way to propagate variegated forms. Use these plants to add foliage interest to mixed plantings and containers. Trailing types are effective cascading out of hanging baskets and large tubs.

P. amboinicus

p. am-BOY-nih-kus. Mexican Mint, Cuban Oregano, Indian Borage, Spanish Thyme. A 1-foot-tall tender perennial, spreading to 3 feet or more, with hairy, fleshy, rounded, 1¾-inch-long, aromatic leaves used in cooking for their spicy flavor, which has been likened to a mix of savory, thyme, and oregano. Bears 12- to 16-inch-long spikes of ½-inch-long lilac flowers. A form with white-edged leaves is available as 'Variegatus' or 'Marginatus'. Tender perennial or warm-weather annual.

P. argentatus P. 161

p. are-jen-TAY-tus. An erect, tender shrub, to 2 to 3 feet tall and wide, with ribbed, scallop-edged, gray-green, 2- to 4½-inch-long leaves. Produces 1-foot-long spikes of bluish white, ½-inch-long flowers. Tender perennial or warm-weather annual.

P. forsteri P. 162

p. FOR-ster-eye. Also listed as *P. colioides.* A 10-inch-tall tender perennial that can spread to 3 feet or more with hairy, rounded, scalloped-edged, 2½- to 4-inch-long leaves and 6- to 8-inch-long racemes of tiny, pale pink or white flowers. 'Marginatus', also sold as 'Iboza', bears white-edged leaves. Tender perennial or warm-weather annual.

P. madagascariensis

p. mad-ah-gas-car-ee-EN-sis. Mintleaf. A tender, 1-foot-tall perennial with brown stems that can spread 3 feet or more. Fleshy, rounded, scallop-edged, 1½-inch-long leaves smell of mint when crushed. Bears 4- to 6-inch-long flower spikes of pale lavender or white blooms. 'Variegated Mintleaf' bears white-edged leaves. Tender perennial or warm-weather annual.

Polygonum *see Persicaria*

Portulaca

por-tyew-LAC-ah. Purslane family, Portulacaceae.

Of the 100 species that belong to *Portulaca,* one is a popular annual grown for its showy, satiny-looking flowers, which can be single or double. *Portulaca* species are erect or trailing annuals, or sometimes perennials, with small, fleshy, flat to cylindrical leaves. Purslane *(P. oleracea)* also belongs here. It is a common garden weed with edible, iron-rich leaves that are harvested for use in salads or as a potherb.

HOW TO GROW

These tough, easy-to-grow plants thrive in full sun and poor, well-drained soil. They grow well in sandy, dry conditions as well, and may not flower well in wet summers. Sow seeds outdoors after the last spring frost date. Or sow indoors in individual pots 6 to 8 weeks before the last frost date at 55° to 65°F. Transplant with care. When sowing, just press the seeds onto the soil surface, as light is required for germination. Use portulacas in tough, dry sites where few annuals will grow. They are useful as edgings, in rock gardens, along walls, and in mixed plantings and also make ideal container plants. Plants self-sow.

P. grandiflora P. 162

p. gran-dih-FLOOR-ah. Portulaca, Moss Rose, Rose Moss. A spreading, 4- to 8-inch-tall annual with cylindrical leaves and single or double, 1-inch-wide flowers in an array of bright colors including hot pink, red, purple, yellow, and white. The flowers normally open only in sunny weather. Sundial Series plants bear double flowers that tend to stay open longer than other selections. Warm-weather annual.

Primula

PRIM-you-lah. Primrose family, Primulaceae.

This large genus of popular garden plants contains some 425 species of tender and hardy perennials commonly called primroses or primulas. They produce rosettes of narrow to broad, rounded leaves and clusters of flowers that are usually salverform, meaning they have a slender tube at the base and an abruptly flared and flattened face. Some species bear tubular, bell-shaped, or funnel-shaped blooms. While most primroses are grown as hardy perennials, a few are tender perennials commonly grown as annuals. The botanical name alludes to the early-blooming nature of many primroses — it is taken from the Latin *primus,* or "first."

HOW TO GROW

The species listed here need partial shade and rich, evenly moist, well-drained soil, as well as cool conditions, to grow well. In areas with cool summers, they can be grown in full sun. All are commonly grown as florists' pot plants and treated as annuals. *Primula* Polyanthus Group plants also can be grown as perennials from Zone 6 south, but the other two species will succeed outdoors only on the Pacific Coast, where summers are cool and rainy. Sow seeds indoors about 12 weeks before the last spring frost date; just press the seeds onto the soil surface. Refrigerate the sown pots for 3 weeks before moving them to a warmer (60° to 65°F) spot for germinating. Use primroses to add spring color to beds and borders as well as plantings of woodland wildflowers. Or use them in containers.

P. malacoides

P. 163

p. mal-ah-COY-deez. Fairy Primrose. A 6- to 8-inch-tall tender perennial, hardy only from Zone 8 south, with tiers of whorled, ½-inch-wide, single or double flowers in shades of lavender-purple, reddish pink, or white. Tender perennial or cool-weather annual.

P. obconica

P. 163

p. ob-CON-ih-kah. Fairy Primrose, German Primrose. A 9- to 16-inch-tall tender perennial, hardy only in Zones 10 and 11, with tiers of whorled, 1- to 2-inch-wide flowers that sometimes have frilled petal edges. Flowers come in shades of pink, red, lilac-blue, and white. Touching the foliage can cause a skin rash. Tender perennial or cool-weather annual.

P. Polyanthus Group

These hybrids are also listed as *P.* × *polyanthus* and are crosses between various hardy primroses. Depending on the cultivar, they can be hardy to Zone 3, but florists' types are usually less hardy—to Zone 6. Plants bear clusters of showy, 1- to 2-inch-wide flowers on 6-inch-tall stems in a wide range of colors, including pale to deep yellow, red, orange, violet-blue, white, and pink, and often have yellow eyes. Harden off plants purchased from a florist before trying them in the garden. Hardy perennial or cool-weather annual.

Proboscidea

pro-bos-SIH-dee-ah. Pedalium family, Pedaliaceae.

Both the common and botanical names for *Proboscidea* species are based on their woody seed capsules, which have hornlike beaks or protrusions at one end. The botanical name is from the Greek *proboskis*, "snout" or "nose," and common names include unicorn plant, devil's claw, ram's horn, elephant's tusk, and proboscis flower. The genus contains nine species of annuals and perennials native to the Americas. They are grown for their tropical foliage, racemes of five-lobed, funnel- to bell-shaped flowers, and interesting seedpods.

HOW TO GROW

Select a site in full sun to very light shade and rich, well-drained soil. Established plants tolerate dry soil but do better with regular watering during dry spells. Sow seeds indoors 6 to 8 weeks before the last spring frost date at 70° to 75°F. Transplant a few weeks after the last frost date, once the weather has settled and temperatures remain above 50°F. In areas with long growing seasons, roughly Zone 8 south, sow outdoors a week or two after the last frost date. Use these annuals to add a lush, tropical effect to mixed plantings. The seedpods are attractive in dried arrangements.

P. louisiana P. 164

p. loo-ee-see-AN-ih-kah. Unicorn Plant, Devil's Claw. Sometimes listed as *P. jussieui*, *P. proboscidea*, and *Martynia fragrans*. An erect to spreading annual that can reach 1½ feet tall and spread to 3 feet. Bears softly hairy, 2½- to 8-inch-long leaves and funnel-shaped, 1½- to 2-inch-long, creamy white to purplish flowers with yellow throats and spotted with red-purple. The flowers are followed by curved, 4- to 8-inch-long seedpods. Warm-weather annual.

Psylliostachys

sil-ee-oh-STACK-eez. Plumbago family, Plumbaginaceae.

Psylliostachys contains from six to eight species of annuals that once belonged to *Limonium*, better known to gardeners as statice. They bear deeply lobed to rounded or lance-shaped leaves that generally are clustered in a rosette at the base of the plant. From summer to fall, they produce branched or unbranched panicles of tiny, pink or white, tubular flowers.

HOW TO GROW

Grow statice in full sun and average, well-drained soil. Plants grow well in sandy soil and are good choices for seaside gardens. Sow seeds indoors 6 to 8 weeks before the last spring frost date at 65° to 75°F. Germination takes 2 to 3 weeks. Or sow outdoors after the last frost. Add statice to mixed plantings. They are ideal candidates for cutting gardens and are top-notch dried flowers. Harvest when most of the flowers in the spray have opened fully, and hang in small bunches in a warm, dark place to dry.

P. suworowii

PP. 164, 165

p. suh-vo-ROW-vee-eye. Rattail Statice, Russian Statice. Formerly *Limonium suworowii* and *Statice suworowii.* A 1- to 1½-foot-tall annual producing narrow, 8-inch-long, branched, cylindrical spikes of rose-pink flowers from summer to early fall. 'Pink Poker', sometimes used as a cultivar name, actually is another common name for the species. Warm-weather annual.

Quamoclit *see Ipomoea*

Rehmannia

reh-MAH-nee-ah. Figwort family, Scrophulariaceae.

Native to China, the 10 species of *Rehmannia* are tender perennials that gardeners grow for their showy racemes of foxglove-like, two-lipped flowers. They bear a rosette of large leaves that are rounded or oblong, toothed or lobed.

HOW TO GROW

Select a site in full sun to dappled shade with average to rich, evenly moist, well-drained soil. Plant them in a sheltered site. *Rehmannia* species require cool conditions: Grow them as perennials in areas with cool summers and mild winters (Zone 9 south)—the Pacific Northwest and California. Elsewhere, grow them as biennials or tender perennials. Sow seeds 6 to 8 weeks before the last spring frost date at 60° to 65°F. Or propagate by root cuttings in fall or cuttings taken from shoots at the base of the plant. Take cuttings either before flowering in spring or from new shoots that arise when the plants are cut down after flowering. To overwinter, pot up or propagate plants and keep them in a bright, cold (40° to 45°F) spot. Keep plants on the dry side (but not completely dry) during the winter. Water regularly when plants are actively growing, and feed at least monthly. Use *Rehmannia* species in mixed plantings and in containers.

R. elata

P. 165

r. ee-LAH-tah. Chinese Foxglove. Also listed as *R. angulata.* A tender, 3- to 5-foot perennial with racemes of tubular rosy purple flowers with red-spotted throats. Biennial or tender perennial.

Reseda

reh-SEE-dah. Mignonette family, Resedaceae.

One of the 55 to 60 species of annuals and perennials in this genus is an old-fashioned annual beloved for its intensely fragrant flowers. Native from the Mediterranean to North Africa and central Asia, plants in this genus bear clusters of star-shaped, greenish, yellow, or white flowers from spring to fall.

HOW TO GROW

Grow mignonette in partial shade and average, well-drained soil. Plants prefer cool conditions and will stop blooming when hot weather arrives. They will grow in full sun in areas with cool summers, but elsewhere a site that receives dappled shade during the hottest part of the day is best. Plants prefer, but do not require, an alkaline pH. Sow seeds outdoors several weeks before the last spring frost date, when the soil is still cool. Sow new crops every 3 weeks until early summer for a long season of bloom. Or sow indoors in individual pots 6 to 8 weeks before the last spring frost date at 55° to 60°F. From Zone 9 south, sow seeds outdoors in late summer or fall for bloom the following spring. When sowing, just press the seeds into the soil surface, as light is required for germination. Pinch seedlings to encourage branching and bushy growth. Use mignonettes in mixed plantings and to provide cut flowers for fresh and dried bouquets. The flowers, which are attractive to bees and butterflies, hold their fragrance even when dried. For drying, harvest when most of the flowers have opened but before those at the bottom of the stalk have started to fade.

R. odorata P. 166

r. oh-dor-AH-tah. Common Mignonette. An erect to spreading, 1- to 2-foot-tall annual with rounded spikes of ¼-inch-wide flowers in yellowish green, white, or reddish green. Newer cultivars with brighter-colored flowers usually are less fragrant than the species. Cool-weather annual.

Rhodanthe

row-DAN-thee. Aster family, Asteraceae.

Commonly called strawflowers or everlastings, *Rhodanthe* species are annuals and perennials from Australia grown for their daisylike flower heads that are outstanding for dried bouquets. They bear linear to rounded leaves that often are gray-green in color. The flower heads consist of all disk florets — they lack the ray florets, or "petals," of many aster-family plants. The showy "petals" in this case are papery, petal-like bracts in yellow, pink, or white that surround yellow centers.

HOW TO GROW

A site with full sun and poor to average, well-drained soil is ideal for these drought-tolerant plants, which also grow well in sandy soil. Sow seeds indoors in individual pots 6 to 8 weeks before the last spring frost date at 60° to 70°F. Germination takes 2 to 3 weeks. In the South, where summers are long, strawflowers can be sown outdoors in spring. When sowing, just press the seeds into the soil surface, as they need light to germinate. Wait to transplant until after the last frost, once the soil has warmed up, and handle them with care. Stake with twiggy brush. To dry the flower heads, pick them before they are fully open, then hang them in small bunches in a warm, dark, dry place. Or simply pull up the entire plant and hang to dry.

R. chlorocephala ssp. *rosea* P. 166

r. chlor-oh-SEFF-ah-lah ssp. ROSE-ee-ah. Formerly *Helipterum roseum* and *Acroclinium roseum.* A fast-growing, 1- to 2-foot-tall annual with 1- to 3-inch-wide, papery daisies that close in cloudy weather. Flower heads have white or pink bracts surrounding yellow centers in summer. Warm-weather annual.

R. manglesii

r. man-GLEH-see-eye. Swan River Everlasting. Formerly *Helipterum manglesii.* A bushy, 2-foot-tall annual producing clusters of 1¼-inch-wide flower heads with yellow centers and white, pink, or red bracts. Warm-weather annual.

Rhodochiton

rho-doe-KYE-ton. Figwort family, Scrophulariaceae.

Three species of climbing perennials, commonly called purple bell vines, belong to this genus of unlikely looking snapdragon relatives. Both the common and botanical names — *Rhodochiton* is from the Greek *rhodon,* "rose," and *chiton,* "cloak" — refer to unusual pendent flowers. Each bloom has an inflated, cup- or bell-shaped calyx (sepals) from which a tubular corolla (petals) emerges. The "bell," or calyx, opens before the corolla, which forms the "clapper." The bell-like calyx also remains on the plant after the corolla drops. The leaves are heart-shaped or roughly triangular, and the plants climb by both twining leafstalks and stems.

HOW TO GROW

These vines require full sun and rich, evenly moist, well-drained soil, as well as a trellis, strings, or other supports upon which to climb. They grow in light, sandy soil as well. Sow seeds indoors 6 to 8 weeks before the last spring frost date at 60° to 65°F. Seeds can be slow to germinate, taking from 12 to 40 days; fresh ones germinate fastest. From Zone 9 south, seeds can be sown outdoors after the last frost date. Seedlings will need thin stakes upon which to climb. While purple bell vines are most often grown as annuals, they can be treated as tender perennials. They are hardy from about Zone 10 south but may overwinter (but be killed to the ground) in warmer parts of Zone 9 if given a protected, south-facing site and covered with a dry mulch such as salt hay or weed-free straw over winter. In the north, pot-grown plants can be overwintered in a bright, cool (60° to 65°F) spot. Water regularly during the summer months, but keep them barely moist over winter. Cut plants back and repot in spring. Plants also can be propagated by cuttings taken in spring or summer, which can be used to overwinter the plants. Use these vines to cover trellises or other supports. They also are attractive in hanging baskets.

R. atrosanguineum P. 167

r. ah-tro-san-GWIN-ee-um. Purple Bell Vine. Also listed as *R. volubile.* A tender vine that commonly reaches 10 feet in northern gardens, more in frost-free regions. Bears 1¾-inch-long, dark maroon-purple flowers with lighter, mauve-pink calyxes from summer to fall. Tender perennial or warm-weather annual.

Ricinus

rye-SINE-us. Euphorbia family, Euphorbiaceae.

Castor bean, the only species in this genus, is a tender shrub of considerable commercial importance as well as a dramatic addition to ornamental gardens. In gardens, it is valued primarily for its large, glossy, palmately lobed leaves. The small, cup-shaped, greenish yellow flowers are borne in spikes but are fairly insignificant, although the spiny, round, red-brown seed capsules are interesting and attractive. All parts of the plant, especially the seeds, are quite poisonous if ingested.

HOW TO GROW

A site with full sun and rich, well-drained soil is ideal, although plants also tolerate partial shade. Castor beans grow in a range of soils, but poor, infertile soil yields plants that bear small, less attractive foliage. A protected site is best; otherwise stake plants to help them withstand wind. Sow seeds indoors in individual pots 6 to 8 weeks before the last spring frost date at 70°F. Germination takes 2 to 3 weeks. From Zone 8 south, sow outdoors after the last frost date. Before sowing, soak seeds in warm water for 24 hours to speed germination. Transplant seedlings a few weeks after the last frost date once the weather has settled and temperatures remain above 50°F. Castor beans are shrub-size annuals that add a lush, tropical look to mixed plantings. They also can be grown in containers.

R. communis P. 167

r. com-MUE-nis. Castor Bean. A tender shrub, hardy from Zone 9 south, that can reach 6 to 10 feet in a single season. The leaves have 5 to 12 lobes, range from ½ to 1½ feet long, and come in green, red-purple, or bronze-red. 'Carmencita' bears bronze-red leaves. 'Zanzibarensis' bears green leaves that can reach 3 feet across. Tender perennial or warm-weather annual.

Rosmarinus

rose-mah-RINE-us. Mint family, Lamiaceae.

Of the two species of shrubs that belong to this genus, rosemary *(Rosmarinus officinalis)* is by far the better known. Native to the Mediterranean region, both species are tender evergreen shrubs with aromatic, needlelike leaves. They bear delicate-looking whorls of small, two-lipped flowers in summer.

HOW TO GROW

Plant rosemary in full sun and poor to average soil that is evenly moist yet well drained. A spot with good air circulation is best. Where hardy, grow it outdoors year-round as a shrub; in areas where it is marginally hardy, try a site against a south-facing wall for extra winter protection. In the North, grow it in large containers year-round and overwinter it indoors in a bright, cool (45° to 56°F) spot; or simply buy new plants annually. Plants resent disturbance and are best not moved after planting. Keep the soil evenly moist but never wet. Sinking the pots to the rim in the garden helps keep the soil moist and reduces the need for constant monitoring. Feed monthly during the growing season. Over winter, water sparingly and do not fertilize. Rosemary is seldom grown from seeds: propagate by cuttings in summer. Pinch and prune plants as necessary to shape them immediately after the flowers fade.

R. officinalis

P. 168

r. oh-fish-in-AL-iss. Rosemary. A tender shrub that can reach 5 or 6 feet tall in frost-free climates and spread as far. The species and most cultivars are hardy in Zones 8 to 10; 'Arp' is hardy to Zone 7. Bears clusters of ½-inch-long, lavender-blue flowers in summer. Tender perennial.

Rudbeckia

rude-BECK-ee-ah. Aster family, Asteraceae.

Commonly known as black-eyed Susans, orange coneflowers, or simply rudbeckias, these aster-family plants native to North America are grown for their showy, summer-borne, daisylike flowers. Some 20 species of annuals, biennials, and perennials belong to the genus, all of which bear flower heads consisting of ray florets, or "petals," surrounding spiny black, brown, or green centers of disk florets, which produce the seeds. Most have petals in shades of yellow to yellow-orange, but one popular species commonly grown as an annual comes in a wider range of colors, including yellows as well as red-brown and rusty orange.

HOW TO GROW

Give coneflowers full sun to light shade and average to rich soil. While evenly moist soil is ideal, plants are drought-tolerant once established. Sow seeds 6 to 8 weeks before the last spring frost date at 70° to 75°F. Germination takes 1 to 2 weeks. Or sow outdoors 2 weeks before the last frost date. Either way, just press the seeds into the soil surface, as light is required for germination. Water plants in dry weather. Deadhead to prolong bloom. Plants self-sow.

R. hirta

P. 168

r. HUR-tah. Black-eyed Susan. An erect, well-branched biennial or short-lived perennial ranging from 1 to 3 feet in height. Bears hairy, ovate to lance-shaped leaves and 3- to 6-inch-wide, single or semidouble flowers from summer to early fall. Many cultivars are available, and old-fashioned, 3-foot-tall gloriosa daisies belong here. Gloriosa daisies bear 3- to 6-inch-wide flowers in shades of red-brown, yellow, gold, bronze, and rusty orange; many flowers have bicolor petals. 'Becky Mixed' is a dwarf mix, to 1 foot tall, that comes in colors similar to gloriosa daisies. 'Indian Summer' bears golden yellow, 6- to 9-inch-wide blooms. 'Toto' bears golden flowers on 10-inch-tall plants. Short-lived perennial, biennial, or cool-weather annual.

Salpiglossis

sal-pig-LOSS-iss. Nightshade family, Solanaceae.

Two species belong to the genus *Salpiglossis,* both annuals or short-lived perennials native to the southern Andes in Chile. They have oval to lance-shaped leaves covered with sticky hairs, and funnel-shaped, velvety-textured flowers in a rich array of colors, including yellow, red, purple-pink, and orange, from summer to fall. In many cases, the blooms are striped or veined with contrasting colors. One species, commonly known as painted tongue, is a popular bedding plant.

HOW TO GROW

Select a site with full sun and average to rich, well-drained soil that is evenly moist. Plants grow best in areas where summers are not excessively hot. In areas with hot summers, start plants early so they have time to bloom before warm weather arrives; also give them a spot with light shade during the afternoon to help them cope with heat. Sow seeds indoors in individual pots 8 to 10 weeks before the last spring frost date at 70° to 75°F. Germination takes 1 to 4 weeks. Hardened-off seedlings can be moved to the garden 2 weeks before the last frost date, but transplant with care, as they resent being moved. Or sow outdoors on or just before the last frost date. When sowing, just press the tiny seeds into the soil surface, but since they need darkness to germinate, cover them with black plastic or an overturned seed flat until seedlings appear. Mulch plants when they are several inches tall to help keep the soil cool. Let the soil dry out slightly between waterings. Stake plants with twiggy brush. Deadhead regularly. Use painted tongues in mixed plantings and containers. They are excellent cut flowers.

S. sinuata P. 169

s. sin-yew-AH-tah. Painted Tongue. An erect, somewhat weak-stemmed annual bearing five-lobed, 2-inch-wide flowers from summer to fall. 'Casino Mix' plants are densely branched and 1½ to 2 feet tall, with flowers in a full range of rich colors. Cool-weather annual.

Salvia

SAL-vee-ah. Mint family, Lamiaceae.

The salvia clan is a large one, comprising some 900 species of widely distributed annuals, biennials, perennials, and shrubs. Commonly called sages as well as salvias—the culinary herb common sage *(Salvia officinalis)* is a popular perennial that belongs here—they are treasured by gardeners for their erect spikes of tubular, two-lipped flowers in shades of violet, purple, lilac, mauve-purple, scarlet, pink, white, and rich true blue. Each flower has a tubular, bell- or funnel-shaped calyx at the base, which in some species is quite showy in its own right. Like other mint-family plants, most species feature square stems. Leaves are usually simple, ranging from linear and lance-shaped to ovate and heart-shaped. They are generally toothed or scalloped and are often aromatic and hairy.

HOW TO GROW

Grow salvias in full sun to partial shade and average to rich, well-drained soil that is evenly moist. In areas with hot summers, a site with afternoon shade is best. Species with densely hairy leaves, such as silver sage *(S. argentea)* need very well drained soil and are best in full sun. Where hardy, grow salvias outdoors as perennials or shrubs; in areas where they are marginally hardy, try a site against a south-facing wall for extra win-

Salvia farinacea

ter protection. In the North, grow them as bedding plants replaced annually or as tender perennials overwintered indoors. To grow them as annuals, sow seeds indoors 6 to 8 weeks before the last spring frost date at 65° to 70°F. To give mealy-cup sage *(S. farinacea)* a head start so it can bloom the first year from seeds, sow indoors 10 to 12 weeks before the last frost date. Germination takes about 2 weeks. Or, from Zone 9 south, sow outdoors after the last frost date. To grow salvias as biennials or perennials, sow them indoors as you would annuals, or sow outdoors in a nursery bed, in pots set in a sheltered location, or where the plants are to grow anytime from spring until two months before the first fall frost. When sowing, just press the seeds into the soil surface, as light is required for germination. Perennial salvias are easy to grow from cuttings taken from spring through early fall; use cuttings to propagate plants for the garden or for overwintering. Set plants in a sunny, cool (60°F) spot during the winter, and keep them on the dry side. Use salvias in bedding displays, mixed plantings, and containers. Some species are suitable for herb gardens. Their flowers attract hummingbirds as well as butterflies and are attractive cut flowers. *S. farinacea, S. leucantha,* and *S. viridis* make fine dried flowers.

S. argentea P. 169

s. are-JEN-tee-ah. Silver Sage, Silver Salvia. A biennial or short-lived perennial, hardy in Zones 5 to 8, grown for its rosette of large, rounded, 8-inch-long, gray-green leaves covered with silvery hairs. Bears white to pinkish flowers on 2- to 3-foot-tall spikes in summer. Plants do not tolerate wet soil in winter. Warm-weather annual or biennial.

S. buchananii

s. bue-kah-NAN-ee-eye. A tender, 2-foot-tall perennial, hardy from Zone 9 south, with a somewhat sprawling habit. Bears loose racemes of 2-inch-long, magenta-red flowers from summer to fall. Tender perennial or warm-weather annual.

S. coccinea P. 170

s. cock-SIN-ee-ah. A bushy, 1½- to 3-foot-tall annual with spikes of ¾-inch-long flowers that have flaring lower lips. Flowers are borne from summer to fall and come in pink, red, or white. 'Coral Nymph', also sold as 'Cherry Blossom', bears flowers with a white upper lip and a salmon pink lower one. 'Lady in Red' bears scarlet flowers. Both are compact, 1½-foot-tall selections. Warm-weather annual.

S. elegans

s. EL-eh-ganz. Pineapple Sage. A shrubby tender perennial, hardy from Zone 8 south, ranging from 3 to 6 feet or more in height. Bears softly hairy, pineapple-scented leaves and loose panicles of 1-inch-long scarlet flowers in late summer and fall. 'Scarlet Pineapple' has more strongly scented leaves than the species and larger, 1½-inch-long flowers. Tender perennial or warm-weather annual.

S. farinacea P. 170

s. fair-ih-NAY-cee-ah. Mealy-cup Sage. A bushy, 2-foot-tall tender perennial, hardy from Zone 8 south. Bears dense spikes of ¾-inch-long flowers on purple stems from summer to fall. Flowers come in violet, violet-blue, or white. *S.* 'Indigo Spires', a hybrid of this species and *S. longispicata*, bears spikes of purple, ½-inch-long flowers with blue bracts. The spikes can reach as much as 3 feet in length. Warm-weather annual or tender perennial.

S. greggii P. 171

s. GREG-ee-eye. Gregg Sage, Autumn Sage. A 1- to 2-foot shrub or perennial, hardy from Zone 7 south, with ¾-inch-long flowers in shades of red, purple, violet, pink, or yellow from late summer to frost. Warm-weather annual or tender perennial.

S. guaranitica P. 171

s. gwar-ah-NIH-tih-cah. A shrubby, 5-foot-tall perennial, hardy from Zone 8 south. Bears deep blue, 2-inch-long flowers with purple-blue calyxes from late summer to fall. Tender perennial or warm-weather annual.

S. leucantha P. 172

s. lew-CAN-tha. Mexican Bush Sage. A 2- to 3½-foot-tall subshrub, hardy only from Zone 10 south, with gray-green leaves. Bears dense spikes of white or purple, ½- to ¾-inch-long flowers with showy purple calyxes in fall. Tender perennial or warm-weather annual.

S. patens

s. PAY-tens. Blue Sage, Gentian Sage. A tender, 1½- to 2-foot perennial, hardy from Zone 8 south. Bears loose racemes of 2-inch-long deep blue flowers from midsummer to fall. Tender perennial or warm-weather annual.

S. splendens PP. 172, 173

s. SPLEN-denz. Scarlet Sage. A tender, 1- to 2-foot perennial, hardy from Zone 10 south, popular as an annual bedding plant. Bears dense spikes of ½- to 2-inch-long flowers with showy bracts from summer to fall in scarlet, mauve-purple, creamy white, and pink. Sizzler Series plants reach 16 inches and come in a wide range of colors, including red, salmon, burgundy, pink, lavender, and purple. 'Red Hot Sally' bears scarlet flowers on 10-inch plants. 'Van Houttei' bears rose-red flowers with burgundy calyxes on 4-foot plants. Red-flowered forms are best in full sun, while pastels benefit from partial shade. Warm-weather annual or tender perennial.

S. uliginosa P. 173

s. yew-lih-gih-NO-sah. Bog Sage. A tender, shrubby perennial, hardy from Zone 8 south, from 4 to 6 feet tall and spreading to 3 feet. Bears spikes of ¾-inch-long, sky blue flowers from late summer to fall. Plants thrive in moist, well-drained soil but also do well in wet conditions. Tender perennial or warm-weather annual.

S. viridis

s. VEER-ih-dis. Annual Clary Sage. Formerly *S. horminum.* A bushy, 1½- to 2-foot-tall annual with spikes of insignificant, pink to purplish flowers and showy, 1½-inch-long bracts. The bracts are mauve-pink, purple, or white and have darker veins. Warm-weather annual.

Sanvitalia

san-vih-TAL-ee-ah. Aster family, Asteraceae.

Sanvitalia contains seven species of creeping annuals and perennials with oval leaves and small daisylike flowers, all native to the southwestern United States and Mexico. One species is an easy-to-grow annual with tiny zinnia- or sunflower-like blooms.

HOW TO GROW

Give creeping zinnia *(S. procumbens)* a site with full sun and average to rich, well-drained soil. Plants tolerate dry and sandy soil. Sow seeds outdoors several weeks before the last spring frost date. From Zone 9 south, sow outdoors in fall for bloom the following spring. Or sow indoors in individual pots 6 to 8 weeks before the last spring frost date at 70°F. Germination takes 2 to 3 weeks. Transplant with care. Outdoor sowing is generally best, since plants resent being disturbed. When sowing, just press the seeds into the soil surface, as light aids germination. Use creeping zinnias as edgings, in rock gardens, as ground covers, and in mixed plantings. They are attractive container plants and will trail over the edges of a hanging basket.

S. procumbens P. 174

s. pro-CUM-benz. Creeping Zinnia. A mat-forming annual that reaches 6 to 8 inches in height and can spread 2½ feet. Bears ¾-inch-wide daisylike flowers with black centers and golden ray florets, or "petals," from early summer to fall. Warm-weather annual.

Satureja

sah-tur-EE-jah. Mint family, Lamiaceae.

Commonly known as savories, *Satureja* species are aromatic-leaved annuals, perennials, and subshrubs with spikes of tiny, two-lipped, tubular flowers. The pungent leaves are linear, lance-shaped, or rounded. About 30 species belong to the genus. One, summer savory *(S. hortensis)*, is a fragrant annual herb.

HOW TO GROW

Grow summer savory in full sun and loose, average to rich, well-drained soil. A neutral to slightly alkaline pH is best. Sow seeds outdoors beginning several weeks before the last spring frost date. Continue sowing new crops every 3 to 4 weeks for a continued harvest. Or sow indoors in individual pots 4 weeks before the last frost date at 60° to 70°F. Germination takes 2 to 3 weeks. Harvest fresh leaves anytime during the season. For drying, cut just before flowering occurs, and hang bunches to dry in a warm, dry, dark place. Use summer savory in herb gardens and mixed plantings. Its flowers are attractive to bees.

S. hortensis P. 174

S. hor-TEN-sis. Summer Savory. A 10-inch-tall annual with fragrant, lance-shaped leaves with a peppery, thymelike flavor. Bears small spikes of ¼-inch-long, white or pink flowers in summer. Cool-weather annual.

Scabiosa

scab-ee-OH-sah. Teasel family, Dipsacaceae.

Commonly known as pincushion flowers or scabious, *Scabiosa* species are annuals, biennials, or perennials. As their common name suggests, they bear rounded flower heads that somewhat resemble pincushions. The blooms, which can be single or double, also look somewhat like daisies and other aster-family plants, and actually are constructed in a somewhat similar fashion, with small central florets that form the "pincushion" surrounded by larger petal-like florets. The leaves are either entire, lobed, or deeply cut in a featherlike fashion.

HOW TO GROW

Pincushion flowers thrive in full sun and average, well-drained soil. A neutral to slightly alkaline pH is best. Sow the annuals listed here indoors 4 to 5 weeks before the last spring frost date at 70° to 75°F. Germination takes about 2 weeks. Or sow outdoors after the last frost date. From Zone 8 south, sow outdoors in fall. Stake plants with twiggy brush. Deadhead regularly to encourage new flowers to form. Use pincushion flowers in mixed plantings, cottage gardens, and containers. Both hummingbirds and butterflies visit the blooms. The seed heads of *S. stellata* are attractive in dried arrangements.

S. atropurpurea P. 175

s. ah-tro-pur-PUR-ee-ah. Sweet Scabious, Pincushion Flower. A 2- to 3-foot annual with feathery leaves and fragrant, 2-inch-wide flower heads in shades of purple, lavender, white, pink, or purple-blue. 'Dwarf Double' bears 1½-foot-tall, double-flowered plants. Warm-weather annual.

S. stellata P. 175

s. stel-LAH-tah. Star Flower. A 1½-foot-tall annual with wiry stems and rounded, 1¼-inch-wide, pale bluish white or pink flowers. The flowers are followed by round, 3-inch-wide seed heads consisting of cup-shaped, creamy tan to brown bracts. Warm-weather annual.

Scaevola

skuh-VOL-ah. Goodenia family, Goodeniaceae.

Some 96 species of tender perennials, climbers, shrubs, and small trees belong to this genus of plants that are found from Australia to Polynesia in a wide range of habitats, including coastal dunes and beaches and damp, subalpine mountains in the tropics. They bear unusual fan-shaped flowers with five fingerlike lobes, or "petals"; the botanical name *Scaevola* is from the Latin *scaeva,* meaning "left-handed," and is a reference to their one-sided, handlike shape. Flowers are carried either singly or in small clusters.

HOW TO GROW

Give fan flower *(S. aemula)* full sun or dappled shade and average, evenly moist soil that is well drained. In Zones 10 and 11, it can be grown outdoors as a perennial; in the North, grow it as a bedding plant replaced annually or as a tender perennial. They are easy to grow from cuttings taken in summer, which can be used to overwinter the plants. Sow seeds indoors 6 to 8 weeks before the last spring frost date. To overwinter, take cuttings or pot up plants; keep them barely moist over winter. Use fairy fan flower in mixed plantings and in containers.

S. aemula P. 176

s. eye-MULE-ah. Fan Flower, Australian Blue Fan Flower, Fairy Fan Flower. A sprawling, ½- to 2-foot-tall perennial that can spread from 4 to 5 feet. Bears spoon-shaped leaves on succulent stems and racemes of 1-inch-wide, purple-blue flowers in summer. 'Blue Wonder' bears an abundance of ½-inch-wide, lilac-blue flowers. Tender perennial or warm-weather annual.

Schizanthus

skih-ZAN-thus. Nightshade family, Solanaceae.

Schizanthus species are annuals and biennials with deeply cut, fernlike leaves and clusters of tubular, two-lipped flowers. From 12 to 15 species belong here, all of which are native to Chile. Their showy flowers have been compared to various butterflies and orchids—thus the common names butterfly flowers or poor-man's orchids—despite the fact that they are more closely related to petunias (*Petunia* spp.) and flowering tobaccos (*Nicotiana* spp.).

HOW TO GROW

Select a site in full sun with rich, evenly moist, well-drained soil. They grow well only in areas with cool summers, where night temperatures consistently drop below 65°F. Sow seeds indoors 8 to 10 weeks before the last spring frost date at 60° to 65°F. Germination takes from 1 to 3 weeks. From Zone 9 south, sow seeds outdoors in spring, several weeks before the last frost date. When sowing, barely cover the seeds with soil, as darkness is required for germination. Pinch seedlings to encourage branching and bushy growth. Stake with twiggy brush. Water regularly. Use butterfly flowers in mixed plantings as well as containers.

S. pinnatus **P. 176**

s. pin-AY-tus. Butterfly Flower, Poor-man's Orchid. A ½- to 1½-foot-tall annual with fernlike leaves and clusters of tubular, 3- to 4-inch-wide flowers with flaring lips in shades of pink, purple, red, yellow, or white. The blooms often have throats marked in contrasting colors. Cool-weather annual.

Senecio

seh-NEE-cee-oh. Aster family, Asteraceae.

Senecio is a large, diverse genus of over 1,000 species of annuals, biennials, perennials, climbers, shrubs, and small trees found all around the world. The genus contains species grown as bedding plants, tender perennials, and houseplants, as well as weeds, all of which bear daisylike flowers. The flowers are usually carried in clusters, but sometimes are borne singly, and consist of densely packed centers, or eyes, of disk florets that produce seeds. In most, but not all, species, the eyes are surrounded by ray florets, or "petals." Foliage is especially diverse, and leaf shapes include rounded, triangular, and deeply cut or fernlike. Foliage also can be fleshy or succulent, and several species bear hairy to woolly white leaves.

HOW TO GROW

The *Senecio* species listed here grow in full sun to very light shade and average to rich, well-drained soil. Sow seeds indoors 6 to 8 weeks before the last spring frost date at 65° to 70°F. Damping off is a common problem, so sow in a sterile seed-starting mix and water from below, keeping the medium barely moist, never dry or wet. Or sow outdoors several weeks before the last frost date. From Zone 9 south, sow seeds outdoors in fall. When sowing, just press the seeds into the soil surface, as light is required for germination. To overwinter perennial species, consider taking cuttings in mid- to late summer. Keep them on the dry side over winter, and grow them in a bright, cool (minimum 45° to 50°F) spot. Use these plants in mixed plantings or in containers. Dusty miller *(S. cineraria)* is a good edging plant and also adds texture to other plant combinations. Give vining types a trellis to climb, or let them cascade out a hanging basket.

S. cineraria P. 177

s. sin-eh-RARE-ee-ah. Dusty Miller. Formerly *S. maritima.* A tender, 1- to 2-foot-tall shrub, hardy from Zone 8 south, grown for its deeply cut, woolly white leaves. Plants bear clusters of 1-inch-wide, mustard yellow flower heads, which many gardeners remove. 'Silver Dust' is a 12-inch-tall cultivar with very lacy white leaves; 'Silver Queen' bears similar foliage on 8-inch-plants. Cool-weather annual or tender perennial.

S. confusus P. 177

s. con-FEW-sus. Orange Glow Vine. Formerly *Pseudogynoxys chenopodioides.* This tender climber, hardy from Zone 10 south, can reach 20 feet in frost-free climates. It bears thick, toothed, lance-shaped leaves and in summer produces clusters of fragrant, 2-inch-wide, orange flower heads that fade to red. Tender perennial.

S. elegans

s. EL-eh-ganz. Purple Senecio, Purple Ragwort. A 2-foot-tall annual with lobed or toothed leaves and 1-inch-wide flower heads with yellow eyes and petals that are purple, red-purple, or sometimes white. Cool-weather annual.

Setaria

seh-TAIR-ee-ah. Grass family, Poaceae.

About 100 species of annual and perennial grasses belong to the genus *Setaria.* They bear leaves that range from linear or narrow and lance-shaped to ovate. Narrow, arching flower heads with prominent bristles are carried above the foliage in summer. The botanical name is derived from the Latin *seta,* "bristle."

HOW TO GROW

Give these grasses full sun to partial shade and average to rich, well-drained soil. Sow seeds outdoors after the last spring frost date. When sowing, just press the seeds into the soil surface, as light is required for germination. Use foxtail millet *(S. italica)* in informal plantings or meadow gardens. The seed heads are attractive to birds and can be added to dried arrangements.

S. italica

P. 178

s. ih-TAL-ih-kah. Foxtail Millet. A 3- to 5-foot annual with linear leaves and brownish to purplish, cylindrical flower heads that reach 1 foot or more in length. Warm-weather annual.

Setcreasea purpurea *see Tradescantia pallida*

Silene

sy-LEE-nee. Pink family, Caryophyllaceae.

Commonly known as campions or catchflies, *Silene* species are annuals, biennials, or perennials found mostly in the Northern Hemisphere, especially in the Mediterranean. They bear flowers with five notched or cleft petals in shades of pink, white, and red. The flowers are carried singly or in clusters, and in many species have an inflated calyx at the base of the corolla (petals). Leaves are opposite and linear to rounded. *Silene* species are quite similar to *Lychnis* species, which are also commonly called campions and catchflies.

HOW TO GROW

Select a site in full sun or partial shade with average, well-drained soil. Neutral to slightly alkaline pH is best; plants tolerate dry soil as well. Sow seeds outdoors in spring several weeks before the last spring frost date or in fall. Or sow indoors in pots 8 to 10 weeks before the last spring frost at 60° to 70°F. Barely cover the seeds with soil. Germination takes 1 to 3 weeks. Use these plants in mixed beds and borders as well as cottage-style gardens. They attract hummingbirds and also make charming cut flowers. Plants self-sow.

S. armeria

P. 178

s. are-MEER-ree-ah. Sweet William Catchfly. This gray-green–leaved annual is 1 foot tall and bears showy, rounded clusters of deep magenta-pink, ½-inch-wide flowers in late summer. Cool-weather annual.

S. coeli-rosa **P. 179**

s. KOE-lee ROE-sah. Rose of Heaven. Formerly *Agrostemma coeli-rosa* and *Lychnis coeli-rosa.* A 10- to 20-inch-tall annual with gray-green leaves and loose clusters of 1-inch-wide, rose-pink flowers with white centers and deeply notched petals. Cool-weather annual.

Silybum

sih-LIH-bum. Aster family, Asteraceae.

Spiny leaves and thistlelike flower heads characterize the two species that belong to this genus. *Silybum* species are annuals or biennials with a rosette of glossy, prickly leaves topped by rounded, spiny, purple-pink flower heads. One species is grown in gardens for its ornamental leaves.

HOW TO GROW

Give *Silybum* full sun and poor to average, well-drained soil. Neutral to slightly alkaline pH is best, and plants prefer cool weather. Sow seeds indoors 6 to 8 weeks before the last spring frost date at 55° to 60°F. Germination takes 2 to 3 weeks. Plants started early bloom the first year. Or sow outdoors in spring after the last frost date or in early summer. If you want plants to overwinter, be sure drainage is perfect, as they resent wet soil in winter. Some gardeners remove flowers as they appear to show off the foliage to best effect. Plants self-sow and can become weedy; deadheading helps control them. Use these plants to add interesting foliage texture and color to mixed plantings.

S. marianum **P. 179**

s. mare-ee-AY-num. Mary's Thistle, Our Lady's Thistle, Holy Thistle, Milk Thistle. A biennial with a low rosette of spiny, dark green leaves attractively veined and mottled with white. In summer, it bears 2-inch-wide, purple-pink flower heads on stems that can range from 2 to 5 feet tall. Cool-weather annual.

Solanum

so-LAH-num. Nightshade family, Solanaceae.

Both vegetable and ornamental gardeners have reason to grow members of this genus, which contains some 1,400 species of annuals, biennials, perennials, shrubs, trees, and climbers. Along with a number of species grown as ornamentals, *Solanum* contains two well-known vegetable crops—eggplant and potato. Plants in the genus bear entire, lobed, or pinnate leaves and clusters of small, five-lobed flowers that can be bell-, trumpet-, or star-shaped and come in shades of lavender-blue, purple, lilac, or white. The flowers are followed by fruit (berries) that are sometimes ornamental. Keep in mind that all parts of these nightshade-family plants can be poisonous if ingested; the vegetable members of the genus are happy exceptions.

HOW TO GROW

Select a site in full sun with average to rich, well-drained soil that remains evenly moist. Neutral to slightly alkaline pH is ideal. Climbers require a trellis or can be trained over shrubs. Sow seeds indoors 6 to 10 weeks before the last spring frost date at 65° to 70°F. Germination takes 1 to 2 weeks. Transplant after the last frost date, once the soil has warmed to 60°F and the weather has settled. Stake plants, and tie climbers to supports as they grow. Water regularly and feed monthly during the growing season. To overwinter perennial species, consider taking cuttings in mid- to late summer. Keep them on the dry side over winter, and grow them in a bright, cool (50°F) spot.

S. aviculare

S. ah-vih-cue-LAH-ree. Kangaroo Apple. A tender shrub, hardy from Zone 10 south, that can reach 6 to 11 feet in frost-free areas. Bears small clusters of 1½-inch-wide, bluish purple or white flowers in spring and summer. Flowers are followed by ½-inch-long, oval fruit that turns from green to yellow. Tender perennial or warm-weather annual.

S. jasminoides

P. 180

S. jazz-mih-NOY-deez. Potato Vine. A scrambling climber, hardy from Zone 8 south, that can reach 20 feet in warm climates. Bears small clusters of fragrant, 1-inch-wide, bluish white flowers from summer to fall followed by small black berries. 'Album' bears white flowers. 'Aurea' bears leaves variegated with green and yellow. Tender perennial or warm-weather annual.

Solenopsis

so-leh-NOP-sis. Bellflower family, Campanulaceae.

Solenopsis contains some 25 species of annuals and perennials native to Central and South America as well as Australia. They bear lobed to deeply cut, fernlike leaves and salverform flowers, which have a slender tube with a flattened "face" consisting of five narrow lobes, or "petals," arranged in a star-shaped pattern.

HOW TO GROW

Select a site in full sun with average, well-drained soil. Grow *Solenopsis* species as bedding plants replaced annually or as tender perennials overwintered indoors. In frost-free areas, they can be grown outdoors year-round. Sow seeds indoors 8 to 10 weeks before the last spring frost date at 65° to 75°F. Transplant a few weeks after the last frost date, once the weather has settled and temperatures remain above 40°F. Perennials also can be propagated from cuttings taken in summer, which can be used to overwinter the plants. Or keep them in containers year-round. To overwinter, set plants in a bright, cool (50°F) spot, and keep them on the dry side while they are dormant. Use *Solenopsis* species in mixed plantings or in containers.

S. axillaris P. 180

s. ax-il-LAIR-iss. Formerly *Laurentia axillaris* and *Isotoma axillaris*. A 1-foot-tall tender perennial, hardy only from Zone 10 south, with lacy, fernlike leaves. Bears an abundance of starry, 1½-inch-wide flowers in pale to deep lavender-blue from early summer to fall. Tender perennial or warm-weather annual.

Solenostemon

so-leh-NAH-stem-on. Mint family, Lamiaceae.

The plants in this genus of 60 species of tender, subshrubby perennials are far better known by their former botanical name *Coleus,* which no doubt will continue to serve as the common name for both gardeners and nongardeners alike. Native to tropical Africa and Asia, they bear opposite, rounded, generally toothed leaves on square stems. Spikes of tiny, two-lipped, tubular flowers appear in summer. The cultivars of one species are grown for their wonderfully varied, colorful leaves.

HOW TO GROW

Give coleus a site in partial shade to full sun with rich, well-drained soil that is evenly moist. A site protected from wind is best, and in areas with hot summers the plants benefit from shade during the hottest part of the day. Coleus can be grown as perennials only in Zones 10 and 11. In the North, grow them as bedding plants replaced annually or as tender perennials. Sow seeds indoors 10 to 12 weeks before the last spring frost date at 65° to 70°F. Germination takes about 2 to 3 weeks. In areas with very long summers—Zone 9 south—seeds can be sown outdoors after the last frost date. When sowing, just press the seeds into the soil surface, as light is required for germination. Coleus are extremely easy to propagate from cuttings, which will root in water or any conventional medium for cuttings, such as a 50-50 mix of peat and perlite. Since young plants are most vigorous—the older ones become woody—consider growing new ones from cuttings taken annually or every other year. Also, many of the best cultivars can be grown only from cuttings. Take cuttings in late summer for overwintering, or from overwintered plants in winter or early spring, to grow plants for the garden. Wait to transplant plants until after the last frost date once temperatures remain above about 50°F. Pinch plants to encourage branching. Water container-grown plants regularly, and feed at least monthly. Remove flowers when they appear. To overwinter, take cuttings or bring container-grown plants indoors in fall and keep them in a bright, warm (60° to 65°F) place. Water regularly, and watch for signs of pests such as aphids. Use coleus to add foliage color to mixed plantings, in containers, or as specimen plants.

S. scutellarioides P. 181

S. skew-tel-air-ee-OY-deez. Coleus, Flame Nettle, Painted Nettle. Formerly *Coleus blumeii* var. *verschaffeltii.* A bushy, 1- to 3-foot-tall tender perennial with leaves that are usually toothed and sometimes heart-shaped at the base. Cultivars come with leaves in a mix of colors and patterns, usually with two or more colors as edgings, irregular splotches, or veining. Colors include green, cream, chartreuse, maroon, purple-black, red, orange, and pink. Bears 6-inch-tall spikes of ½-inch-long, pale purple-blue or white flowers, which are usually removed. Many cultivars are available. 'Wizard Mix' is a dwarf (to 10 inches), seed-grown strain that comes in a full range of colors. 'Rainbow Blend', also in a range of colors, reaches 1½ feet. The selection of cultivars that are cutting-propagated—some named, others unnamed—is seemingly endless. 'The Line' has chartreuse leaves with a maroon stripe down the center; 'India Frills' bears small, deeply lobed leaves marked with rose-purple, green, and yellow on compact, 8- to 10-inch plants. Tender perennial or warm-weather annual.

Strobilanthes

stro-bih-LAN-theez. Acanthus family, Acanthaceae.

Strobilanthes contains some 250 species of tender perennials and shrubs from Madagascar and Asia, most of which grow naturally on woodland edges. They bear clusters of tubular to funnel-shaped, two-lipped flowers and lance-shaped to rounded leaves. While some are grown for their flowers, the most popular species is primarily valued for its silver-and-purple-patterned foliage.

HOW TO GROW

Give Persian shield *(S. dyeranus)* a site in partial shade to full sun with rich, well-drained soil that remains evenly moist. Rich soil and even moisture yield lush growth and thus the best foliage display. This species thrives in heat and humidity but benefits from a spot with some shade during the hottest part of the day, especially in areas with hot summers. North of Zone 10, grow Persian shield as bedding plants replaced annually or as tender perennials. Plants usually are grown from cuttings. Since young plants have the best foliage—the older ones become woody-stemmed—consider growing new ones from cuttings taken annually or every other year in spring or early summer. Try taking cuttings in mid- to late summer for overwintering; bottom heat will speed rooting. Pinch to encourage branching. Water container-grown specimens regularly and feed at least monthly. To overwinter, bring plants indoors in fall and keep them in a bright, warm (minimum 60° to 65°F) place. Prune overwintered plants in early spring, as necessary to shape them. Use Persian shield to add foliage color to mixed plantings or in containers.

S. dyeranus P. 182

s. dy-er-AY-nus. Persian Shield. A tender shrub that can reach 4 feet in frost-free climates but is usually smaller when grown in the North. Bears toothed, 6-inch-long, dark green leaves marked with purple and overlaid with a silvery sheen. Bears small spikes of 1¼-inch-long, pale lilac-blue flowers in fall. Tender perennial.

Sutera cordata see *Bacopa* sp.

Tagetes

TAH-jeh-teez. Aster family, Asteraceae.

Tagetes species, better known as marigolds, are a familiar sight in summer gardens everywhere. Approximately 50 species of annuals and perennials belong to this genus, most with aromatic foliage deeply cut in a feather-like fashion. With the exception of one species, which is native to Africa, all are native from New Mexico through Central and South America. Like other aster-family plants, marigolds bear flower heads with disk florets and larger, petal-like ray florets. Flowers can be single, semidouble, or double and are borne either singly or in clusters. Colors include yellow, orange, mahogany, rust, maroon, and creamy yellowish white.

HOW TO GROW

Give easy-to-grow marigolds a spot in full sun with average, well-drained soil. In areas with hot summers, a site with afternoon shade is best. Plants tolerate drought but bloom best with regular watering. Too-rich soil yields plants with plenty of foliage but few flowers; it also makes the plants more prone to disease. Too much water causes similar problems. Sow seeds indoors 6 to 8 weeks before the last spring frost date at 70° to 75°F. Germination takes 1 to 2 weeks. Or sow seeds outdoors around the last spring frost date. Plants grown from indoor sowings bloom earlier in the season, and indoor sowing is best with African-type marigolds, which are slow to bloom from seeds. Pinch plants to promote branching and bushy growth. Deadhead regularly to encourage new buds to form. Some marigolds, especially French types, stop blooming during very hot weather; keep them watered, and they will resume blooming when cooler fall weather arrives. African marigolds may rot in wet, humid weather. Use marigolds in mixed plantings, as edgings, in containers, and as cut flowers. Signet marigolds also are attractive for summer color in herb and rock gardens. Both butterflies and hummingbirds will visit marigold flowers.

T. erecta P. 182

t. eh-REC-tah. African Marigold, American Marigold. A Central American, not African, species with pinnate leaves on 1½- to 3-foot-tall plants. Bears showy, carnation-like, double flowers that are 4 to 5 inches across in shades of yellow, gold, and orange. Compact cultivars stay under 1½ feet tall and include Gold Coin Series, Inca Series, and Lady Series. Warm-weather annual.

T. patula P. 183

t. PAH-tyew-lah. French Marigold. A compact, 6- to 12-inch-tall, well-branched species with pinnate leaves and usually double flowers, although cultivars with single, semidouble, and crested flowers are available. French types include Hero Series, Bonanza Series, and Janie Series. Warm-weather annual.

Triploid Marigolds

These are vigorous hybrid plants developed by crossing African and French marigolds. They have more dwarf, French-type habits (to about 1 foot in height) and single or double flowers that range from 2 to 3 inches across. They don't set seeds and thus continue blooming even in hot weather or other stressful conditions. Zenith Series and Nugget Series are triploid selections. Warm-weather annual.

T. tenuifolia P. 183

t. ten-you-ih-FOE-lee-ah. Signet Marigold. Bushy, mound-forming, 9- to 12-inch plants with lacy, finely divided leaves. Bears an abundance of dainty, single, ¾-inch-wide flowers. Gem Series cultivars, in gold, lemon yellow, or orange, are most common. Warm-weather annual.

Thunbergia

thun-BER-gee-ah. Acanthus family, Acanthaceae.

Many of the 100 species of annuals and perennials that belong to *Thunbergia* are twining climbers, although a few shrubs are classified here as well. Native to tropical and southern Africa, as well as Madagascar, they bear ovate to nearly round leaves and tubular flowers that are trumpet-shaped or salverform, meaning they have a tubular base with a flattened "face" consisting of five spreading lobes, or "petals."

HOW TO GROW

Select a site in full sun with rich, evenly moist, well-drained soil. In hot climates, a spot that receives partial shade in the afternoon is best. Sow seeds indoors 6 to 8 weeks before the last spring frost date at 60° to 70°F.

Germination takes 2 to 3 weeks. Water regularly throughout the growing season; container-grown plants may need daily watering in hot weather. Commonly grown *Thunbergia* species are perennials and can be propagated by cuttings taken from spring to midsummer, as well as by layering. Use cuttings or layers to propagate plants for the garden or for overwintering. Although black-eyed Susan vine *(T. alata)*, the most popular species, is usually treated as an annual, it can be overwintered, and second-year plants are more vigorous than first-year ones. Overwinter in a sunny, warm (60° to 70°F) spot. Prune as necessary in early spring before new growth begins. Use these vines to cover trellises or other supports. Black-eyed Susan vine is especially effective trailing over the sides of a hanging basket or other container.

T. alata

P. 184

t. ah-LAH-tah. Black-eyed Susan Vine. A tender perennial, hardy only in frost-free climates, that can reach 8 feet in frost-free regions. Bears arrowhead-shaped to triangular leaves and solitary, salverform, 1¼- to 1½-inch-wide flowers from summer to fall. Flowers are orange, orange-yellow, yellow, or creamy white with dark black to brownish black centers. Tender perennial or warm-weather annual.

Thymophylla

tye-mo-FILL-ah. Aster family, Asteraceae.

Daisylike flowers and strongly aromatic foliage characterize the 10 to 12 species of annuals, biennials, perennials, and subshrubs that belong to this genus. Native from prairies and dry slopes in the United States through Central America, they have very finely cut, feathery leaves and produce an abundance of small, yellow to yellow-orange flower heads from spring to summer.

HOW TO GROW

Select a site in full sun with average, well-drained soil that is not too rich. *Thymophylla* species thrive in heat and tolerate dry soil. Sow seeds outdoors a few weeks before the last spring frost date. For earlier flowers, sow indoors 6 to 8 weeks before the last frost date at 50° to 55°F. Use them as edgings, in mixed plantings, in rock gardens, and in containers. Plants self-sow.

T. tenuiloba P. 184

t. ten-yew-ih-LOW-bah. Dahlberg Daisy, Golden Fleece. Formerly *Dyssodia tenuiloba.* A well-branched, mounding, ½- to 1-foot-tall annual or short-lived perennial with fragrant leaves cut into threadlike segments. Bears starry, ½-inch-wide, yellow, daisylike flowers from spring to summer. Cool-weather annual.

Tibouchina

tih-boo-CHEE-nah. Melastoma family, Melastomataceae.

Tibouchina contains about 350 species of perennials, subshrubs, shrubs, and climbers native to the rain forests of South and Central America. They are commonly called glory bushes, and the botanical name is based on a native South American name for these tropical plants. Although many are quite showy, few are cultivated. They bear ovate to lance-shaped leaves and five-petaled, cup- to saucer-shaped flowers from summer to fall.

HOW TO GROW

Select a site in full sun or dappled shade with rich, evenly moist soil. Plants usually are propagated by cuttings taken in spring or summer but also can be grown from seeds sown about 8 to 10 weeks before the last spring frost date at 65° to 70°F. From Zone 10 south, grow *Tibouchina* outdoors as shrubs; where marginally hardy, try them in a protected, south-facing site and mulch over winter. In the North, grow them in containers either set on terraces or sunk to the rim in the soil over the summer. They also can be treated as bedding plants replaced annually, but plants treated as tender perennials will be showier and make outstanding specimens. They also can be trained as standards. Water regularly during the summer months, and feed pot-grown plants monthly. Overwinter them indoors in a bright, somewhat cool (50° to 60°F) spot, and keep them on the dry side over winter. Prune to shape plants in late winter or early spring.

T. urvilleana P. 185

t. ur-vill-ee-AH-nah. Glory Bush, Brazilian Spider Flower. Sometimes listed as *Pleroma macrantha* and *T. semidecandra.* A tender shrub that can range from 10 to 20 feet in frost-free regions. Bears dark green, 2- to 3-inch-long leaves covered with velvety hairs and satiny-textured, 2-inch-wide, violet-purple flowers. Tender perennial or warm-weather annual.

Tithonia

tih-THOW-nee-ah. Aster family, Asteraceae.

Commonly called Mexican sunflowers, *Tithonia* species are native from Mexico through Central America. About 10 species belong to this genus, most of which are annuals, although some are perennials or shrubs. One is a popular annual. Mexican sunflowers, or tithonias, as they also are called, bear entire or lobed leaves and daisylike flower heads in shades of yellow, orange, or red from late summer to fall.

HOW TO GROW

Give Mexican sunflower *(T. rotundifolia)* full sun and poor to average, well-drained soil. Plants thrive in heat. Too-rich soil yields abundant foliage but few flowers. Sow seeds indoors 6 to 8 weeks before the last spring frost date at 60° to 70°F. Germination takes 1 to 2 weeks. Or sow seeds outdoors after the last frost date. Stake plants to keep them erect during windy weather. Deadhead regularly to encourage new flowers to form. Water during dry weather. Use these plants at the back of perennial borders or mixed plantings. Butterflies and hummingbirds are attracted to these plants, which also make excellent, long-lasting cut flowers.

T. rotundifolia

P. 185

t. roe-tun-dih-FOE-lee-ah. Mexican Sunflower. A vigorous, somewhat coarse, 3- to 6-foot-tall annual bearing 3-inch-wide daisies in shades of orange or orange-red from late summer to frost. 'Torch' bears 4-inch-wide orange-red flowers. 'Goldfinger' bears burnt orange flowers on compact, 30-inch-tall plants. Warm-weather annual.

Torenia

tor-REE-nee-ah. Figwort family, Scrophulariaceae.

Of the 40 to 50 species that belong to the genus *Torenia,* two are commonly grown in gardens. All *Torenia* species bear clusters of tubular flowers that somewhat resemble monkey flowers (*Mimulus* spp.). They have two flaring, lobed lips and are marked with combinations of violet, purple, pink, white, and yellow. Leaves are ovate to lance-shaped.

HOW TO GROW

Select a site with partial shade and rich, well-drained, evenly moist soil. Plants that receive shade in the afternoon tend to have brighter flowers.

Sow seeds indoors 6 to 8 weeks before the last spring frost date and germinate at 65° to 70°F. Germination takes 1 to 4 weeks. Grow seedlings at about 55°F to keep them compact. Or sow outdoors a week before the last frost date. When sowing, just press the seeds into the soil surface, as light aids germination. Transplant seedlings about 2 weeks after the frost date, once the weather is settled. Pinch plants when they are 2 to 3 inches tall to encourage branching and bushy growth. Use *Torenia* species in shady gardens as well as containers. Hummingbirds will visit the flowers.

T. fournieri P. 186

t. FOUR-nee-AIR-ee. Wishbone Flower. An erect, 1-foot-tall annual with 1½-inch-long purple flowers with deep violet lobes and a yellow blotch on the throat. 'Clown Mix' bears lavender and white, violet and purple, and pink and white flowers, all with yellow throats, on 8-inch-tall plants. Warm-weather annual.

T. flava

t. FLAY-vah. Yellow Wishbone Flower. Also listed as *T. baillonii.* An 8- to 12-inch-tall annual with ¾- to 1-inch-long, golden yellow flowers that have dark purple-red throats. 'Suzie Wong' bears 1-inch-long flowers on 8-inch plants. Warm-weather annual.

Trachelium

tray-KEL-lee-um. Bellflower family, Campanulaceae.

Trachelium contains seven species, all tender perennials, that are native to the Mediterranean. They bear tubular flowers with five spreading "petals," more properly called lobes, and leaves that range from lance-shaped to nearly round. They are commonly called throatworts, and the botanical name is from the Greek *trachelos,* "neck." Both names are references to the plants' supposed virtues for treating diseases of the trachea.

HOW TO GROW

Give blue throatwort *(T. caeruleum)* full sun to partial shade and average, very well drained soil that remains evenly moist. A spot that receives shade during the hottest part of the day is best. This species can be grown as an annual or a biennial. To grow it as an annual, sow seeds indoors 8 to 10 weeks before the last spring frost date at 55° to 60°F. Germination takes 2 to 3 weeks. To grow it as a biennial, sow seeds in midsummer into pots, then overwinter the plants in a bright, cool (45°F) spot. Transplant to the garden after the last frost the following spring. Water regularly in dry weather. These plants also can be propagated by cuttings taken in early summer. Use throatworts in mixed plantings. They also make attractive cut flowers.

T. caeruleum P. 186

t. see-RUE-lee-um. Blue Throatwort. An erect, 3- to 4-foot tender perennial, hardy from Zone 9 south. Bears dense, flattened clusters of starry, ¼-inch-wide, violet-blue, white, or lavender-mauve flowers that have a slight fragrance. Warm-weather annual or biennial.

Trachymene

tray-KEH-men-ee. Carrot family, Apiaceae.

Native to Australia and the islands of the western Pacific, *Trachymene* species are annuals, biennials, and perennials with three-part leaves that usually have narrow leaflets and dainty umbels of tiny, star-shaped flowers. About 12 species belong to the genus, one of which is grown for its lacy flowers.

HOW TO GROW

Give blue lace flower *(T. coerulea)* full sun and average, well-drained soil. The plants tolerate dry soil but grow best in evenly moist, not wet, conditions. A site sheltered from wind is best. Sow seeds indoors in individual pots 8 to 10 weeks before the last frost date at 60° to 70°F. Germination takes 2 to 4 weeks. Transplant with care. Or sow outdoors after the last frost date. When sowing, barely cover the seeds with soil, as darkness is required for germination. Pinch seedlings when they are several inches tall to encourage branching. Stake with twiggy brush. Use blue lace flower in beds and borders. It is an excellent cut flower.

T. coerulea P. 187

t. see-RUE-lee-ah. Blue Lace Flower. Formerly *Didiscus coeruleus.* A 2-foot-tall annual or biennial with lacy, 2-inch-wide umbels of lightly fragrant, lavender-blue flowers in summer. Warm-weather annual.

Tradescantia

tray-des-CAN-tee-ah. Spiderwort family, Commelinaceae.

Tradescantia contains some 65 species of perennials, both hardy and tender, that are native to the Americas. The genus contains well-known, clump-forming hardy perennials such as spiderworts (*T.* Andersoniana

Group) as well as trailing tender species grown for their colorful foliage both as houseplants and as tender perennials. The plants bear fleshy leaves that are lance-shaped, linear, or ovate and three-petaled flowers that usually are borne in clusters that arise from boat-shaped bracts.

HOW TO GROW

Give the tender perennial species covered here a spot in partial shade to full sun with rich, moist soil. They are most often grown from cuttings, which can be taken anytime and will root in water or any mix designed for rooting cuttings. Move cutting-grown plants to the garden a few weeks after the last frost date, once the weather has settled and temperatures stay above 50°F. Pinch plants regularly to encourage bushy growth. To overwinter the plants, take cuttings in fall and grow them in a bright, cool (50° to 60°F) spot. You can also grow them as houseplants in warmer spots. Use these plants to add summer-long foliage interest to mixed plantings as well as in containers.

T. fluminensis

t. flu-mih-NEN-sis. Wandering Jew. A trailing, 6-inch-tall tender perennial, hardy in Zones 10 and 11, with ovate, 1- to 4-inch-long leaves that are green on top and flushed with purple on the bottom. Flowers are white and relatively insignificant. Variegated cultivars are most popular: 'Albovittata' bears green leaves striped with white; 'Variegata' has green leaves striped with cream, purple, and/or white. Tender perennial.

T. pallida 'Purpurea'

P. 187

t. PAL-lih-dah. Purple Heart. Also listed as *Setcreasea purpurea* and *T. pallida* 'Purple Heart'. A trailing, 8-inch-tall tender perennial, hardy in Zones 10 and 11, with narrow, V-shaped, 4- to 6-inch-long leaves. Both stems and leaves are rich, deep violet-purple. Bears clusters of small pink flowers in summer. Tender perennial.

Tripteris *see Osteospermum*

Tropaeolum

tro-pee-OH-lum. Nasturtium family, Tropaeolaceae.

The genus *Tropaeolum* contains from 80 to 90 species of annuals and perennials native from Mexico to Chile. The plants can be bushy, trailing,

Tropaeolum majus

or climbing, and many have tuberous roots, which can be lifted for overwintering. Commonly called nasturtiums, they are grown for their showy, spurred, five-petaled flowers, usually in shades of red, scarlet, orange, yellow, or cream. The leaves are rounded or lobed and peltate, meaning the stem is attached near the center of the leaf, rather than on the edge. In a confusing twist of nomenclature, nasturtium is the botanical name for watercress, *Nasturtium officinale.* Like watercress, *Tropaeolum* species bear edible leaves that have a peppery taste. The flowers are edible and also attract hummingbirds.

HOW TO GROW

While all *Tropaeolum* species grow in full sun, soil preferences vary. Plant common nasturtiums *(T. majus)* in poor, well-drained soil; rich soil yields foliage but few flowers. Give flame nasturtium *(T. speciosum)* well-drained, evenly moist soil that is rich in organic matter; it also will grow in partial shade. Plant the other species in well-drained, evenly moist soil of average fertility. *Tropaeolum* species are best in areas with relatively cool summers and do not grow well in the hot, humid Southeast. Where hardy, grow the perennials outdoors. In the North, treat these plants as annuals or tender perennials. Sow seeds outdoors 1 week after the last spring frost date. Or sow indoors in individual pots 4 to 5 weeks before the last frost date at 55° to 65°F. Transplant with care. Seeds of perennial species often germinate erratically. Plants also can be propagated by cuttings taken in spring or early summer to propagate plants for the garden, or in late summer to overwinter the plants. Double-flowered forms must be propagated by cuttings. Or propagate tuberous-rooted species by dividing the tubers in fall. Overwinter perennials by bringing pot-grown plants indoors and growing them in a sunny, cool (50° to 60°F) spot. Or dig the tubers in fall and store them in a frost-free spot, as you would dahlias. Use common nasturtiums as edgings, to trail over the edge of a raised bed or wall, in mixed plantings or containers, in rock gardens, or as a temporary ground cover on a slope or other site. Train climbing types onto strings, trellises, shrubs, or other supports.

T. azureum

t. ah-ZUR-ee-um. A tender perennial climber, hardy from Zone 9 south, with palmate or palmately lobed leaves. Plants climb to 7 feet and bear short-spurred, pale blue, ½- to ¾-inch flowers in late spring. Warm-weather annual or tender perennial.

T. majus P. 188

t. MAY-jus. Common Nasturtium, Indian Cress. A climbing annual with nearly round, wavy-margined leaves. Bears 2- to 2½-inch-wide, long-spurred flowers from summer to fall in shades of red, orange, or yellow. Both bushy and climbing cultivars are available; many are hybrids with other species and sometimes are listed as *T. nanum.* Whirlybird Series plants are bushy, rather than climbing, 10-inch-tall plants that bear spurless flowers well above the foliage. Alaska Series plants reach 1 foot tall and bear leaves variegated with cream. Gleam Series plants are about 1½ feet tall and trail to 2 feet wide. 'Jewel of Africa' climbs to 8 feet and has leaves variegated with creamy white. 'Tip Top Mahogany' bears chartreuse leaves with mahogany flowers on foot-tall plants. 'Empress of India' bears semidouble scarlet blooms on 1-foot plants. Warm-weather annual.

T. peregrinum P. 189

t. peh-reh-GRY-num. Canary Vine, Canary Creeper. A vigorous annual or tender perennial, hardy from Zone 9 south, that climbs to 12 feet in a single season. Leaves are lobed and grayish green. Bears yellow, 1-inch-wide flowers with fringed petals from summer to fall. Tender perennial or warm-weather annual.

T. polyphyllum P. 189

t. pol-ee-FILL-lum. A trailing annual or tender perennial, hardy from Zone 8 south, with a fleshy, rhizomelike tuber and deeply lobed, blue-green leaves. Plants are 2 to 3 feet tall and spread to 3 feet. Bears spurred, 1½-inch-wide, deep yellow flowers over a long season in summer. Warm-weather annual or tender perennial.

T. speciosum P. 190

t. spee-cee-OH-sum. Flame Flower, Flame Nasturtium. A tender climbing perennial, hardy from Zone 8 south, that climbs to 10 feet and has a fleshy rhizome. Bears palmate, dark green leaves and brilliant scarlet flowers from summer to fall. Warm-weather annual or tender perennial.

Tulbaghia

tul-BAHH-ee-ah. Lily family, Liliaceae.

About 24 species, all native to tropical and southern Africa, belong to the genus *Tulbaghia.* They produce grassy to strap-shaped leaves that have a garlic- or onionlike odor, along with dainty umbels of starry, tubular flowers in lilac-purple or white.

HOW TO GROW

Select a site in full sun and average to rich, well-drained soil. Where hardy, grow *Tulbaghia* species outdoors; in areas where they are marginally hardy, try a site against a south-facing wall for extra winter protection. In the North, grow them in containers either set on terraces or sunk to the rim in the soil. Water regularly in summer and feed pot-grown plants monthly. Gradually withhold water in fall, and keep them nearly dry over winter. Overwinter them in a bright, cool (40° to 50°F) spot, and water sparingly until active growth resumes in spring. Propagate by dividing the clumps or sowing seeds (germinate at 55° to 60°F). Repot or divide in late winter or early spring as necessary.

T. violacea P. 190

t. vee-oh-LAY-cee-ah. Society Garlic, Pink Agapanthus. A clump-forming, 1½- to 2-foot-tall, tender perennial, hardy from Zone 7 south, with linear, gray-green leaves. Bears small umbels of fragrant, ¾-inch-long, lilac flowers from midsummer to fall. 'Variegata' or 'Silver Lace' bears leaves striped in gray-green and cream. Tender perennial.

Tweedia

TWEE-dee-ah. Milkweed family, Asclepiadaceae.

A single species belongs to this genus: *Tweedia caerulea,* which is native to Brazil and Uruguay. The plants are shrubby at the base but bear twining stems higher up on the plant, and are grown for their clusters of sky blue flowers.

HOW TO GROW

Select a site in full sun with average to rich, evenly moist, well-drained soil. Plants tolerate poor, dry soil. Sow seeds 6 to 8 weeks before the last spring frost date at 60° to 70°F. Germination takes 2 to 3 weeks. Pinch seedlings once or twice to encourage branching and bushy growth. Move them to the garden a few weeks after the last frost date, once the weather has settled and temperatures remain above 40°F. Twining stems require a trellis or other support. Water regularly and feed monthly, especially container-grown specimens. Grow *Tweedia* as an annual or a tender perennial overwintered indoors. Take cuttings in spring to propagate plants for the garden or in summer to bring them in for overwintering. To bring container-grown specimens indoors, dry them off gradually in fall and keep them on the dry side over winter. In winter, give plants a bright, cool (55° to 65°F) spot. Prune plants as necessary in early spring.

T. caerulea P. 191

t. see-RUE-lee-ah. Formerly *Oxypetalum caeruleum* and *Amblyopetalum caeruleum*. A 2- to 3½-foot tender subshrub, hardy in Zones 10 and 11, with oblong to lance-shaped leaves that have heart-shaped bases. Bears three- to four-flowered clusters of five-petaled ¾- to 1-inch-wide flowers that are pinkish in bud and open to sky blue. Warm-weather annual or tender perennial.

Ursinia

ur-SIH-nee-ah. Aster family, Asteraceae.

Commonly called African daisies, *Ursinia* species are annuals, perennials, or subshrubs grown for their showy, daisylike flowers. The 40 species in the genus are found growing in dry grasslands, mostly in South Africa, but also Namibia, Botswana, and Ethiopia. The leaves are usually cut or divided in a fernlike fashion and often are aromatic. The flower heads are borne on tall stems above the foliage, usually singly but sometimes in small clusters. They come in shades of yellow, red, or orange. The flowers close at night and also tend to close during overcast weather.

HOW TO GROW

Select a site in full sun with poor to average, light, very well drained soil. Plants are drought-tolerant. They do not grow well in heat and humidity, so in areas with hot summers, start them early enough to bloom before hot weather arrives, then pull them up and replace them when they begin to die out. Sow seeds indoors 6 to 8 weeks before the last spring frost date at 55° to 60°F. Germination takes 2 to 4 weeks. Or sow outdoors after the last frost. Deadhead to prolong the bloom season. Plants need staking, especially in rich soil. The species listed here is an annual, but perennial species are hardy in Zones 10 and 11, where they can be grown outdoors. In the North, start perennials each year from seeds, or overwinter them indoors by digging the plants or taking cuttings in summer. Keep overwintered plants barely moist. Use *Ursinia* species in beds and borders as well as in containers.

U. anthemoides **P. 191**

u. an-them-OY-deez. A 1- to 1½-foot-tall annual with aromatic, deeply cut leaves and 2½-inch-wide daisies in summer. Flowers are yellow-orange with purple centers. Warm-weather annual.

Venidium fastuosum *see Arctotis fastuosa*

Verbascum

ver-BAS-kum. Figwort family, Scrophulariaceae.

Commonly known as mulleins, most *Verbascum* species are grown for their spirelike clusters of blooms. The erect bloom stalks of most species are densely covered with flowers that have a short, tubular base and five spreading lobes or petals. About 360 species belong to this genus, and most are biennials, although the genus also contains some annuals, perennials, and subshrubs. Most species have hairy to woolly leaves borne in a large rosette at the base of the plant. Mulleins are native from Europe to northern Africa and Asia and also are widely naturalized in North America.

HOW TO GROW

Select a site in full sun with poor to average, well-drained soil. Neutral to slightly alkaline pH is ideal. Established plants tolerate dry soil. The species listed here are grown as annuals or biennials. Sow seeds indoors in individual pots 6 to 8 weeks before plants are scheduled to go into the garden, which means midsummer sowing for plants that are to be moved to the garden in early fall; winter sowing to produce seedlings for spring planting. Germination takes 2 to 4 weeks at 55° to 60°F. Transplant with care, as plants have a taproot. Outdoors, sow seeds in spring or summer up to 2 months before the first fall frost. Plants self-sow. Use mulleins in mixed plantings, cottage gardens, and naturalized or informal areas.

V. blattaria

v. blat-TAIR-ee-ah. Moth Mullein. A 3- to 7-foot-tall species, hardy to Zone 6, with hairless, oblong to lance-shaped leaves and loose racemes of 1-inch-wide, yellow or white flowers in summer. Biennial or warm-weather annual.

V. bombyciferum P. 192

v. bom-bih-SIFF-er-um. Turkish Mullein. A 5- to 8-foot-tall species, hardy from Zone 4 south, with woolly white leaves. Bears erect spikes of 1½-inch-wide, saucer-shaped, yellow flowers in summer. 'Arctic Summer' is a 5-foot selection with felted leaves and yellow flowers. Biennial or short-lived perennial.

Verbena

ver-BEE-nah. Vervain or Verbena family, Verbenaceae.

Some 250 species of annuals, perennials, and subshrubs, both hardy and tender, belong to the genus *Verbena*. Most are native to the Americas, although a few species are found in southern Europe. They have square stems and usually opposite leaves that range from toothed to deeply lobed. Their small flowers are salverform, meaning they have a slender tube at the base and an abruptly flared and flattened face, which has five lobes, or "petals." Blooms are carried in showy spikes or clusters over a long season and come in shades of purple, violet, pink, cream, scarlet, and magenta.

Verbena sp.

HOW TO GROW

Select a site in full sun with average, well-drained soil that is evenly moist. A site with dappled shade during the hottest part of the day is best in the South. Grow verbenas as bedding plants replaced annually or as tender perennials. Where marginally hardy, select a sheltered, south-facing site, and protect plants with a dry mulch such as salt hay or weed-free straw over winter. In the North, overwinter plants in a sunny, cool (50° to 55°F) spot. Sow seeds indoors 8 to 10 weeks before the last spring frost date at 65° to 70°F. Germination takes 2 weeks to a month or more, depending on the species. Or sow outdoors after the last frost date. When sowing, barely cover the seeds with soil, as darkness is required for germination. *V. bonariensis* and *V. rigida* benefit from a period of cool, moist stratification before germination: sow the seeds 2 weeks earlier and set the sown pots in the refrigerator for that period before moving them to a warmer spot for sprouting. Pinch seedlings to encourage branching and bushy growth. Wait to transplant until a few weeks after the last frost date, once the weather has settled and temperatures remain above 50°F. Established plants tolerate drought but perform best with regular watering. Deadhead regularly to encourage repeat bloom. Perennials can be propagated by cuttings taken in late summer, which can be used to overwinter the plants. Use verbenas in beds, borders, and containers. Low-growing types make attractive edgings. The flowers attract hummingbirds and butterflies and make handsome cut flowers. Some species self-sow, including *V. bonariensis.*

V. bonariensis P. 192

v. bon-air-ee-EN-sis. Formerly *V. patagonica.* A tender, shrubby perennial hardy from Zone 7 south. It reaches 6 feet in southern areas but is about 3 feet tall in the North. The lance-shaped leaves are borne at the base of the plant and topped by erect, branching stems with 2-inch-wide clusters of ¼-inch-wide purple flowers from midsummer to fall. Tender perennial or warm-weather annual.

V. × hybrida P. 193

v. × HY-brih-dah. Common Garden Verbena. Also listed as *V. × hortensis.* A tender 1½-foot-tall perennial, hardy from Zone 9 south, that can be erect and bushy or mat-forming, depending on the cultivar. Leaves are oblong and toothed. Flowers are borne in rounded, 3-inch-wide clusters from summer to fall. Individual flowers are ½ to 1 inch wide and come in violet, purple-blue, scarlet, rose, wine red, and white, most with a white eye. Some cultivars are fragrant. 'Peaches and Cream' bears pastel apricot and salmon flowers on 9-inch-tall plants. Romance Series and Novalis Series bear flowers in a range of colors on 10-inch-tall plants. Tender perennial or warm-weather annual.

V. rigida **P. 193**

v. RIH-jih-dah. Vervain. Also listed as *V. venosa.* A 1½- to 2-foot-tall tender perennial, hardy from Zone 8 south, with oblong, toothed leaves and loose, 2-inch-wide clusters of fragrant, purple or magenta, ¼-inch-wide flowers. Tender perennial or warm-weather annual.

V. tenuisecta **P. 194**

v. ten-you-ih-SECK-tah. Moss Verbena, Cut-leaf Verbena. A 1½-foot-tall annual or tender perennial, hardy from Zone 8 south, with aromatic, three-lobed leaves and 3-inch-wide clusters of flowers in lavender, mauve, purple, lilac-blue, and white from summer to fall. 'Alba' bears white flowers on 6-inch plants. Warm-weather annual or tender perennial.

Vinca

VINK-ah. Dogbane family, Apocynaceae.

Commonly called periwinkles or simply vincas, the seven species that belong to the genus *Vinca* are hardy or tender subshrubs native from Europe and northern Africa to central Asia. They bear opposite, ovate to lance-shaped leaves and salverform flowers, meaning they have a slender tube at the base and an abruptly flared and flattened face. The flowers have five lobes, or "petals." Variegated forms of one species are popular tender perennials.

HOW TO GROW

Plant vincas in full sun or partial shade; they will grow in any type of soil. Grow greater periwinkle *(V. major)* as a bedding plant replaced annually or as a tender perennial. Where hardy, it can be grown as a ground cover but tends to be quite invasive. *Vinca* species are propagated by cuttings or division (rather than seeds), which can be used to propagate plants for the garden or bring them indoors for overwintering. Take cuttings in summer, divide clumps in spring or fall, or separate and dig up small plants anytime where stems have touched the soil and rooted. Cut plants back hard in spring to shape them and control their spread. Let greater periwinkle spill out of containers and hanging baskets.

V. major

P. 194

v. MAY-jor. Greater Periwinkle. A tender, 1½-foot-tall perennial, hardy to Zone 7, that can spread indefinitely in frost-free areas. Bears purple-blue, 2-inch-wide flowers from spring to fall but is primarily grown as a foliage plant in variegated forms. 'Variegata' bears leaves with creamy white margins and blotches. 'Maculata' bears leaves with yellow-green centers. Tender perennial or warm-weather annual.

V. rosea see *Catharanthus roseus*

Viola

vy-OH-lah. Violet family, Violaceae.

Viola is a large genus of beloved garden plants commonly known as violets, violas, and pansies. Some 500 species of annuals, biennials, perennials (both hardy and tender), and a few subshrubs belong here. They bear spurred flowers that have five petals—one that forms a lower "lip," two that point up, and two more that point sideways. Leaves range from rounded and toothed or lobed to heart-shaped but also can be cut in a featherlike fashion.

HOW TO GROW

Select a planting site in full sun or partial shade with rich, moist, well-drained soil. In areas with hot summers, partial shade is best, especially during the afternoon. Sow seeds indoors 10 to 12 weeks before the last spring frost date, then set the sown pots in the refrigerator for 2 weeks before moving them to a warmer (65° to 70°F) spot for germination, which takes 2 to 3 weeks. When sowing, barely cover seeds with soil, as they need darkness to germinate. Some gardeners cover the flats with black plastic or newspaper to exclude light. Sow Johnny-jump-ups *(V. tricolor)* outdoors in late summer to fall for bloom the following year. In warm climates, Johnny-jump-ups and pansies *(V. × wittrockiana)* can be sown in midsummer and seedlings planted out in early fall for late-winter to early-spring bloom. (This works for Johnny-jump-ups from about Zone 6 south, and for pansies from Zone 7 south.) Cut Johnny-jump-ups back in midsummer when they get scraggly to encourage new flowers when cooler temperatures return in fall. This encourages more compact growth and curtails reseeding. Plants die out by midsummer in areas with hot summers. Deadhead pansies to keep plants blooming. Use violas in mixed plantings; as edging plants, combined with spring bulbs; and in containers.

V. hederacea

v. hed-er-AY-cee-ah. Ivy-leaved Violet, Tasmanian Violet. A tender, 4-inch-tall perennial, hardy from Zone 8 south, that spreads vigorously by stolons to form a mat. Bears rounded leaves with scalloped margins and 1-inch-wide flowers in shades of cream, white, violet, or lilac-purple in late summer. Tender perennial or cool-weather annual.

V. tricolor PP. 195, 196

v. TRI-cuh-lor. Johnny-jump-up, Hearts-ease. A 3- to 5-inch-tall annual, biennial, or short-lived perennial with 1-inch-wide flowers from early spring to fall marked with deep violet, purple, white, or yellow in a facelike pattern. Cool-weather annual, biennial, or short-lived perennial.

V. × wittrockiana P.

v. × wit-rock-ee-AH-nah. Pansy. A 6- to 9-inch-tall perennial with showy, 2½- to 4-inch-wide flowers in a wide variety of patterns and colors including violet, maroon, bronze, yellow, orange, lavender, wine purple, lilac-blue, and white. Traditional types, such as Swiss Giant Series plants, have a dark, velvety, facelike blotch at the center, but solid colors also are available. 'Padparadja' bears orange flowers. Clear Crystal Series and Crystal Bowl Series plants come in a range of solid colors without faces. Cool-weather annual or biennial.

Xeranthemum

zer-AN-the-mum. Aster family, Asteraceae.

Xeranthemum contains six species of annuals grown for their papery, daisylike flowers, which are used in dried bouquets. The botanical name—from the Greek *xeros,* "dry," and *anthos,* "flower"—refers to the texture of the flower heads, which consist of a cluster of small florets surrounded by showy, stiff, petal-like bracts in pink, mauve, lilac, white, and red. Leaves are entire and linear to linear-elliptic, and both leaves and stems are woolly white.

HOW TO GROW

Select a site in full sun with poor to average, well-drained soil. Plants tolerate dry soil, and too-rich soil yields lots of foliage but few flowers. Sow seeds indoors in individual pots 6 to 8 weeks before the last spring frost date at 60° to 70°F. Germination takes 2 to 3 weeks. Or sow outdoors after the last frost date; plants take about 10 weeks to bloom from seeds, so in areas with short growing seasons, it's best to give them a head start indoors. Stake plants with twiggy brush. They are attractive additions to mixed plantings and are also good for fresh or dried arrangements. Harvest the flowers just before they open fully, and use fresh or hang in bunches in a cool, dry, dark place.

X. annuum P. 196

x. AN-yew-um. Immortelle. A 1- to 3-foot-tall annual with silvery leaves and 2-inch-wide, single or double flower heads in shades of bright pink, purple, or white from summer to fall. *X. cylindraceum* is a 1½- to 2-foot annual with pink flowers. Warm-weather annual.

Zea

ZEE-ah. Grass family, Poaceae.

Although commonly known only as an agricultural or vegetable-garden crop, corn *(Zea mays)* is sometimes grown as an ornamental—especially variegated-leaved cultivars. The genus *Zea* contains four species of annuals, or sometimes perennials, with lance-shaped leaves. The plants bear separate male and female flowers: The female flowers, which develop into individual kernels, are enclosed in spathe-like bracts, called the husks, and have long silky styles (the silks) that stick out the top. The male flowers, referred to as the tassels, are borne at the top of the plant.

HOW TO GROW

Select a site in full sun with rich, well-drained, evenly moist soil. Sow seeds outdoors after the last frost date, once the soil has warmed up to at least 55°F. Germination takes about 2 weeks. Or sow indoors in individual pots 4 to 6 weeks before the last frost date at 70°F. If you want ears to form, plant in drifts or blocks to encourage wind pollination, or hand-pollinate by dusting pollen from the male flowers onto the silks. Water during dry weather, and mulch plants to keep the soil evenly moist. Use corn as a tall backdrop behind plantings of annuals and perennials.

Z. mays P. 197

Z. MAYS. Corn. A 4- to 12-foot-tall annual with lance-shaped, 3-foot-long leaves. 'Variegata' is a 3- to 5-foot-tall cultivar with leaves striped in cream and white. 'Harlequin' is about the same size and has leaves striped with green, red, and cream. Warm-weather annual.

Zinnia

ZIN-nee-ah. Aster family, Asteraceae.

Few flowers are as familiar or as easy to grow as zinnias. The genus contains about 20 species of annuals, perennials, and subshrubs that are primarily native to Mexico but also southwestern North America, as well as farther south in Central and South America. They bear leaves that range from linear to ovate or rounded, and showy, daisylike flowers that can be single or double. Hot colors predominate in the zinnias: they come in shades of orange, red, bronze, hot pink, orange-red, and yellow-orange, as well as cooler colors such as white, pale pink, cream, and green.

HOW TO GROW

Select a site in full sun with average to rich, well-drained soil. A site with good air circulation is best; otherwise, powdery mildew can be a problem. Gardeners in areas with hot, humid summers should consider some of the newer disease-resistant selections. Sow seeds outdoors after the last frost date. Or sow indoors 6 to 8 weeks before the last frost at 60° to 65°F. Transplant with care. For season-long bloom, sow new crops of seeds every 3 to 4 weeks until midsummer. Pinch plants to encourage branching, unless you are growing exclusively for cut flowers and want long stems. Tall plants may need staking. Use zinnias in mixed plantings or in cottage gardens. Dwarf types make great edging plants and can be used in containers. The flowers attract both hummingbirds and butterflies and also make excellent cut flowers.

Z. elegans PP. 197, 198

Z. EL-eh-gans. Common Zinnia. A bushy, ½- to 4-foot-tall annual with lance-shaped leaves. Many cultivars are available, with single or double flowers ranging from 1½ to 5 inches wide. Cactus-flowered cultivars, including Zenith Series, bear double and semidouble, 4-inch-wide flowers with narrow, curved petals, generally on 2½- to 3-foot plants. Dahlia-flowered cultivars have semidouble to double, 3- to 5-inch-wide blooms in both full-size and dwarf plants. 'Blue Point Mix' bears 5- to 6-inch dahlia-like blooms on 4-foot plants. Dasher Series and Dreamland Series bear 3½- to 4-inch-wide, double blooms on compact, 10- to 12-inch-tall plants. Oklahoma Series plants bear double, 2½-inch-wide flowers and were developed for their "cut and come again" performance as cut flowers. Pulchino Series plants are 1 to 1½ feet tall with 2- to 3-inch-wide flowers; they are more disease-resistant than most cultivars. Warm-weather annual.

Z. haageana PP. 198, 199

z. haa-gee-AH-nah. Narrow-leaved Zinnia, Mexican Zinnia. Also listed as *Z. angustifolia* and *Z. linearis.* A bushy, 1- to 2-foot-tall annual with outstanding resistance to diseases as well as heat and drought tolerance. Bears linear to lance-shaped leaves covered in bristly hairs, and daisylike, 1½-inch-wide flower heads in summer. Star Series plants bear 2-inch-wide flowers in gold, orange, and white. Profusion Series produces 2- to 2½-inch-wide flowers in cherry pink and orange. Warm-weather annual.

Z. peruviana P. 199

z. per-oo-vee-AH-nah. Formerly *Z. pauciflora.* A 2- to 3-foot-tall annual with linear to lance-shaped leaves that resist mildew. Bears 1- to 1½-inch-wide, daisylike flowers with dark centers and red or yellow petals. 'Bonita Red' has brick to soft orange-red blooms, while 'Bonita Yellow' bears yellow to gold blooms. Warm-weather annual.

Photo Credits

KAREN BUSSOLINI: 32 top, 64, 82, 112, 131, 133, 151

DAVID CAVAGNARO: 6, 9, 18, 36 top, 37 top, 38 bottom, 39 top, 41 top, 44 bottom, 45 bottom, 49 top, 50 top, 51 top, 51 bottom, 53 bottom, 56 top, 63 bottom, 64 top, 69 top, 70 bottom, 75 bottom, 78 top, 80 top, 85 top, 88 top, 90 bottom, 94 bottom, 97 top, 97 bottom, 99 bottom, 109 top, 110 top, 111 bottom, 113 bottom, 114 bottom, 115 top, 115 bottom, 116 top, 117 top, 118 bottom, 131 top, 132 top, 136 bottom, 139 top, 140 top, 141 top, 148 top, 155 top, 164 top, 173 bottom, 175 top, 178 top, 181 top, 181 bottom, 188 bottom, 197 bottom, 199 top, 199 bottom

KEN DRUSE: 105 top

BARBARA ELLIS: 65 bottom

THOMAS ELTZROTH: 11, 12, 35 bottom, 46 top, 48 bottom, 54 bottom, 57 bottom, 58 top, 61 top, 61 bottom, 62 bottom, 66 bottom, 78 bottom, 79 bottom, 81 bottom, 83 top, 83 bottom, 84 top, 84 bottom, 87 bottom, 95 top, 100 top, 104 top, 117 bottom, 120 bottom, 127 top, 128 top, 134 top, 134 bottom, 136 top, 156 bottom, 161 top, 162 bottom, 165 top, 168 top, 175 bottom, 179 top, 183 top, 184 bottom, 192 top, 194 bottom, 200–201

DEREK FELL: 5, 15, 32 bottom, 33 top, 33 bottom, 39 bottom, 41 bottom, 44 top, 47 top, 47 bottom, 48 top, 54 top, 58 bottom, 59 top, 59 bottom, 62 top, 66 top, 68 bottom, 73 bottom, 76 top, 81 top, 82 top, 86 top, 89 top, 98 top, 99 top, 101 top, 101 bottom, 103 bottom, 108 top, 109 bottom, 110 bottom, 113 top, 114 top, 126 top, 130 bottom, 133 top, 138 top, 141 bottom, 142 bottom, 143 top, 143 bottom, 145 bottom, 146 top, 147 bottom, 152 top, 157 bottom, 166 top, 166 bottom, 167 bottom, 169 top, 174 bottom, 180 top, 182 bottom, 186 bottom, 187 top, 190 top, 191 top, 191 bottom, 197 top

CHARLES MARDEN FITCH: 22, 35 top, 42 top, 42 bottom, 55 bottom, 56 bottom, 60 top, 60 bottom, 63 top, 68 top, 71 bottom, 74 bottom, 75 top, 77 bottom, 90 top, 103 top, 107 bottom, 126 bottom, 146 bottom, 156 top, 164 bottom, 176 bottom, 177 bottom

DENCY KANE: 34 top, 65 top, 87 top, 92 top, 112 top, 184 top, 186 top, 189 top

CHARLES MANN: 16, 21, 40 bottom, 52 top, 70 top, 73 top, 76 bottom, 77 top, 79 top, 93 bottom, 102 top, 105 bottom, 116 bottom, 119 bottom, 125 bottom, 129 bottom, 130 top, 132 bottom, 135 bottom, 142 top, 152 bottom, 153 top, 163 bottom, 164 top (inset), 168 bottom, 179 bottom, 185 top, 189 bottom, 192 bottom, 195 top, 195 bottom

NANCY J. ONDRA: 135 top

JERRY PAVIA: ii–iii, vi–1, 3, 4, 10, 30–31, 34 bottom, 36 bottom, 37 bottom, 38 top, 40 top, 43 bottom, 45 top, 46 bottom, 49 bottom, 50 bottom, 52 bottom, 53 top, 55 top, 57 top, 67 top, 67 bottom, 69 bottom, 71 top, 72 top, 72 bottom, 74 top, 80 bottom, 85 bottom, 86 bottom, 88 bottom, 89 bottom, 91 top, 91 bottom, 92 bottom, 93 top, 94 top, 95 bottom, 96 top, 96 bottom, 98 bottom, 100 bottom, 102 bottom, 104 bottom, 106 top, 106 bottom, 107 top, 108 bottom, 111 top, 118 top, 119 top, 120 top, 121 top, 121 bottom, 122 top, 122 bottom, 123 top, 123 bottom, 124 top, 124 bottom, 125 top, 127 bottom, 128 bottom, 129 top, 137 top, 137 bottom, 138 bottom, 139 bottom, 140 bottom, 144 top, 144 bottom, 145 top, 147 top, 148 bottom, 149 top, 149 bottom, 150 top, 150 bottom, 151 bottom, 153 bottom, 154 top, 154 bottom, 155 bottom, 157 top, 158 top, 158 bottom, 159 top, 159 bottom, 160 top, 160 bottom, 161 bottom, 162 top, 163 top, 165 bottom, 167 top, 169 bottom, 170 top, 170 bottom, 171 top, 171 bottom, 172 top, 172 bottom, 173 top, 174 top, 176 top, 177 top, 178 bottom, 180 top (inset), 180 bottom, 182 top, 183 bottom, 185 bottom, 187 bottom, 188 top, 190 bottom, 193 top, 193 bottom, 194 top, 196 top, 196 bottom, 198 top, 198 bottom

JOANNE WALKOVIC: 43 top

Index

Page numbers in italics refer to illustrations.

TITLES AVAILABLE IN THE TAYLOR'S GUIDE SERIES:

Taylor's Guide to Annuals 0-395-94352-3

Taylor's Guide to Perennials 0-395-40448-7

Taylor's Guide to Roses 0-395-69459-0

Taylor's Guide to Bulbs 0-395-40449-5

Taylor's Guide to Ground Covers 0-395-43094-1

Taylor's Guide to Houseplants 0-395-43091-7

Taylor's Guide to Shrubs 0-395-43093-3

Taylor's Guide to Trees 0-395-46783-7

Taylor's Guide to Gardening in the South 0-395-59681-5

Taylor's Guide to Shade Gardening 0-395-65165-4

Taylor's Guide to Herbs 0-395-68081-6

Taylor's Guide to Container Gardening 0-395-69829-4

Taylor's Guide to Heirloom Vegetables 0-395-70818-4

Taylor's Guide to Fruits and Berries 0-395-71806-3

Taylor's Guide to Orchids 0-395-67726-2

Taylor's Guide to Seashore Gardening 0-395-73532-7

Taylor's Guide to Ornamental Grasses 0-395-79761-6

Taylor's Master Guide to Gardening 0-396-64995-1

Taylor's Guide to Growing North America's Favorite Plants 0-395-76535-8

At your bookstore or by calling 1-800-225-3362